LEARNING RESOURCES CTR/NEW ENGLAND TECH

3 0147 1000 399

S0-BSS-609

TX 652.7 .A3 1963

Adams. Charlotte, 1899-

1

NEW ENGLAND INSTITUTE
OF TECHNOLOGY
LEARNING RESOURCES CENTER

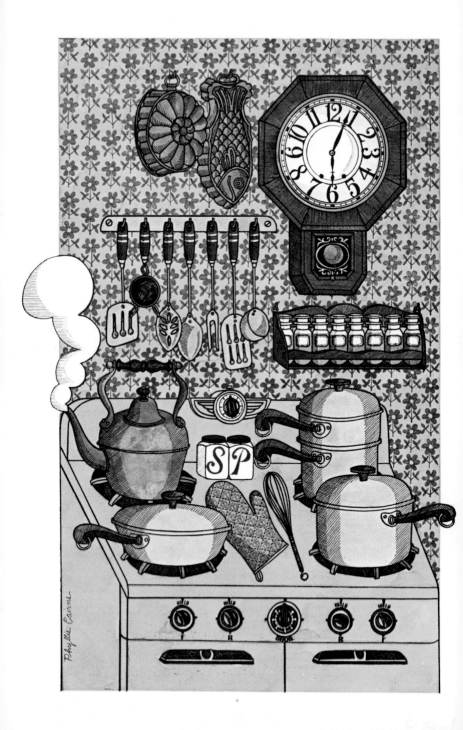

1001 Questions Answered About Cooking

BY CHARLOTTE ADAMS

WITH DRAWINGS BY JAMES MACDONALD

DODD, MEAD & COMPANY
NEW YORK

NEW ENGLAND INSTITUTE
OF TECHNOLOGY
LEARNING RESOURCES CENTER

1-98

#492126

For

Mary Lyon Williams

with love

The frontispiece is reproduced through
the courtesy of Ladies' Home Journal

COPYRIGHT © 1963 BY CHARLOTTE ADAMS

ALL RIGHTS RESERVED

NO PART OF THIS BOOK MAY BE REPRODUCED IN ANY FORM
WITHOUT PERMISSION IN WRITING FROM THE PUBLISHER

PRINTED IN THE UNITED STATES OF AMERICA

INTRODUCTION

Cooking is one of the most delightful, creative experiences anyone can have. It has always made me sad when a woman said to me, "You see, I don't like to cook." "Poor you!" is my invariable answer. Happily for the human race, of course, we are not all alike. But when the potential for great pleasure and excitement is right there, it seems a shame that anyone who has to cook whether she wants to or not cannot achieve the point of view which shows her the joy of providing people with interesting, delicious meals. Sometimes, it seems to me, this lack of interest in cooking, or downright dislike of it, comes from too little information and knowledge. This book is presented in the humble hope that it may fill that gap, at least in part.

The material included here has been gathered from questions asked me over a period of years, during which I have been a newspaper and magazine writer, a lecturer on food, and the author of cookbooks. Out of such experience I know that the most common query, from the experienced cook as well as the novice, is "How do you make all the dishes in a meal come out at the same time?" I have endeavored to answer that by explaining my own solution which, it seems to me, is based on logic as well as experience.

There are, of course, *hundreds of thousands* of questions which could be asked about food—and often are! I have tried to gather together the thousand-odd most often asked by the average home cook and to answer them in a way which can be helpful to her. The book is intended to be used for reference—by the bride who wants to avoid pitfalls or rescue herself from disasters, by the food writer who wants to make sure of a fact, by the knowing cook who wants to check the authenticity of one dish or the basic proportions involved in another.

The most knowledgeable cook does not try to keep in her head all the recipes she likes to make. She may, in fact, cook a good deal by instinct, as her grandmother did. But sometimes, she likes to check herself on a matter like—how much of a stick of butter makes a quarter cup? The answers to such questions are included here.

This is not a recipe book. In some very few, basic instances, quantities are given, as in Cream Sauce and Hollandaise. But it is taken for granted that anyone interested in cooking, whether from necessity or from sheer joy in the process, owns at least one basic cookbook. If you do not own one, you should proceed at once to acquire it! Also, if you are especially interested in the dishes of other countries, I expect that you will have given yourself the pleasure of acquiring books which give you complete instruction in making them. In this book you can check to see what various names of foreign dishes mean. If the contents intrigue you, you will then go to your foreign cookbooks for their recipes.

You will find here a minimum of questions on nutrition. Because this has been arranged very purposefully, I should like to explain why. Nutrition is a rapidly, and marvelously, growing science. The best of the nutritionists are the first to tell you that we have learned a great deal in the past few decades—and have probably barely scratched the surface of what we shall one day know. As research goes on, nutrition information changes constantly. In my opinion, the best way to keep up with its findings is through newspapers, government pamphlets, the *Journal of the American Medical Association,* and similar current publications. It is also my premise that one reads such material with care and interest, being sure to discover, if possible, whether findings are absolute, controversial, or frankly "iffy," as they sometimes are. One waits for the absolute before changing the whole family's pattern of eating. Pity the poor family run by a hypochondriac, forced to give up everything which *may* be dangerous or bad for it, and to eat every new fad food which comes along the way!

Foods fads and fad diets are another of my pet dislikes. I have included none in this book. These fads are not only foolish, but may be downright dangerous to health. The American public, unhappily, contains entirely too many people who are ready to jump at the first quack diet or pill purporting to thin them down or make them young and vigorous—or whatever may be their ambitions of the moment. A lot of illness, and even hospitalization due to malnutrition, results from such jumping at magic cure-alls.

So in the nutrition chapter of this book you will find only answers to things we really know—long proven and scientifically accepted. For example, is there more nutritional value in a white or in a brown egg? *Your* answer may depend on which part of the country you come from, but *the* answer is that there is no difference.

Choosing and answering these 1001 Questions has been a delight, and it is my great hope that it will be as useful to others as I know it is going to be to me!

CONTENTS

INTRODUCTION iii

GLOSSARY OF COOKING TERMS 1

TABLES OF EQUIVALENT WEIGHTS AND MEASURES 7

I COOKING EQUIPMENT 9

II MENU PLANNING AND NUTRITION 29

III SOUPS AND CHOWDERS 49

IV MILK, BUTTER, CHEESE, AND EGGS 54

V MEATS 79

VI POULTRY AND GAME 103

VII FISH AND SHELLFISH 120

VIII VEGETABLES 129

IX PASTA AND RICE 137

X SALADS 142

XI SAUCES 149

XII DESSERTS AND FRUIT 159

XIII BEVERAGES 172

XIV BAKING 176

XV COOKING WITH HERBS, SPICES, AND WINES 189

XVI CANNED FOODS 196

XVII FROZEN FOODS 200

RECOMMENDED COOKBOOKS 209

INDEX 210

1001 Questions
Answered
About
Cooking

GLOSSARY OF COOKING TERMS

Bake: To cook in the oven (when referring to meats, this is called roasting). Also, occasionally applied to top-of-the-range cooking, as in *baking* pancakes or waffles.

Barbecue: To cook meats over an open fire, indoors or out. Many very complete modern kitchens contain charcoal broilers for such cooking. Meats are sometimes marinated in a sauce before being barbecued.

Baste: To pour or brush melted fat, water, wine, or other liquid over food. This is sometimes done before cooking, to inject flavor and to tenderize meat. It is often done during the cooking process, to keep foods moist and to add flavor.

Beat: To mix briskly with a spoon, rotary beater, or electric beater. A good beating thoroughly mixes all ingredients involved.

Beat lightly: This is a term usually applied to eggs, involving sufficient light beating with a fork to mix yolks and whites completely.

Beat stiff: This is applied to egg whites. Beat with electric or rotary beater until almost dry and until peaks will hold their shape when the beater is lifted up through the whites. It cannot be done with a blender.

Also applied to whipping cream. Beat until cream holds definite peaks, but be *very careful* not to overbeat or you will have the beginnings of butter. In beating cream with a blender, turn it on and off pretty constantly to avoid such a contingency. With an electric beater or rotary beater, cream takes longer to reach the desired consistency, but should be checked frequently after it begins to thicken.

Beat until peaks are formed: This is applied to egg whites. Beat with electric or rotary beater until soft peaks are formed when the beater is lifted up through the whites. At this point the beaten whites will still be moist and shiny. This cannot be done with a blender because its action is too severe to beat egg whites.

Bind: To hold foods together with a sauce so that they form a cohesive mass.

Blanch: To immerse foods briefly in boiling water. In preparing many fresh vegetables for freezing, for instance, they are first blanched to hold the color and flavor by stopping or slowing the action of enzymes. Nuts, tomatoes, and other fruits are blanched by being plunged into boiling water for from 1 to 3 minutes to loosen their skins. They are then drained, rinsed in cold water, and the skins slipped off easily.

Blaze: To pour *warmed* liquor over food and set it aflame.

Blend: To incorporate several ingredients completely into one another with a spoon. Or to whirl in an electric blender to achieve the same result.

Boil: To cook in boiling water (212° F. at sea level). So long as bubbles rise to the top and break, the water is boiling. The fastest is a "full, rolling boil." Slowest is a low boil, which is just above a simmer.

Braise: To brown meat or vegetables in hot fat. A small amount of liquid is then added, and the food is cooked covered, long and slow.

Bread: To roll in crumbs. Often food is first dipped in beaten egg, then rolled in crumbs.

Broil: To cook under (range broiler or portable electric broiler) or over (open fire or grill) direct heat.

Brush: To coat food with melted fat or liquid. A pastry brush is most satisfactory for accomplishing this job.

Candy: To cook fruit in a heavy syrup, drain, and dry it, as for orange or grapefruit peel. Applied to vegetables, it means to cook them with fat and sugar or corn syrup until they are glazed, as with sweet potatoes or carrots.

Caramelize: To melt sugar over low heat, stirring constantly with a wooden spoon, until it turns liquid and browns to the degree desired.

Chop: To cut into fine or coarse pieces, as required by the recipe, with a knife or special chopper. Chopped food is never as finely cut as that which is ground.

Clarify: To clarify stock, broth, or consommé add egg white and egg shell and bring to a rolling boil. Strain. Bits of food involved in the original making stick to the egg, and the resultant liquid is entirely clear. (For clarifying butter see Question 205.)

Coat: To cover food thoroughly with seasoned flour or with crumbs. Also: custard is cooked "when the mixture 'coats' the spoon," that is, forms a film on it.

Coddle: To cook gently below the boiling point, as for fruit or eggs.

Cream: To mix fat and sugar together with the back of a spoon until they are smooth and creamy.

Crisp: To place in ice water until crisp and well chilled, as for vegetables. To place in a low oven until brown and crisp, as for making thin bread into Melba toast.

Cube: To cut into small, equal squares.

Cut: 1. To divide food into pieces with a knife or kitchen shears. 2. To mix fat into dry ingredients with two knives or a pastry blender, as for making pie crust.

Degrease: To remove accumulated fat from the surface of hot liquid (from the French "dégraisser"). This can be done with a slotted spoon or with paper towels. In the case of fat drippings from a roast, the fat can be removed with a bulb baster.

Devil: To prepare food with hot seasonings, or to serve cooked food with a hotly spiced (deviled) sauce.

Dice: To cut food into very small cubes.

Disjoint: To cut a chicken, turkey, or other bird into pieces at the joints. Easiest with poultry shears—or even better, have your butcher do it.

Dot: To scatter small bits of fat (usually butter) over food before cooking.

Dredge: To cover food completely with a dry ingredient, such as flour or crumbs. It can be done by shaking the food to be dredged in a paper bag with the dry ingredients (and seasonings, if desired), or by using a shaker designed for the purpose (some containers are made with shaker tops).

Dust: To sprinkle food lightly with a dry ingredient.

Fillet: To cut a piece of fish or meat into the desired shape, removing all bones. Easiest to have your fish market or butcher shop do it.

Flake: To break food into (not necessarily even) flat pieces, usually with a fork.

Flambé: The French equivalent of blaze.

Fold: The gentle combining of two or more ingredients with a spoon, a spatula, or the hand. This process usually involves a mixture which would be flattened and ruined by hard beating. Whatever instrument you use, put it down through the mixture to the bottom of the bowl, across, and up to the top. This is continued until the ingredients are well mixed but still retain air.

Fricassee: A stew, or stewing. The main ingredient of the dish is browned or not, as desired, then cooked long and slow in liquid.

Fry: To cook, partly or wholly immersed in fat, either in a skillet containing 1 to 2 inches of fat or in a deep-fat fryer with lots of fat. These can be top-of-the-range utensils, or electrically controlled ones.

Garnish: To decorate, usually with other foods.

Glaze: To give food a shiny finish, as: vegetables, in butter and sugar; meat, with a sauce, usually containing some sugar; or cold foods, by covering with aspic.

Grate: To pulverize food by rubbing it against a rough surface (grater). The same result can be achieved with many foods by whirling them in the blender.

Grill: To broil—referring to the rack on which food is cooked.

Grind: To reduce food to small particles by friction, as with a grinder, a mortar and pestle, or a blender.

Julienne: Food cut into match-like strips.

Knead: To fold, turn, and press down on a dough with the hands until it becomes smooth and elastic. There are dough-hook attachments for some electric mixers which accomplish the task of kneading without much use of muscle.

Lard: To place broad or narrow strips of fat (usually salt pork or bacon) over the top of meat or birds, or insert them into the meat with a larding needle or a skewer. This is usually done to very lean meat which needs fat added in order that it may not dry out in cooking.

Marinade: Usually a mixture of oil, acid (wine or vinegar), and seasonings, in which food is soaked prior to cooking, to season it and sometimes to tenderize it.

Marinate: To soak food in a marinade.

Mask: To cover food completely with mayonnaise, a thick sauce, or aspic.

Mince: To cut or chop into very small pieces.

Parboil: To cook food in boiling water until partially done. The cooking is usually finished by putting the parboiled food into a casserole, by frying or sautéing it, or by some other means of cooking.

Panbroil: To cook, uncovered, in a hot skillet with no grease added, pouring off fat rendered from the meat as it accumulates.

Panfry: To cook, uncovered, in a hot skillet with a very little grease added.

Pare: To remove an outer skin. To peel.

Poach: To simmer food gently in a hot liquid.

Purée: To force food through a sieve, or whirl it in the blender until it is completely smooth.

Reduce: To boil a liquid until it reaches the quantity required in a recipe, thus concentrating the flavor.

Render: To melt fat down so that any connective tissue may be removed.

Roast: To cook in an oven. The term is usually applied to meat. (See Bake.)

Roux: A mixture of flour and butter cooked together for a few minutes before any liquid is added. For a white sauce this is done over low heat so that it will not brown. For a brown sauce the mixture is browned before liquid is added.

Sauté: To cook food on top of the range in a small amount of fat, for whatever time the recipe requires. Sometimes the food is sautéed to brown it, sometimes not.

Scald: To heat liquid (such as milk) to the boiling point, but not let it boil. A few tiny bubbles will appear on top when the right point is reached.

Score: To make slashes in food with a sharp knife. This can apply to meat and to bread or cakes before baking.

Sear: To brown fast over high heat or in the oven. Usually refers to meat. The process seals in the juices and adds to flavor.

Shuck: To remove a natural outer covering from food, such as shells from oysters or husks from corn.

Sift: To put dry ingredients through a sieve or a sifter.

Simmer: To cook gently in liquid below the boiling point. There should be only barely observable bubbles coming to the top of the liquid. Used in long, slow cooking as a rule.

Skewer: To put meat and/or other foods on thin metal or wooden pins for broiling (or, occasionally, for sautéing). Also, to hold meat together with short metal pins.

Skim: To remove scum, fat, or other floating substances from a liquid. It is usually done with a spoon, or a slotted spoon known as a "skimmer." For removing fat, it is often best to lay a paper towel over the surface. Also: to take cream from the top of milk.

Sliver: To cut food into thin pieces, as for nuts.

Steam: To cook food over boiling water which does not touch it.

There are special pots for steaming, also racks to put into any pot which will lift the food above the water. Sometimes used also with reference to food cooked in a very little liquid or fat, as with onions to get them "soft but not brown."

Steep: To extract the essence from a food by soaking in hot liquid. Most commonly used in reference to tea, but applicable to many leaves, such as saffron and other herbs.

Stew: To cook long and slow in liquid.

Stir: To blend ingredients with a circular motion. Less vigorous than beating.

Truss: To tie the wings and legs of a bird to the body so that shape is not lost in cooking. A ball of white string in the kitchen for such purposes is indispensable.

Try out: To remove fat from such meats as salt pork and bacon. The liquid fat is then usually used for frying and the solid pieces for toppings and the like. (See Render.)

Whip: To beat rapidly in order to incorporate air and expand the ingredients, such as eggs, cream, and gelatin dishes.

TABLES OF EQUIVALENT WEIGHTS AND MEASURES

Equivalent Weights and Measures

Familiar Designation	Equivalent	Weight in Ounces
Dash or pinch	A very small amount; vague—better to add ingredient "to taste"	
1½ teaspoons	½ tablespoon	¼ fluid ounce
1 tablespoon	3 teaspoons	½ fluid ounce
¼ cup	4 tablespoons	2 ounces
⅓ cup	5 tablespoons, plus 1 teaspoon	4½ ounces, plus
⅜ cup	¼ cup, plus 1 tablespoon	2½ ounces
⅝ cup	½ cup, plus 2 tablespoons	5 ounces
⅞ cup	¾ cup, plus 2 tablespoons	7 ounces
1 cup	16 tablespoons or ½ pint	8 ounces (about)
1 pint	2 cups	1 pound (about)
1 quart	2 pints or 4 cups	2 pounds (about)
1 gallon	4 quarts	8 pounds (about)
1 liter (fluid)	1.057 liquid quarts	
1 ounce	28.35 grams	
1 pound	16 ounces or .454 kilograms	
1 gill	½ cup	4 fluid ounces
1 centiliter	2 teaspoons	.338 fluid ounces

Equivalent Weights and Measures of Specific Foods

Food	Weight of One Cup in Ounces (about)	Measurement of One Pound in Cups (about)
Cottage or cream cheese	8	2
Liquid fats and oils	8	2
Solid fats (butter, margarine, lard)	8	2
Hydrogenated fats	6⅔	2½
Dry bread crumbs	3¼	5
Soft, fresh bread crumbs	1½	10
Corn meal	5	3
Macaroni	4	4
Noodles	2⅔	6

Food	Weight of One Cup in Ounces (about)	Measurement of One Pound in Cups (about)
Spaghetti	3⅓	4¾
Flour	4	4
Whole wheat flour	4¼	3¾
Cake flour	3⅓	4¾
Apples, peeled and diced	3⅓	3¾
Bananas, mashed	8	2
Bananas, sliced	7¼	2¼
Coconut (canned, moist)	3	5⅓
Almonds (blanched, whole)	5½	3
Filberts	4¾	3⅓
Peanuts	5	3¼
Pecans, halved	3¾	4¼
Walnuts, halved	3½	4½
Seedless raisins, whole	5¾	2¾
Chocolate, melted	9	1¾
Cocoa	4	4
Coffee	3	5⅓
Meat, ground raw	8	2
Kidney and Lima beans (dried)	6½	2½
Split peas (dried)	7	2¼
Sugar, brown and granulated	7	2¼
Sugar, superfine	7	2⅓
Sugar, confectioner's, sifted	4½	3½
Corn syrup	11½	1⅓
Honey	12	1⅓
Maple syrup	11	1½
Molasses	11½	1⅓
Cabbage, shredded, packed down	2½	6
Carrots, cut up	3¾	3¾
Mushrooms, cut up	3	5
Onions, sliced or diced	4	4
Potatoes, sliced or diced	4	4
Rice, raw	8	2

I. COOKING EQUIPMENT

1. What small equipment is needed for an average kitchen? Defining average as meaning a kitchen which has one oven, a broiler, and four top-of-the-range units, here is my complete list. Let me point out that no two cooks would make exactly the same requirements, so I may list some things you would have no use in the world for, and leave out something without which you cannot live. Please leave out mine and get yours, by all means!

French cook's knife
Utility knife
Slicing knife
2 or 3 paring knives
Grapefruit knife
Small cleaver
Knife sharpener
Pancake turner
Narrow metal spatula
Basting spoon
Slotted spoon
Long-handled fork
Ladle
Tongs
Wire whisks, small and large
3 rubber spatulas, narrow and broad
Set of wooden spoons in different sizes
Stainless steel flatware for kitchen use
Apple corer
Cheese grater
Garlic press
Small funnel
Kitchen shears
Game scissors
Vegetable-cleaning brush
2 sets of measuring spoons
Bulb baster
Pastry brush

2 1-cup measuring cups
1 2-cup measuring cup
Can opener
Jar-top opener
Lid lifter
Corkscrew
Bottle opener
2 or 3 strainers in different sizes
Colander
Biscuit cutter
Cookie cutters
Pastry board
Rolling pin
Pastry cloth
Pastry blender
Flour sifter
Salt and flour shakers
Pepper grinder
Cannister set for flour, sugar, coffee, and tea
2 or 3 chopping boards
Rotary beater
6 custard cups
2 muffin pans
1 or 2 loaf pans
2 layer-cake pans
2 pie pans
1 cake-cooling rack
Set of mixing bowls in graduated sizes
2 cookie sheets
Pans for special cakes (angel, cheese, etc.)

Wooden chopping bowl
Chopper
1 or 2 large casseroles with covers
4 to 6 individual casseroles
1 soufflé dish
Shallow baking pan
Meat thermometer
Roasting rack
Shallow roasting pan
Dutch oven
1 large skillet with lid
2 or 3 smaller skillets with lids
Omelet pan
2 or 3 saucepans, in graduated sizes, with lids
1 or 2 double boilers
Frying basket
Griddle
Meat grinder
Ricer, or food mill
Juicer or reamer
Coffee pot
Tea kettle
Timer
1 or 2 kitchen platters
4 to 6 kitchen plates
Quart pitcher
Ice crusher

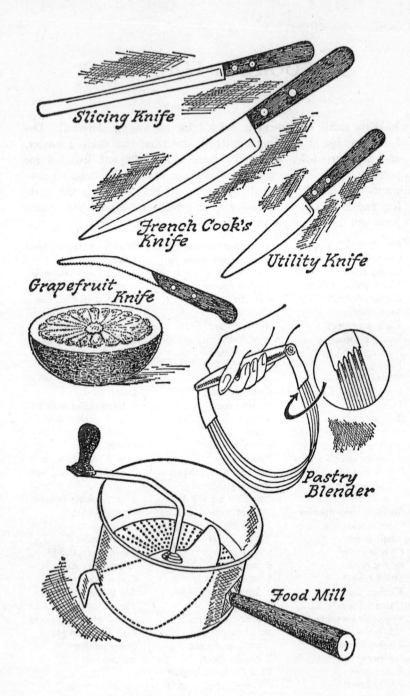

Slicing Knife

French Cook's Knife

Utility Knife

Grapefruit Knife

Pastry Blender

Food Mill

Small Electrical Equipment (not absolutely essential, but very helpful)

Toaster	Mixer	Rotisserie
Blender	Skillet	
Portable mixer	Saucepan	

2. Does it pay to buy expensive cooking equipment?   If it is equipment you use a lot, it is a sound investment to buy the best you can afford. Cheap equipment which is used infrequently for easy tasks may be adequate, though even cookie cutters, for instance, work better if they are sturdy and won't bend, for which asset you have to pay extra.

3. Is it important that the bottom of pans be flat?   It is very important, because if they are uneven the heat will be unevenly distributed and the foods may burn in places, be undercooked in others. Discard pans with dented or otherwise uneven bottoms. If you buy good, sturdy cookware, it is not likely to get into such a condition.

4. Is wrought aluminum better than cast aluminum for cookware?   Yes, because it is more highly purified than cast aluminum and resists corrosion better.

5. Can aluminum cookware contaminate food?   No. The use of aluminum cooking utensils is in no way injurious to health. Most of the propaganda against them has come from manufacturers of competing types of utensils.

6. What makes dark stains on aluminum pans?   The alkalies in boiling water, vegetables, and melting soap.

7. How can I best remove dark stains from my aluminum pans?   Cook highly acid foods in them, like tomatoes or rhubarb; or cook a weak solution of vinegar and water in them.

8. If you make applesauce in a darkened aluminum kettle and it becomes clean and shiny, is the applesauce fit to eat?   Yes. Applesauce is an acid food and has caused the pan to shine, but has in no way been contaminated in the process.

9. Do you approve of copper cooking utensils? Oh, yes! They conduct and hold heat beautifully, and are beautiful to look at *if* they are kept polished—otherwise they should be kept out of sight. Also, since they are lined with tin it is necessary to have them relined periodically, and in these days it is sometimes quite a chore to find anyone who knows how to do this job. So, unless you love to polish copper, or have someone to do it for you, I suggest that you buy pots and pans of other, usually far less expensive, materials.

10. Should one polish the copper bottoms of stainless steel pans? If you do not, you should keep them out of sight, as tarnished copper is not very attractive. There is a school which announces firmly that unpolished copper-bottomed pans hold the heat better than polished ones. I have used them in both conditions and must say that I see very little difference in their effectiveness.

11. Is glass cookware good? Yes, but I like best glass ovenware, such as pie and loaf pans. Of course a glass double boiler has the advantage of letting you see (if you keep looking) whether there is still water in the bottom, but I do not think it is compensated for by the fact that the utensil is so much more easily broken than a metal one. The only top-of-the-range glass utensil I really like is a coffee-maker, which is easy to keep absolutely clean—an essential for coffee-makers, which is difficult to achieve with metal, and even earthenware, ones.

12. Is enamel-covered iron cookware good? I think it is fine, but it is also relatively expensive, and food seems to stick in the skillets more than it does in those of other materials. One great advantage of this type of cookware is that it is so handsome that one can cook and serve in it and only add to the attractiveness of the table.

13. What is the advantage of enamelware? Its greatest advantage is that it is so easy to clean.

14. Is it dangerous to cook in chipped enamelware? No. The possibility of swallowing small chips is so remote that it is not regarded as a hazard. On the other hand, enamelware which has been chipped so that the iron underneath is exposed may unpleasantly affect the flavor and color of certain foods.

15. Do you approve of tin cooking ware?   Its greatest disadvantage is that it bends and dents too easily. Foods baked in it brown well, so it is good for muffin tins and cake pans. But aluminum is much more substantial and, in the long run, more satisfactory.

16. How can you prevent tin pans from rusting?   By making sure that they are always thoroughly dried.

17. Of what material should cookie sheets be made?   Stainless steel is by far the most satisfactory. Tin ones bend and dent and thus do a bad job of browning the cookies or whatever you put on the sheets.

18. What kind of pans should one buy for making layer cake?   I like the kind with a false bottom, as it is thus possible to get the cake out neatly. They should be sturdy pans of heavy aluminum or steel.

19. What is the best kind of omelet pan?   Cast aluminum is the best material for an omelet pan. It should have gently rounded sides, with no sharp division between them and the bottom. It should also have a heatproof handle. (See Questions 263 through 266.)

Omelet pan

20. What is a Dutch oven?   A deep, heavy pot with a lid, used for making stews and such dishes. Dutch ovens come in many materials, but the best one is still the heavy iron. If you can find it, get one lined with stainless steel, which will not rust and is much easier to clean. An enameled iron one is perhaps even better.

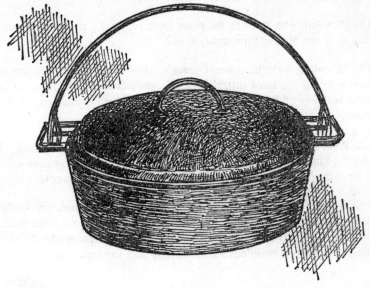

Dutch oven

21. Do you approve of pressure cookers?   I do not. It is impossible to get consistent results with them. For instance, if you buy peas in the market it is quite difficult to know how old they are, how long they have been in transit, and other factors bearing on the length of time they should be cooked. If you cook them in a pan, with or without a lid, in which you can test them periodically to see whether they are done, all is well. Doing them in a pressure cooker, however, you cannot be sure whether you will get little bullets or what is practically a purée. Even stews, in the making of which a pressure cooker saves a great deal of time, do not turn out as well when made by this method as they do when cooked long and slow with loving care in a Dutch oven.

22. What is a flan ring? It is a French pastry ring with no bottom, used for making tart shells. The ring is set on a baking sheet, the pastry molded into it and baked. When the tart shell is done the ring is removed and the shell slid from the baking sheet to a rack or a serving dish.

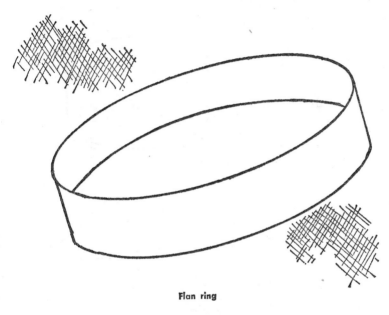

Flan ring

23. What is a spring-form pan? It is a pan for baking which has a fastener on the side, to be opened when the cake is done and lifted off without touching the cake, which is left on the bottom of the pan. Sometimes these pans have just a plain flat bottom, sometimes they come with a plain bottom, a fluted one, and a tube one.

24. What is a bulb baster? It is a tube of glass or metal with a rubber bulb on the end of it which is used to draw up juices from a pan and pour them back over the meat or whatever is cooking.

25. What kind of spatula should one buy? The most important are a narrow metal one with flexible blade, either square or rounded at the end, for taking cookies off a cookie sheet, spreading icing on

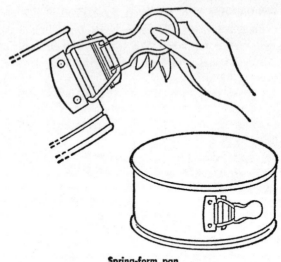

Spring-form pan

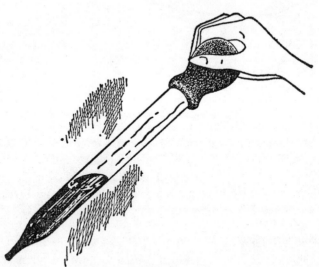

Bulb baster

cakes, et cetera; and rubber ones of varying size for mixing, scraping food from the sides of a beating bowl, and such operations. There are metal spatulas of various sizes and shapes which, if you become a devotee, you may wish to buy.

26. Is a meat grinder necessary?   It is for most people. Even if you only use it for grinding leftover meat, there is no other way to accomplish the job. And if you really love to cook and want to make dishes like fish puddings (see Question 554) and quenelles (see Question 543) you must have a meat grinder. Even a blender cannot take over all the tasks of a meat grinder. There is one sad thing about modern kitchens. There is never any place to screw on the meat grinder, because all counters are so flush with their cupboards. An attempt to solve this problem has been made by constructing a meat grinder with suction cups to hold it to the counter. So far, I am unhappy to report, this has not worked out very well. The grinder inevitably "walks" about on the counter after a few grinds.

27. Are measuring spoons really necessary?   Absolutely. Many recipes, particularly those for baking, have been scientifically worked out, and if you do not measure accurately, the end product will be ruined.

28. Should one buy only stainless steel knives?   I think so. Though some people cling to old knives which are not stainless because they think it is possible to keep a better edge on them, this is really a superstition. Stainless steel is easiest to clean, will not rust, and retains its edge beautifully. In any case, buy good knives. Cheap ones are useless and a waste of money.

29. How do good knives best retain an edge?   By being given proper care. Never throw good knives into a drawer in a jumble with each other and with other utensils. They should be kept on a rack: either one of the glass-fronted wooden variety with slits for knives of varying sizes, or a magnetic rack to which they cling, or a wooden wall rack in which they rest on their handles with the blades protected in slots. Knives should be sharpened before they show signs of dullness. A dull kitchen knife is a disgrace and a great handicap to the cook.

30. What is the best kind of knife sharpener?   If you have been taught to sharpen knives properly with a hone, you will think that is best, but few people have this skill. I like a small wall-mounted sharpener, through which I draw the knife down between two little round wheels. Mine is attached to the side of my glass-fronted knife rack, and I draw each knife gently through every time I put it away. Electric knife-sharpeners can do an excellent job, but the novice must be careful not to wear the knives away with it.

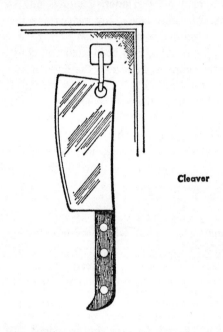

Cleaver

31. What is a cleaver good for? A cleaver, even the small home-kitchen type, will cut through bones of poultry or meat as no other knife can. It is also useful for pounding meat to make it thinner (with the flat) and for crushing a clove of garlic or a slice of ginger so that the flavor will be sure to be brought out when it is cooked and yet it can be easily identified and removed from a dish, if desired.

32. How do you use a garlic press? If you are smart and care about your hands, you will put an unpeeled clove of garlic into the press, squeeze it, and discover that the crushed garlic comes through, leaving the skin inside. It is easy to remove the skin with the point of a knife.

33. Is it really necessary to own a reamer? This seems to mean that since the advent of frozen fruit juices no reamer is necessary. However, lemon and lime juice are called for in many recipes and must be squeezed fresh if the dishes are to have proper flavor. If you try to do this by just squeezing the fruit with your hand, you will be very wasteful, so a reamer is really needed for cooking, as well as for making fresh fruit juice if you go to that trouble.

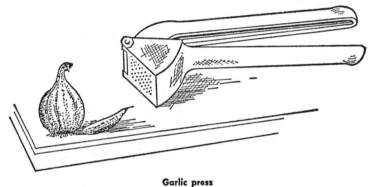

Garlic press

34. What is the best kind of scissors to buy for the kitchen? While any ordinary scissors will do, I am particularly devoted to the type, specifically made for the kitchen, which comes apart completely in

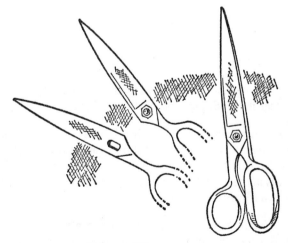

Scissors which come apart

two pieces for washing. This is especially handy when you have been cutting foods with these scissors. And they are perfectly good for cutting kitchen string and for such other uses.

35. What is the best type of flour sifter?   The small one, through which you sift flour into a cup by squeezing the handle. It is so handy for measuring your sifted flour, and it is perfectly adequate for sifting in any quantity, though if you prefer, you can own a big one for bigger jobs.

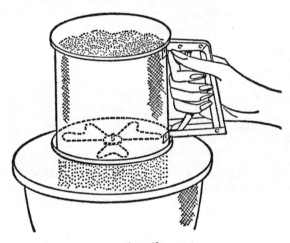

Flour sifter

36. What is a jar-top opener?   It is a metal gadget with grips which can be opened or closed by means of a wooden handle on top, to grip the top of a jar and then turn it. For people whose fingers are not as strong as steel it is indispensable in the kitchen.

37. What is a wire whisk?   It is a hand beater made of thin wires, with a sturdy handle, and is wonderful for beating sauces and the like. Some people refuse to use anything else for beating egg whites, but I think that is making life hard when they can be beaten without effort in jig time with a rotary or an electric beater.

38. Does it pay to buy an expensive rotary beater?   Yes, indeed it does. This is a tool you use a great deal. A cheap, wobbly one with tin beaters that rust is an abomination. The more expensive ones are far easier to use, since the best have ball bearings and practically work themselves. Their beaters are made of stainless steel and thus are very easy to clean.

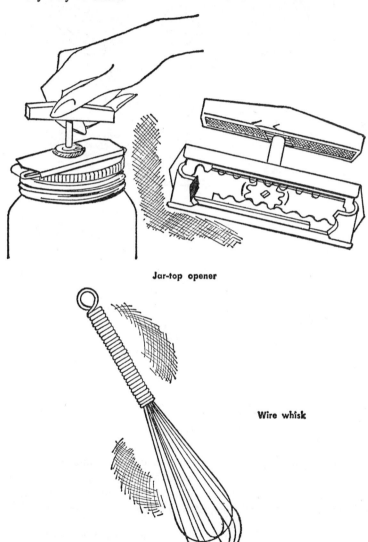

Jar-top opener

Wire whisk

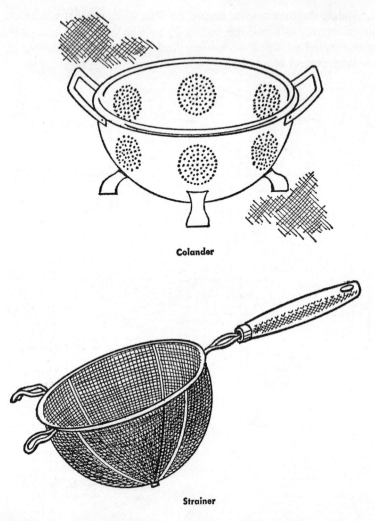

Colander

Strainer

39. What is the difference between a colander and a strainer?
Strainers have a fine mesh. The colander has much larger, coarse holes
in it. The colander also has legs so that it can stand on its own while
foods drain. The strainer must, of course, be set over a pan to drain.

40. Are parsley mincers good?   No, because they crush the parsley,
rather than mince it. A French knife minces parsley fast and well.

41. What is the best type of chopper?   This is probably a matter of opinion, but my own favorite is the kind with three blades, the center one controlled by a spring. Whatever kind you buy, be sure that it has stainless steel blades so they will not rust.

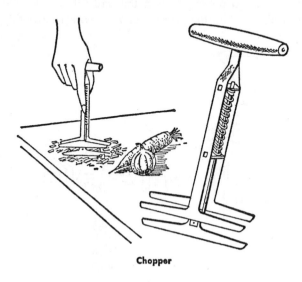

Chopper

42. What is the use of game shears?   They are exceedingly handy as an aid in carving a duck, for one thing, as they will cut through

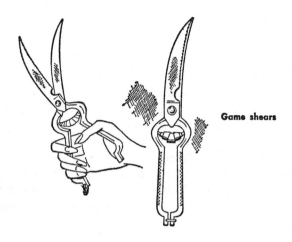

Game shears

bone and gristle easily. They are also useful in cutting up poultry or game birds before cooking them.

43. What is the best type of corkscrew? The kind which has a pair of "wings" which go up as you turn the screw down into the cork. You then push down on the "wings" and the cork is smoothly lifted

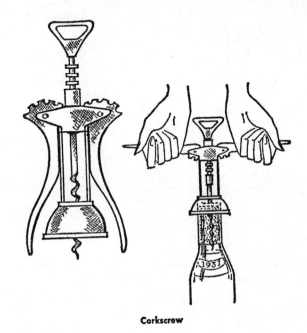

Corkscrew

from the bottle. I will say, in all frankness, however, that I have never had, or heard of, a corkscrew which did not eventually get out of whack and have to be replaced, and you may, in the process of such replacements, have found or be about to find one which will suit you far better than the one described suits me.

44. What is the best type of grater? The French Mouli is something no household should be without. It eliminates grated fingers and nails and does a splendid job. It is also very easy to clean. Also, do not forget that you can "grate" hard substances like cheese and nuts with a blender.

45. What is the best kind of can opener? The wall kind, with a magnet to catch and hold the lid of the can when it is entirely cut. Of course there are electric can openers and they work very well, but they seem to me a rather large investment for the amount of use they get—unless you eat entirely out of cans!

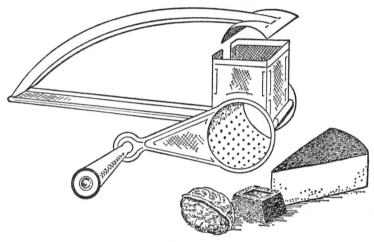

Mouli grater

46. What kind of ice crusher should one buy? One of the best inventions for crushing just a little ice is a long-handled gadget with a round spoon-like arrangement at the end. When you whack a cube of ice with this, it is crushed in no time. Another possible arrangement is a sturdy canvas bag and a mallet for pounding the ice. *Never* let anyone crush ice in your tea towels. They will be destroyed in no time. One of the blenders has an ice-crushing attachment, which is well worth the investment if you use a great deal of crushed ice.

47. What kind of coffee-maker is best? In my opinion a drip pot makes the best coffee, but I have tasted excellent coffee made in just about all the ways there are. The glass coffee-makers which require the use of folded papers to hold the grounds through which hot water is poured are really a form of drip pot and are my favorite type. Many people much prefer an electric coffee-maker, which works on the percolator system.

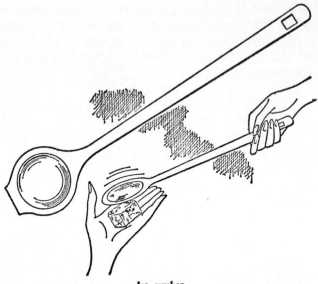

Ice crusher

48. What points should one consider in buying portable electric appliances?   Check the warranty on the appliance and ascertain whether servicing of the item is readily available. Look for the Underwriters' Laboratories seal of approval. Check all automatic features and ease of operating. The controls should be easy to read and set. Heating appliances should have a heat-resistant base or legs, handles, and controls. Note whether the appliance is going to be easy to clean, inside and out.

49. Is a blender useful?   Next to a toaster it seems to me the most important electrical appliance one can own. A blender can do jobs which are hard, if not impossible, to do one's self. On the other hand, one can accomplish with other tools anything an electric mixer can do, though it may be harder! Therefore, if I had to choose between the mixer and the blender, I would take the blender.

50. Is an electric portable mixer useful?   If you are very limited in space and cannot store a full-sized one, a portable hand mixer is exceedingly useful. It is much easier to use than even the best rotary beater. It can be hung on the wall.

51. What should one look for in buying a portable electric mixer?
Be sure that it is comfortable to hold and well balanced. It should
have a steady heel rest. It should have fingertip speed control. The
beater ejector should be conveniently located. The motor should be
permanently lubricated.

52. Is an electric saucepan a good buy? To my mind, it is one of
the best. For making stews and doing deep-fat frying, the controlled
heat is most important, and the electric saucepan will give you perfect
results. Though not as many people have them as own electric skillets,
they are to me a much more important kind of pan.

53. Is a rotisserie a good buy? If you have space to store it and
you cook a lot of roast meat, a rotisserie is a fine thing to own. Meat
and poultry roasted this way are about the best. But it takes up a
lot of room and is heavy, so it should really stay in the place where
you use it, if possible. You can also broil in most rotisseries, but in
my opinion they do no better job in this respect than your range can
do.

54. Is an electric skillet a good buy? Most people who have them
would not be without them. The controlled heat is a great asset. If
you can afford to buy one, the only thing which should stop you is
not having room to store it.

55. What should one look for in buying an electric skillet? Be
sure that it is completely immersible for washing. It should have a
temperature chart to indicate the settings for various foods. It should
have an indicator light which goes out when the desired temperature
is reached, then goes on and off to maintain temperature. It should
have an adjustable steam vent in the cover. It should be well balanced.

56. Why does the outside of an electric skillet get discolored? This
is largely due to the "burning on" of grease vapors or drippings which
were not completely removed when the skillet was washed. Lots of
times this comes from grease in the dish water. The exterior of the
skillet, as well as the inside, should be thoroughly scoured after each
use with soap-filled steel-wool pads, then thoroughly rinsed and dried.
If this is not done, the grease is not removed, and the next time the

skillet is used it burns onto the outside of the skillet and becomes increasingly difficult to remove.

57. What should one look for in buying an electric coffee-maker? It should have balanced construction and be comfortable to hold and pour from. There should be a brew selector for making mild, medium, or strong coffee. The maker should keep the coffee at serving temperature when it is made. It should be easy to clean. The cup markings should be easily visible. It should have the safety feature of a cutoff control in case the coffee-maker runs dry.

58. Why does a toaster make bread too dark at the top? During baking certain breads dry out at the top. Try putting the slices in with the top down.

59. Why do waffles stick or break in an electric waffle baker? This can be caused by opening the baker before the waffle is done. Always wait for the light to go out before opening the baker. If you use a packaged mix or a recipe which does not call for shortening, add at least ¼ cup of melted shortening or oil, to prevent sticking. Use unsalted shortening to season grids. Do not wash the grids. Brush out crumbs, then wipe with a dry soft cloth or paper towel. Let the baker cool with the top up.

II. MENU PLANNING AND NUTRITION

60. In what order should one proceed when planning menus?
First, check your refrigerator to see what leftover foods might be incorporated into your plans. Then decide what else is needed to make them into tasty dishes. Check your newspapers and radio reports for plentiful foods. Read your cookbooks for inspiration. As you do all these things, make lists of foods needed. When you decide to make a specific recipe, list every ingredient required to prepare it. Then check your staple shelves and refrigerator to be sure you have all the items required. Now make your market list, including every staple and fresh food you require.

61. Is it a good idea to plan a week's meals in advance? Yes, if you leave leeway for changes due to unexpected factors, such as bargains in the market, last-minute guests, or last-minute invitations for yourself. It is perhaps easiest for the housewife with a large family to plan meals for a week because the number of people to be fed is relatively constant in her setup. In reverse, the woman or man who lives alone, unless a misanthrope, is likely to be invited out to dinner unexpectedly with frequency. Therefore, for her or for him, planning and marketing far ahead is likely to waste food.

62. Is it necessary to plan all three meals for each day, or only dinner? It is absolutely necessary to plan all three meals if you really expect your family to eat them. Breakfast is, for instance, an exceedingly important meal. It gives you the impetus for the morning's work, a right start for the day. Therefore, variety is important, to offer the essential appetite appeal. Though you may proceed for breakfast on the conventional plan of fruit, cereal or eggs, toast and coffee, the meal can be varied by serving different kinds of fruit in season; sometimes cold cereals, sometimes hot; cooking the eggs in different ways; serving them sometimes with bacon or sausage or scrapple; and offering muffins or coffee cake sometimes instead of toast, which can be varied itself if you provide different kinds of bread. Planning for lunch is equally important. To be sure, lunch offers a fine opportunity to use up leftovers, which make some of the best dishes in the world if combined and cooked properly. But you cannot always count on having leftovers, so you must be prepared at least with canned or frozen foods which you can produce for lunch at a moment's notice.

63. What is the best way to keep track of food bargains available? Most newspapers give excellent information on what foods are plentiful nationally and locally. Many big chain stores issue weekly fliers, listing bargains in canned goods and other produce. There are also often local radio programs which give such information. Learn all your local sources of food information and follow them carefully. It pays, both in easing the budget problem and in adding variety to your meals.

64. How can one avoid running out of staples? The best way I know is to keep a pad, fastened somewhere in the kitchen, on which you write down every staple you use, when you find it is dwindling. Only you can know whether in your house you should buy more flour if you have only five pounds left—or if you have only a cup (in some houses a cup might last weeks). But if you do keep this running list and check it every time you are making a market list, you should never run out of anything.

65. What should be included in a basic list of foods to consult for menu planning and shopping?

Check List of Meats

Beef

Corned beef
All-beef frankfurters
Ground beef
Pot roasts
Roasts
Steaks
Stews and ragouts
Short ribs

Veal

Chops: loin, kidney

Cutlet or steak
Leg or loin roast
Stew

Pork

Bacon
Butt
Canadian bacon
Chops: loin or shoulder
Frankfurters
Fresh ham
Smoked ham

Loin roast
Pig's feet or knuckles
Sausage meat
Sausage links
Smoked picnic ham
Spareribs

Lamb

Chops: rib, shoulder, or loin
Crown roast
Leg roast

Roast saddle Shoulder roast	*Kidneys*	*Heart*
	Beef	Beef
Liver	Lamb	Lamb
	Veal	Veal
Calf		Pig
Lamb	*Tongue*	
Beef	Beef	
Chicken	Veal	
Pork	Lamb	

Check List of Vegetables

Asparagus	Celery root	Peas
Artichokes	Collards	Peppers, sweet green or red
Beans, green	Corn	Sauerkraut
Beans, Lima	Cucumbers	Shallots
Beans, wax	Eggplant	Spinach
Beets	Kale	Squash, acorn
Broccoli	Kohlrabi	Squash, summer
Brussels sprouts	Leeks	Squash, winter
Cabbage, red	Mushrooms	Swiss chard
Cabbage, white	Okra	Tomatoes
Chinese cabbage	Onions	Turnips
Carrots	Oyster plant (Salsify)	Zucchini
Cauliflower	Parsley	
Celery	Parsnips	

Check List for Salads

Avocados	Lettuce:	Radishes
Chicory	bibb	Scallions
Dandelion	Boston	Sorrel
Endive	iceberg	Watercress
	romaine	

Check List of Potatoes and Other Starchy Foods

Beans, dried	Potatoes:	Macaroni
Hominy	white	Spaghetti
Lentils	sweet	Noodles
Peas, dried	yams	Cornmeal

Check List of Fruits

Apples	Grapes	Honeyballs	Pears
Apricots	Grapefruit	Honeydew	Pineapples
Bananas	Lemons	Persian	Plums
Blackberries	Limes	Spanish	Raspberries
Blueberries	Melon:	Watermelon	Rhubarb
Cherries	Cantaloupe	Nectarines	Strawberries
Cranberries	Casaba	Oranges	Tangerines
Figs	Crenshaw	Peaches	

66. Should one plan meals, course by course, in the sequence in which the food will be eaten?   No. It is best to plan away from the most important or the richest dish you intend to serve in a meal. This may be a first course, a main dish, a salad, or a dessert. To illustrate, here are four sample dinner menus. In each, the dish from which planning started is starred:

I

Cold Cream of Avocado Soup*
Broiled Chicken
Green Peas
Chiffonade Salad
Lemon Ice with Plain Cookies

II

Hot Clam Bouillon
Beef Stew in Red Wine with Vegetables*
Mashed Potatoes
Tossed Green Salad
Caramel Custard

III

Vichyssoise
Roast Leg of Lamb
Green Beans with Mushrooms
Salad Niçoise*
Coeur à la Crème with Strawberries

IV

California Salad
Sautéed Veal with Lemon
Hashed Brown Potatoes
Asparagus
Chocolate Bavarian Cream*

In Menu I the cold cream of avocado soup is made with cream which, added to the avocado, makes it exceedingly rich. All else is simple.

In Menu II the beef stew is rich and can be made richer by the serving of cold sour cream to put on top of it. Therefore the rest of the meal is quite plain.

In Menu III the salad niçoise is much more substantial than most and rich in its inclusion of ripe olives, anchovies, and tuna fish. Also, it might be pointed out that no potato dish is suggested because the vichyssoise contains potato.

In Menu IV the chocolate Bavarian cream is rich with cream and eggs and thus demands a light, uncluttered menu to precede it.

67. How can one avoid getting into ruts in menu planning?   One excellent way is to read cookbooks and find new and interesting recipes, then build the menu away from one of them. Try at least one new recipe a week, picked from your cookbooks, magazines, or newspapers. Never serve the same meal every Sunday—or every any-other-day! (When I was a child we had roast lamb for Sunday dinner one week and roast beef the next, all year long.) Keep track of the foods which are in season and liven your menus by including them. Use the check list of foods (see Question 65) to remind yourself of things you have not served in a long time which will add variety and interest to your menus.

68. What are the most important points to keep in mind in planning menus? Color, texture, nutritional values, variety, bulk, and attractive presentation.

69. Why is color important in menu planning? Because eye-appeal is closely related to appetite. A meal with foods all of one color, such as halibut in a cream sauce, mashed potato, and cauliflower, is uninviting. Change the sauce to Hollandaise, hash-brown the potatoes, and substitute brussels sprouts for the cauliflower—and while you have approximately the same food values and flavors, you have a far more appetizing and attractive meal. Also, if you are careful to vary the colors in a meal, you will almost undoubtedly make for nutritional balance.

70. Why is the texture of food important in menu planning? Because it is unappetizing to be confronted with a meal which is all soft, or all crisp, or all chewy, is it not? Steak gives you something to chew on. French fried potatoes are crisp if they are properly cooked. Peas are rather soft. The three go together beautifully, and part of the reason is the variation in texture.

71. Why is bulk a factor in menu planning? A meal must have some bulk in order to satisfy appetites. On the other hand, if your main course contains meat, macaroni and cheese, and a vegetable, it is perhaps best not to serve bread or rolls, on the premise that they would make the course too bulky. Also, because macaroni and cheese is so hearty and bulk-providing, it might be well to serve fruit for dessert—again, to keep the bulk down.

72. What specifics go into attractive presentation of food? Food should be arranged neatly on plates or platters. It should never look heaped or crowded. Hot food should be served on hot plates, cold food on chilled plates. Foods of clashing colors should not be served together, such as bright red tomatoes and purple beets.

73. How can one plan to use leftover foods? Every day before you prepare meals check the refrigerator to see what leftover foods are available. Then, perhaps, change the menu slightly in order to use them. No thrifty cook fails to use up every bit of food. And many of the best dishes ever made are concocted of leftover foods. One has to experiment a little to find which combinations of food are most acceptable to the family. Since leftovers are likely to come in small quantities, they must usually be combined with other foods to make a dish. One quickly learns that putting leftover beets into a casserole stains the whole dish dark red so that it does not present a very appetizing appearance. (However, beets are the one absolutely necessary ingredient for a chiffonade salad.) Also, strong-flavored foods, like those of the cabbage family, are likely to overwhelm any delicate foods with which they may be combined, so caution has to be exercised in their use. And speaking of planning in connection with leftovers, it is often a good idea to *plan to have them*. In other words, buy more than is needed of meat or fish or vegetables in order to have some left over. For instance, when you are having chicken fricassee, deliberately buy and cook too much chicken. You can use what is left over later in the week by combining it in a sauce with vegetables, covering it with pastry, and serving up a chicken pie—or do a thousand other things with it, as your imagination happens to dictate.

74. Is there any way to be absolutely sure of being able to feed unexpected guests? Yes, indeed. Have a shelf in a cupboard devoted to canned goods especially put there to serve in an emergency. Fasten to the inside of the cupboard door two or three menus, the ingredients for which are there on the shelf. There are many fine entrées in cans, which you can dress up by adding your own imaginative seasonings. Canned soups make wonderful sauces for various fish dishes, and why should not the fish be tuna or salmon straight from the can? You may not like all canned vegetables, but there are many good ones, so see that you have a supply of your favorites which fit well into your tacked-up menus. Canned fruit makes a fine dessert, but if you want to be ready for the fanciest contingency, have canned Crêpes Suzette on hand. They are exceedingly good.

Sample Emergency Menus with Canned Foods

I	II
Clear Consommé	Artichoke Hearts Vinaigrette
Casserole of Tuna Fish in Mushroom Sauce (made from soup)	Tamale Pie (made from corn muffin mix, canned meatballs, and canned corn)
Candied Sweet Potatoes	
Tiny Canned Peas	Tortillas (from can)
Baking Powder Biscuits (from mix)	
	Canned Pears Flambé
Hot Gingerbread (mix) with Apple-sauce	Cookies

75. How can the freezer help with emergency meals? You use the same system you do with your canned goods. Inside or outside your freezer, fasten two or three emergency menus, the ingredients for which you know to be in the freezer because you replace them every time you use them up. I would not suggest that you serve TV dinners to guests, however unexpected. But there are many fine foods which you can keep in your freezer for emergency meals of great elegance. Not, for instance, a roast of beef or a turkey, which take too long to defrost. But frozen lobster or crabmeat in a sauce which can start with a frozen soup and be enhanced by herbs and wine makes food fit for kings in a twinkling. Also, you can have "big cookings" and then freeze things like lasagna, creamed chicken, and many others, heat them up and enchant your guests with them in jig time.

Sample Emergency Menus with Frozen Foods

I	II
Chicken Consommé with Rice	Mixed Fruit Cup
Lobster in Sauce (based on frozen shrimp soup)	Lasagna
	Brown-and-Serve Italian Bread
Frozen Potato Patties	
Frozen Green Beans with Almonds	Ice Cream and Chocolate Cake
Brown-and-Serve French Bread	
Apple Turnovers (buy frozen) with Hard Sauce	

76. In serving emergency meals is it essential to have a salad? No, not if you serve a vegetable or vegetables. However, if yours is the type of family who does not regard a meal as complete without a salad, you will doubtless have the makings always in the refrigerator. If there are sufficient of these greens, you can add a salad to any emergency meal. Also, I take the liberty of supposing that you will have butter, milk, seasonings, and such staples on hand no matter how small your storage facilities may be.

77. How do you get all the dishes in one course finished at the same time? This difficulty is the one most common to all cooks, experienced as well as novice. It may have a lot to do with the original planning of the menu. When you plan a meal, keep in mind the number of top units on your range (and the number of oven dishes), to be sure that the meal does not require more than you possess, or something will have to be done at the last minute when the rest of the food is ready. You must also plan your work schedule. If the cookbook does not tell you, figure out how much time you must allow for the preparation of foods before cooking. As you begin to try to lick this problem, write down all the preparation time you must expect to use in readying the meal to be served. Write down also the cooking times for the dishes if, as is occasionally the case, the recipes do not tell you. For example:

Menu	Preparation	Cooking
Soup	10 minutes	10 minutes (then chill 2 hours)
Broiled Chicken	2–3 minutes	30–40 minutes
Green Peas	5–15 minutes	10–25 minutes
Chiffonade Salad	10–15 minutes	None
Dessert (buy and store)		

In this menu, as in many others, there are foods which must be prepared well ahead so that they may chill (the soup) or crisp (greens for the salad). In the timing for the actual cooking and putting together of the meal, an hour should see it all done expeditiously, including the setting of the table. If your peas are young and uniform in size, put them into the boiling water after the chicken has been in the broiler for 25 minutes. You are thus allowing time for draining them and dressing them with butter. If the chicken is done before 40 minutes is up, you can keep it warm (without drying it up) for whatever time is left before the peas are done.

78. Is it all right, in hot weather, to serve a whole meal of cold food?
No. Every meal should contain at least one hot dish. It may be only
a hot clear consommé at the start, or it may be a soufflé or a hot
berry pudding at the end. Remember that in the hottest countries
great quantities of not only hot, but hotly spiced, food are eaten, on
the theory that they make one feel cooler. Even in hot weather the
stomach is more comforted by hot food than by cold, though cold
dishes are appealing, too.

79. Is it wrong to serve more than one fried food in a meal? It is
not a good idea. First, it makes for monotony in texture. Second,
while fried foods may be delicious, they are not regarded as most
digestible, and so one at a time is best.

80. How much should I spend on food? The best way to calculate
is to allow so much per person per week. This is a figure which varies
quite widely. The cost of food has gone up astronomically during
the past couple of decades. So has average take-home pay. And so,
whereas there was a time when a great many families spent from
25 to 33 per cent of their income on food, the average percentage
is a good deal smaller now. Twenty years ago $5 per person per
week was an adequate budget for medium-cost food. Now it is very
low. Costs will probably continue to change, and probably upward.
Perhaps it would be safe to say that if you spend 25 per cent of income on food at present you ought to be serving your family quite a
lot of elegant treats. And remember, it is no harder to do adequately
by them nutritionally on inexpensive food than on the most expensive.

81. Is it possible to plan interesting meals on a small budget? Of
course it is. You may spend time instead of money—searching out
bargains, doing the long, slow type of cooking which makes inexpensive meats delectable, learning or inventing little touches which make
inexpensive foods of all sorts interesting. You may have to confine
your consumption of broiled foods to fish and chicken and your consumption of beef to stews and pot roasts. You may have to serve
more cabbage than asparagus (if any), but cabbage, properly cooked,
is a dish for the greatest gourmet. If you happen to be a housekeeper
who works for pay outside the home, you will probably have to do
most of your long, slow cooking jobs over the weekend when there

is time. You are lucky in this respect—stews and other meat dishes in sauce are usually only the better for being warmed over, so you can make them in quantity and freeze or refrigerate some for use later in the week.

82. Is it best to buy "large economy sizes" in canned, and sometimes frozen, foods? This depends largely on two things: the size of your family and the extent of your storage space. If there are sales of such items and yours is a large family, chances are you can find a place to store a case or whatever quantity you want to buy. If you are a single person, even the best of refrigerator space may not serve to keep the food in question fit for consumption for the time it will take you to eat it up. That constitutes no bargain!

83. What is impulse buying? It is what happens most often when the master of the house goes to the food market. If he has been given a good list, he may bring home everything on it. If he has no list, he may forget practically everything he was told to buy. *But,* in either case, impulse buying will lead him to throw the food budget completely askew, and he will come home with smoked oysters, caviar (red or black, depending on how strong his impulses are), fancy biscuits, too many kinds of beautiful cheeses, black olives as well as the stuffed ones Mother asked for, and so on and on! There are women who behave this way, too, but men are best at it and are therefore the darlings of food merchants.

84. Should a full-time housekeeper have to go to market every day? If you plan your meals for a week ahead, you should be able to do the bulk of your marketing on one day. Perishable foods and forgotten items (everybody has some of those) will have to be picked up at more frequent intervals, but daily visits to the market should not be necessary if you plan well.

85. Should a working person living alone shop for food daily? Since people living in such circumstances are more free than families to accept (and give) last-minute invitations, it is sometimes best for them to shop daily or almost daily in order not to waste food. This is governed somewhat by what freezing-compartment space is available. If you have that, you can keep always on hand the makings of a meal for one or two. You can do approximately the same thing with canned goods. Perishables are best bought at the last possible moment, no matter how you live.

86. What is the best time of day to go to market? If you are a full-time housewife, either as early in the morning as possible or between 12 and 2, when many people are having lunch. In either case you avoid crowds and can accomplish your job in a reasonable length of time without hurrying. You also help the working people who cannot shop at those times, by not adding to the crowds that appear at the end of the day or in the evening.

87. Is it better to shop in supermarkets, or in small independent stores? There is no one answer to this question. If you find it possible to keep careful track of where bargains are to be had, you will probably find them in both types of store. Often you can get standard foods at exactly the same price in a small independent store as in a supermarket—sometimes even for less. Both types have special sales. Some relatively expensive stores are worth using for special items. Some are expensive and not always to be relied upon. Some stores where merchandise is cheap offer goods of poor quality. However, if you shop in them carefully and in person, you may find real bargains.

88. Is shopping in supermarkets necessarily confusing? Only if you are basically disorganized. You should make a special kind of market list for such shopping, putting together in groups all canned goods, refrigerated foods, frozen foods, fresh fruits and vegetables, condiments, baked goods, seasonings, cleaning aids, and so forth. If you know your supermarket and thus are aware of approximately where each of these items is to be found, you can help yourself even more by writing down the foods in the order in which you will approach the various departments. No matter where they are situated, however, the refrigerated items should be picked up next to last and the frozen last of all.

89. Should one market by telephone? It is really much better to buy food in person if you possibly can. However, if you must save time rather than money, you will frequently have to order food by telephone. If that is the case with you, at least appear in your market often enough at the start so that you get to know the personnel—and they, you. You will thus establish the standard you require, and they will, by and large, do well by your telephone orders.

90. Does food cost more in a store which provides delivery service? Though you can sometimes get bargains in such stores, as in any other, in general the prices must be at least a little higher, since such service requires more personnel, takes more time, sometimes involves the expense of operating a truck. All this, naturally, has to be paid for by the customer. There are, also, some stores (usually small chains) which will send your food at a specific cost per delivery. This is the only instance in which you can tell exactly how much extra it costs you not to collect your food yourself.

91. Is it more expensive to shop in stores where you can have a charge account? Undoubtedly at least a little more, because such stores have to pay bookkeeping costs and cover occasional losses from bad accounts. For some people, however, it is worth the extra cost. People with children can send them to the store without involving them in the business of taking money and returning change. Working people can order and have foods delivered when they are away, without the necessity of having someone there to pay for them.

92. Is it advisable always to shop in the same food stores? It is nice, and in many ways advisable, to shop in stores where you become known. However, it is very foolish not to explore as many food stores as you can so that you do not miss new items and bargains. There is never *one* store which has all of them.

93. Is it best to buy meat from an independent butcher? Though not everyone will agree with me, I think it is very definitely best. I have an absolute horror of the pre-packaged meats in refrigerated chests. Chops turn out not to be of the same size and thickness. The weight or number of items in a package is never exactly what I want. Besides, being friends with one's butcher is one of the great pleasures in life! Dealing with an independent butcher does not at all necessarily mean that you will pay more for your meat. This is again something worth exploring. Find a good butcher who is not expensive. Though it would be fine if all women knew all about cuts and grades of meat, it will be a long, cold day before they do, if ever. The butcher knows. He also learns quite quickly exactly the sort of thing you want. Furthermore, if you would really like to learn about meat and what to buy, your butcher, if you make good friends with him, is the best possible teacher.

94. How can one be sure to achieve nutritional balance in menu planning? By serving foods from each of the four basic groups set up by the National Research Council: (1) milk, cheese, ice cream; (2) meat, poultry, fish, eggs, dry beans and peas, nuts; (3) grain products; (4) vegetables and fruits.

95. How much of the milk, cheese, ice cream group should I serve my family daily? Milk: children: 3 to 4 cups; teenagers: 1 quart or more; adults: 2 or more cups; pregnant women: 1 quart or more; nursing mothers: 1½ quarts or more. On the basis of the calcium they contain, the following are equivalent to an 8-ounce cup of milk: Cheddar cheese, 1⅓ ounces; cream cheese, 1 pound; creamed cottage cheese, ¾ pound; ice cream, 1 pint. These foods may be used as alternates for part of the required milk.

96. Why is milk important in providing good nutrition? First, because it is our leading source of calcium. Further, because it also provides high-quality protein, riboflavin, vitamin A, and many other vitamins and minerals.

97. Is it possible to drink too much milk? Yes, if milk is consumed in such large amounts that it crowds out other essential foods from the diet.

98. What is the nutritional value of yoghurt? Yoghurt has the same food value as the milk from which it is made. When made from partially skimmed milk it has less fat, vitamin A, and calories than when it is made from whole milk.

99. How does low-fat cottage cheese differ in food value from creamed cottage cheese? Low-fat cottage cheese has very little fat and vitamin A. Creamed cottage cheese usually has about 5 per cent fat and therefore furnishes more calories and vitamin A.

100. How much of the meat, poultry, fish, eggs, dry beans and peas, and nuts group should I feed my family?   You should offer two or more servings of such foods daily, including at least one serving of meat, poultry, or fish. Serve each person at least three or four eggs a week. Offer one or two servings a week of dry beans, peas, lentils, soybeans, soya products, peanuts, peanut butter, other nuts.

101. What is the importance of meat, poultry, and fish in good nutrition?   They are important primarily for their high-quality protein. They also provide iron, thiamine, riboflavin, and niacin in varying amounts. Liver is an excellent source of vitamin A also.

102. Which is higher in food value, the liver from beef, pork, lamb, or calf?   All kinds of liver are prime sources of good-quality protein, iron, riboflavin, and niacin.

103. How does the protein content of peanut butter compare with that of meat?   Four tablespoons of peanut butter supply about the same amount of protein as two ounces of lean cooked meat without bone.

104. Is bread advertised as "high protein" a good substitute for meat? No. Many of the breads advertised as "high protein" contain very little more protein than ordinary bread. Four slices of ordinary white bread contain less than half as much protein as an average serving of lean meat (2 to 3 ounces, cooked). The protein in bread must be combined with some protein from foods of animal origin in order to provide all the amino acids needed by the body.

105. Why are eggs required for good nutrition?   They are a source of high-quality protein, iron, vitamin A, riboflavin, and vitamin D. They also provide some calcium and thiamine. (See Question 239.)

106. Do eggs contain as much iron as meat?   Yes. Equal quantities, by weight, of eggs and lean meat contribute about the same amount of iron.

107. Is there any difference in food value between dried and fresh eggs? There is practically no loss from the drying process, and when the dried eggs are reconstituted, they supply nutrients in about the same quantities as the fresh.

108. What is the importance of dry beans and peas and nuts in nutrition? They contain protein which is good but lower in quality than that of milk, meat, and eggs. They also furnish some calcium, iron, thiamine, riboflavin, and niacin.

109. Is there any difference in food value between green and yellow dried peas? Not much, if any.

110. How much of the grain products group should I feed my family? Offer four or more servings daily of bread and other baked goods made with flour or meal from any grain (wheat, corn, oats, buckwheat, rye); cooked or ready-to-eat cereals; rich, barley, hominy, noodles, or macaroni.

111. Why are grain products important in nutrition? Whole-grain products, or those enriched with added vitamins and minerals or restored to whole-grain value, provide significant amounts of iron, thiamine, riboflavin, and niacin. They also help out with protein and calories.

112. How much of the vegetables and fruits group should I feed my family? Offer four or more servings of vegetables and fruits daily. Of these, one or more daily should be citrus fruit or tomatoes, because they are such good sources of vitamin C. Some alternates for ½ cup of orange or grapefruit juice are 2 tangerines; 1¼ cups tomato juice; ½ medium-sized cantaloupe; ½ to ¾ cup fresh strawberries; 1 cup shredded raw cabbage; ½ cup broccoli or ¾ to 1 cup brussels sprouts or dark green leaves such as collards or kale, cooked briefly; ¾ medium green pepper.

You should serve, at least every other day, dark green and deep yellow vegetables such as broccoli, green peppers, greens of all kinds, carrots, pumpkin, winter squash, and sweet potatoes. Serve potatoes or an alternate once a day. Other vegetables and fruits may be used to fill the required four or more servings a day, but they should not be substituted for the citrus and tomato group or for the dark green and deep yellow vegetables.

113. Why are dark green and deep yellow vegetables important in nutrition?   Because they contain vitamin A, which is important to the young for growth and important at any age for normal vision. Vitamin A also helps guard against infection.

114. How do canned and frozen vegetables compare in nutritional value with their fresh equivalents?   Canned and frozen vegetables contain a high proportion of the nutrients originally present if they are prepared commercially or in the home by modern scientific methods.

115. Should vegetables be cooked covered to retain vitamins?   Covering the pan helps to retain some of the vitamins by making it possible to cook vegetables in only a little water. The percentage of water-soluble vitamins dissolved in the cooking liquid is less when a small amount of water is used.

116. How much loss is there when the liquid in canned vegetables is poured off?   Approximately a third of the vitamins and minerals go down the drain, which is why you are urged to save such liquid for use in soups or sauces.

117. Has white cabbage a lower food value than red?   Not necessarily. Some varieties of white cabbage have as much vitamin C (the main nutrient) as red cabbage. The amount present depends in part upon the conditions under which the vegetable has been stored and the length of storage time. The way it is cooked also affects the final value.

118. Why are potatoes important in nutrition?   Because they contain fair amounts of a number of nutrients and can become a quite important source of vitamin C if eaten in sufficient quantity.

119. What makes citrus fruit and tomatoes important in nutrition? The fact that they are rich in vitamin C or ascorbic acid. Body tissues cannot keep in good condition without it. The body cannot store this vitamin, which is why it must be taken daily.

120. Is there as much food value in canned grapefruit sections as there is in fresh grapefruit? Grapefruit, like all citrus fruit, is a stable source of vitamin C. Only small losses occur in canning and during the usual storage periods.

121. Have fresh oranges values that are lost in frozen, condensed orange juice and canned orange juice? Canning and freezing methods now in use cause very little loss. Even vitamin C, which is usually destroyed more quickly than other nutrients, is remarkably stable in these products. The canned juice may lose up to a fifth of its original vitamin C content after long storage at room temperature.

122. How many vitamins are there? There have been about twenty discovered, and there are probably many more, which we consume and which do us good, about which we know nothing. They will undoubtedly be discovered as time goes on, because food scientists are constantly working in this area. For that reason, it pays to keep up with new knowledge in the field, but not to do too much self-prescribing and not to panic when one realizes how vast are the unexplored areas in this field. We have learned a lot. We shall learn a lot more.

123. Why are vitamins essential? Vitamins, although they are required in minute amounts, are essential for growth and reproduction; formation of antibodies; coagulation of the blood; resistance to infection; formation of intercellular substances; and integrity of bones, teeth, skin, blood, and nervous tissue. They also function as coenzymes for innumerable chemical reactions concerned with the metabolism of food, on which the nutrition of the body depends.

124. Should people take vitamins to supplement those they get in their food? The best answer I can make to that is to tell the story of my saying to my doctor once, "If you eat properly, you don't need to take vitamins." He answered: "And who, do you think, eats properly?" Good question! However, if you eat a good variety of well-prepared food, you are likely to do very well, except possibly regarding vitamin D. If, for any reason, you feel that you need to supplement your vitamin intake with pills, ask your doctor whether he thinks so too, and if so, what you should take. Certainly *never* take vitamins *instead* of food!

125. How many calories a day should people consume?   This varies greatly with age, sex, and body build, also with the kind of life people lead—active or sedentary. If you are in any doubt about the number of calories any member of your family should be getting, consult your doctor.

126. What can we eat to give us protein and few calories?   Good sources of protein, relatively low in fat, are skim milk, cottage cheese, eggs, lean meat and fish, chicken, and turkey.

127. Which has more calories—butter or margarine?   As far as calories are concerned, fat is fat, and whether it be butter, margarine, vegetable oil or fat, olive oil, or any other, it contains the same amount of calories as the rest, 9 to a gram, our most concentrated source.

128. Is fat essential in the diet?   Yes. Some fat is necessary for good nutrition, according to our current knowledge. Fat is a concentrated source of calories. Some fats provide vitamins A and D and some are important as sources of essential fatty acids.

129. What is cholesterol?   A crystalline fatty alcohol found especially in nerve tissue, animal fats, blood, and bile.

130. Why is cholesterol harmful in the diet?   This is a highly technical question, to which, in this writer's opinion, the end answer has not yet been found. Those whom I regard as the best men and women in the field of nutrition will tell you that we do not yet know about the effect that cholesterol taken into the body as food has on that body. Bodies make their own cholesterol as well, and the relationship between what the body makes and what it absorbs is still not fully known. There is, however, a strong suspicion, which may in the end prove true, that high cholesterol in the blood has a distinct relationship to the incidence of coronary heart disease. Until the complete story is told, I suggest strongly that you follow your doctor's advice in this area and that you do not allow yourself to become frightened or hypochondriac because of reading stories of extremist theories regarding the matter of cholesterol, which exist even among medical men.

131. Is it possible to cut down the amount of fat used in cooking and still prepare tasty food? Of course it is. Americans use altogether too much fat, by any standard, and if we used half as much in our cooking, our food would be interesting and good to eat. Perhaps you must be more meticulous in your other seasoning if you cut down on fats, but it can be done with no great loss of flavor. However, remember never to cut fat out entirely, unless for some reason your doctor has so prescribed for some member of your family.

132. What is the food value of molasses? Molasses is a concentrated sugar food. Its value in the diet is chiefly for its flavor and for the taste variety it provides. The content of iron and calcium is high, especially in the darker kinds, but because molasses is generally used in small quantities it does not make an important contribution to the ordinary diet.

133. Is there a difference between cane sugar and beet sugar? No. These sugars have the same chemical composition though they come from different sources. The granulated sugar you buy in the store is practically pure sucrose, whether it comes from beet or cane.

134. Has monosodium glutamate any food value? It is used only to emphasize flavor already present in a food, and the amounts consumed are too small to make any worthwhile contribution to the diet. However, MSG is one of the more concentrated sources of sodium and should not appear in low-salt or salt-free diets.

135. Is it possible to make food palatable for a person on a low-sodium diet? It is not easy, which you know if you have been, or tried to feed, a person requiring such a diet. The lack of salt when you are accustomed to it, is a great deprivation. Some people never become resigned to it. Others, however, do. That is usually because there are agreeable ways of seasoning their food with herbs and spices, which are free of sodium. Garlic, onion, pepper, vinegar, and lemon juice are also very helpful. So are salt-free fats, used as seasonings for these diets. And, of course, some people (like me) prefer sweet butter in any case! In cooking for a special diet you should always consult the patient's doctor to learn exactly what foods and seasonings are permitted before you start planning inventions to tempt his palate.

136. Are onions and parsley blood builders? Foods which are good sources of iron or of high-grade protein improve the quality of the blood. Onions provide little of either of these nutrients. Parsley is a good source of iron, but is not likely to be eaten in sufficient quantity to supply the body with a significant amount.

137. Has rhubarb any nutritive value? Rhubarb offers small amounts of several nutrients, including vitamins A and C and the minerals calcium, phosphorus, and iron. There is calcium present also, but it may not be available to the body, as it may be bound by the oxalic acid which is present in the fruit.

138. What is wheat germ? A part of the kernel called the embryo, from which the new plant starts its growth. It is a concentrated source of protein, iron, vitamin E, and the B vitamins. Its nutritional significance in the ordinary diet is limited because such small amounts are eaten, alone or combined with other foods.

139. What is "royal jelly"? Has it any value in nutrition? It is a substance from the salivary glands of bees and is fed by worker bees to the queen bee. No important nutrient has been reported to be present in "royal jelly" that cannot be obtained readily from ordinary foods we eat customarily. Some food faddists claim that "royal jelly" has special health values for human beings, but there is no scientific basis for such claims.

140. Are carbonated beverages good for children? The nutritive value lies largely in their sugar and calories. If children drink too many of them, their diets may be deficient in necessary nutrients.

141. Does beer furnish any nutrients? Beer furnishes calories and very small amounts of some nutrients. The amounts of minerals and vitamins present are too small to be important in an ordinary diet.

III. SOUPS AND CHOWDERS

142. Is there any objection to using canned and dehydrated soups?
Not at all—and it would be futile if there were, since over 90 per cent of the soup consumed in our homes is one or the other. My only caution would be to be sure to add seasonings, toppings, or whatever you feel will enhance and improve the taste. Remember that most foods prepared with the public taste in mind are under-seasoned, rather than over-seasoned. Try combining two canned or dehydrated soups for new and interesting flavors, diluting the cream ones with either milk or light cream, rather than water.

143. How do you make soup from the carcass of roast poultry?
Put the bones, with a little meat clinging to them, into a big pot, cover with cold water, bring to the boil, skim, then simmer for an hour. Now add onion, celery, carrots, and seasonings and simmer for another hour or more. Strain. Before serving, remove fat (it can be kept for cooking) from the top. This is good to serve as a first course, or for use in other soups and sauces.

144. How do you clarify broth?   See Glossary (page 2).

145. What is Scotch Broth?   A broth made from lamb and vegetables.

146. What is Cock-a-Leekie?   A Scottish soup of chicken and leeks.

147. What is a Bisque?   The term originally was applied only to seafood soups, such as lobster and crayfish. It is now given to any creamed soup, including tomato.

148. What are fruit soups?   They are made from dried or fresh fruit and originated in the Scandinavian countries, where they are served either as the main course of a luncheon or supper or for dessert with whipped cream. They have never been very popular in this country. I think this is perhaps because when we have tried serving them at all, we have offered them as a first course, as we would any soup.

149. What is Philadelphia Pepperpot? A soup made from tripe and vegetables, highly seasoned with pepper (and sometimes a touch of Tabasco).

150. What is Minestrone? It is an Italian soup of good strong stock, vegetables, pasta, and sometimes meat, sometimes not.

151. What is Pot-au-Feu? This is a homemade soup containing meat and vegetables, which is simmered long and slow. In French households there is always a pot of it on the back of the range. The soup and its contents are served separately, as two courses. The liquid is also used as stock for various sauces.

152. What is Borsht? A beet soup, Russian in origin, served hot or cold, either with sour cream beaten into it or placed on top. In Russia cold borsht is often served accompanied by a hot boiled potato.

153. What is Consommé Bellevue? Half hot chicken consommé and half hot clam broth, combined and served topped with a dab of salted whipped cream.

154. What is Consommé Double? It is rich beef or chicken consommé which has been boiled down ("reduced") to half its original quantity, thus doubling its strength.

155. What is a Consommé Printanière? Consommé containing a mixture of cooked spring vegetables.

156. What is Consommé à la Reine? Chicken consommé thickened with tapioca or with egg yolks and heavy cream, sometimes with rice added, sometimes not.

157. What is Consommé Royale? Hot consommé served with diced or fancy-cut custard royale floating in it. (See Question 158.)

158. What is Custard Royale? A baked custard made with eggs and beef stock. Chilled, it is cut into fancy shapes or diced and used as a garnish for consommé.

159. What is Madrilène? A clear chicken consommé with tomato pulp cooked in it, served icy cold and jellied.

160. What is Mulligatawny Soup? A chicken consommé, flavored to taste with curry and containing pieces of chicken. It is served over hot rice.

161. What is Petite Marmite? Consommé containing meat and vegetables, and sometimes with chicken added. This is served in individual casseroles or "marmites," accompanied by toast or rusks, which are sometimes spread with beef marrow. It may also be served with a piece of toasted French bread, sprinkled with grated Parmesan cheese, and run under the broiler to brown.

162. What is the soup called Purée Crécy? A purée of carrot soup, sometimes with rice or tapioca added. Any dish with the name Crécy in it is either made of, or garnished with, carrots.

163. What is Potage St. Germain? Green pea soup. Whenever the title of a dish contains the designation St. Germain you may be sure that it has peas involved in it somehow.

164. What is Purée Mongole? It is soup made of split peas cooked with a ham bone and other vegetables, in particular lots of tomatoes —or by combining canned cream of pea soup with canned cream of tomato, thinned to taste with stock and cream.

165. What is Snert? The Dutch pea soup, which is the best in the world. It is made of split peas cooked for hours with pork knuckle, shin beef, and fresh bacon. It is served with slices of smoked sausage floating on top.

166. What is Boula-Boula Soup? This designation is incorrect. The soup was originally called Boula Soup and has nothing to do with Yale University so far as we know. It is half cream of pea soup, half green turtle consommé, mixed well, heated, put into individual flameproof casseroles, topped with salted whipped cream, and run under the broiler to brown.

167. What is Snapper Soup? It is an invention of Philadelphia, where snapping turtles abound, made with the turtle, many vegetables, a veal knuckle, and fine seasonings, including sherry. In most parts of the United States it is impossible to make this soup at home, lacking the snapping turtles, but it can be obtained in cans in specialty food shops and is very, very good.

168. What is a chowder? The old French word for cauldron was chaudière. Vegetables or fish stewed in a cauldron thus became known as chowders in English-speaking nations—a corruption of the name of the pot in which they were cooked.

169. What is New England Clam Chowder? A chowder made from clams, potatoes, onion, salt pork, and milk. The only proper clam chowder.

170. What is Manhattan Clam Chowder? A sort of vegetable soup, containing plenty of tomatoes (or sometimes just their juice) and a few clams.

171. What is a Bouillabaise? A Mediterranean fisherman's soup which contains at least six different kinds of fish and usually some shellfish in the shell, though the latter is not essential. This is indeed a meal in a dish.

172. What is Creole Gumbo? A soup which originated in New Orleans, and which is a meal in a dish. It may be based on chicken or on seafood (usually crabs and shrimp) and contains vegetables and either okra or filé powder (sassafras). It is dark brown and rich and is served over hot rice.

173. What is Billi Bi? A cream of mussels soup, which is served hot or cold, and despite its ridiculous name is delectable.

174. What is Gazpacho? A cold Spanish soup made of tomatoes, well seasoned with garlic and vinegar. It is served with a lump of ice in the middle of the soup plate. Chopped green peppers, tomato, cucumber, and toasted croutons are provided for sprinkling over the top.

175. What is Vichyssoise? It is cold leek and potato soup, cooked with chicken stock, puréed, then blended with cream and served chilled, topped with minced chives. This soup was invented by Louis Diat of the Ritz Carlton Hotel in New York.

176. What is Cold Cream Senegalese? A cold, curried cream of chicken soup with finely chopped cooked white meat of chicken in it.

177. What is Won Ton Soup? Won ton is the Chinese original of ravioli—little dumplings stuffed with pork and/or shrimp and seasonings. In won ton soup they are then cooked in boiling water and served in hot chicken consommé, which usually contains also a bit of spinach and/or Chinese cabbage.

178. What is Shark's Fin Soup? It is clear chicken broth with soft, transparent shark's fin in it and one of the most delicious soups ever invented (it is Chinese). Shark's fins may be obtained in any Chinatown and are very expensive.

179. Is Bird's Nest Soup really made from birds' nests? Yes. The nests are made by swifts on islands in the South Seas and the edible part is a gelatinous substance which has to be very carefully cleaned, but is worth all the work and the cost, as it has a delicate, distinctive flavor which is like nothing else in the world. It is cooked in a chicken broth to make the soup.

IV. MILK, BUTTER, CHEESE, AND EGGS

180. What is raw milk?   Milk in its natural state without any treatment other than cooling.

181. What is pasteurized milk?   Pasteurized milk is raw milk which has been subjected to temperatures no lower than 143° F. for not less than 30 minutes, or to 161° for not less than 15 seconds. It is then promptly cooled to 50° or lower. This process destroys undesirable bacteria.

182. How is milk homogenized?   Milk is homogenized by a mechanical process which breaks up the fat into small particles and distributes them throughout the milk. Cream does not form in homogenized milk, because the fat particles do not rise to the top of the milk.

183. What is skim milk?   Skim milk is raw milk from which most of the fat has been removed. It is then usually pasteurized.

184. What is non-fat dry milk?   A powder resulting from the removal of fat and water from whole milk. It contains other food values in the same relative proportions as fresh milk.

185. What is buttermilk?   In churning milk or cream (sweet or sour) to make butter, the liquid which remains when the fat is removed is called buttermilk. *Cultured* buttermilk is a soured product obtained by treating pasteurized skimmed or partially skimmed milk with a culture of lactic acid bacteria.

186. What is clabber?   Clabber is milk that has soured to the stage where a firm curd has been formed, but not to the point of separation of the whey.

187. If you need sour milk for a recipe, can you make it quickly?
Yes. Milk can be soured artificially by adding 1 tablespoon of lemon juice or vinegar to a cup of milk.

188. What is condensed milk?   Whole milk from which about half the water has been evaporated, with cane or corn sugar added. It is sealed in cans and sterilized.

189. What is evaporated milk?   Whole milk from which about 60 per cent of the water has been removed under vacuum at temperatures below boiling. It is homogenized to distribute fat globules evenly, sealed in cans, and sterilized.

190. Is it safe to use lumpy evaporated milk?   Lumps in evaporated milk are formed by the solids settling during storage. The lumps do not harm the milk. Cans of evaporated milk can be shaken or turned at intervals during storage to prevent lumping.

191. How should milk be stored?   As soon as possible after fresh fluid milk is purchased or delivered the bottle or carton should be rinsed under cold running water, dried, and refrigerated promptly. The ideal temperature for storing milk is 40°, which is about that in most mechanical refrigerators.

Evaporated and condensed milk may be stored at room temperature until the container is opened. Then it should be refrigerated in the same way as fresh fluid milk.

Dry milks will keep for several months at room temperatures of 75° or lower, or they may be kept in the refrigerator. They should be stored in tightly covered containers to prevent moisture absorption, which causes off-flavors and makes reconstitution difficult.

192. Can the various forms of milk be used interchangeably in recipes?
This varies with the type of dish being prepared. For example:

1. Evaporated milk, even when it is diluted, makes a thicker white sauce than any other milk.

2. Fresh skim milk and nonfat dry milk, reconstituted, make the thinnest white sauce.

3. Whole milk makes a sauce that thickens more as it cools, because the fat in the milk becomes firm in cooling.

Thus you may wish to use more or less of which ever type of milk is on hand, depending upon the result you want to achieve.

193. What is yoghurt?   Yoghurt is a custard-like food made by fermenting partly evaporated milk with Bulgarian bacillus. It has a slightly acid taste. In the middle-Eastern countries where it is greatly used, yoghurt is made from buffalo milk and is very rich, quite unlike our pallid counterpart. (See Question 98.)

194. What are the types of sweet cream?

1. Light cream—for coffee and other table uses. Contains at least 18 per cent, but less than 30 per cent milk fat.

2. Medium cream—light whipping cream. Contains at least 30 per cent, but less than 36 per cent milk fat.

3. Heavy cream—whipping cream. Contains not less than 36 per cent milk fat, usually 36 to 40 per cent.

195. What is sour cream?

The sour cream we buy in the markets has been commercially soured and is thick, white, and creamy, only slightly tart in flavor. It is quite different from the sour cream used in Russia and other countries which have long cooked with it. That cream is soured naturally, has a really sour flavor, and is yellowish in color.

196. Why do sauces containing sour cream often crack?

Because they are cooked at too high a heat. Remove the sauce base from the heat and stir in sour cream smoothly. Just before serving, heat gently. *Do not boil.*

197. What is Crème Fraîche?

Crème fraîche, which is obtainable only in France, is cream in which lactic acids have been allowed to ferment naturally until the cream achieves a rather nutty flavor. It is not sour. The nearest we can come to it is to put a teaspoon of buttermilk into a cup of heavy cream and heat it to lukewarm, then let it stand at a temperature of at least 60° until it has thickened. Depending upon the weather, this may take six hours or a day and a half. It is usually served on fruits or fruit tarts.

198. What is Devonshire Cream?

Devonshire cream is made by allowing milk to stand for 6 to 12 hours or until cream rises to the top. Next, the pan is set over *very* low heat until the milk is quite hot, though it must never be allowed to boil. The more slowly this process can be accomplished the better will be the result. As soon as the milk is hot it should be put in a cool place for 24 hours. The thick cream is then skimmed off and stored in jars. It is usually served with fresh fruit.

199. What do United States butter grades mean?

A great deal.

They give you assurance that the butter has been tested by an experienced government butter grader. All butter bearing the United States grade shield is packaged by modern automatic machines in a plant approved by the government. All the plants are maintained in a sanitary manner.

1. Grade AA butter (93 score) has a fresh, pleasant aroma with a delicate, sweet flavor. The texture is smooth and creamy and it spreads well. It is made from high quality fresh sweet cream.

2. Grade A butter (92 score) is made from fresh cream and has good flavor. Although it rates second to AA, it is a fine product.

3. Grade B butter (90 score) is usually made from selected sour cream and is acceptable to many people, though it does not have the fresh flavor of the two top grades.

It seems absurd for consumers to buy ungraded butter, since they have no idea what they will get by way of flavor or quality, whereas if they buy graded butter they know precisely what the product will be.

200. What is sweet butter?　In the United States we have taken to calling unsalted butter "sweet butter." Technically, any butter made from sweet cream is sweet butter, but we use the term sweet as opposed to salty.

201. What is whipped butter?　Butter which has been beaten briskly with a bit of cream added so that it is light and fluffy and considerably increased in bulk.

202. How long can butter be stored in the refrigerator?　It should be used within two weeks of purchase.

203. How should butter be stored?　Butter should be tightly wrapped or put into a covered container in the coldest part of the refrigerator. Keep only as much butter in the butter keeper as is needed for immediate use.

204. Is it all right to keep some butter around at room temperature so it will spread easily?　It should not stand long thus, because exposure to heat and light hastens rancidity.

205. How do you clarify butter?　Melt butter over moderate heat. Skim off the foam and pour the melted butter into a bowl, leaving the milky residue in the bottom of the pan. This residue may be stirred into sauces to enrich them.

206. What is Beurre Noir?   To make beurre noir, clarify ¾ cup of butter and rinse out the pan. Put butter back in the pan, cook over moderate heat, and let it foam up. It will then begin to brown. When brown (not black), remove from heat and pour into another saucepan. Put into the first pan four tablespoons of vinegar or lemon juice and cook it down to one tablespoon. Stir into the browned butter. Add capers, if desired. Use on calves brains, or with broiled fish.

207. What is Beurre Manié?   Half butter, half flour, blended together into a paste and used to thicken sauces by beating it in, a little at a time, with a wire whisk. The liquid to which beurre manié is added should never be boiling.

208. What is Shrimp Butter?   Shells removed from cooked or uncooked shrimp are dried in the oven, then crushed as fine as possible, either in a mortar and pestle or in the blender. They are then added to melted butter in a double boiler, together with a little water, cooked 10 minutes, and strained through cheesecloth. The resultant product is refrigerated so that the butter separates from the liquid and hardens and can easily be lifted off the top for use in sauce, or whatever other dish you wish it for.

209. Is cheese government-graded?   The Dairy Division of the Agricultural Marketing Service, United States Department of Agriculture, offers voluntary inspection and grading services for Cheddar, Swiss, processed, and cottage cheese. However, you will probably have to hunt to find graded cheese, as few makers have taken advantage of the service, and it is not likely that many more will do so without greater consumer demand for the graded product.

210. What is natural cheese?   Most natural cheese is made by separating the milk solids from whole milk through curdling with rennet or bacterial culture or both. The curd is then separated from the whey by heating, stirring, and pressing. Occasionally both milk and cream are used, as is skimmed milk.

Cheeses are then formed into characteristic shapes and given a coat of wax or other protective covering. Then they are allowed to ripen, under conditions of controlled temperature and moisture, until they are ready to eat. In this country, being always in a hurry, we are sometimes inclined not to ripen cheese long enough. Still, we make many excellent ones, like our own original Cheddars, Liederkranz, and copies (in varying degrees of accuracy) of European cheeses.

211. What is processed cheese? It is a product made by mixing a variety of shredded natural cheeses and pasteurizing (heating) them so that no further ripening occurs. Such cheese often contains pimientos, fruits, vegetables, or meats. Most true lovers of natural cheeses regard the processed variety as a leathery abomination, the best part of whose flavor has been destroyed by the pasteurizing process.

There are also pasteurized processed cheese food and pasteurized processed cheese spread, made in much the same manner as processed cheese, but usually in different forms and shapes.

212. What is a ripened cheese? After a cheese has been made and shaped, it is given a protective coating or wrapping and kept at specific temperatures and humidity for varying times, depending upon variety, to ripen and thus reach full flavor and texture. In Europe this is often done in caves. In the United States artificial conditions, arranged to approximate those in caves, are maintained.

213. What is an unripened cheese? Unripened cheeses are those which are consumed soon after they are made. They are relatively high in moisture and most cannot be kept very long—like cottage cheese. Norwegian Gjetost, on the other hand, while it is an unripened cheese, has little moisture in it and may be kept for several weeks without damage to texture or flavor.

214. What are the various types of cheese? Cheeses are often divided into categories such as Cocktail or Appetizer Cheeses, Grating Cheeses, Dessert Cheeses, and Spreading Cheeses. When thus divided, most of them are interchangeable with other classifications, though one cannot grate Camembert, for instance, and it would be difficult to spread Romano.

215. What are the firm, ripened natural cheeses?

Name of Cheese	Place of Origin	Flavor	Consistency
Cheddar	England	Mild to very sharp	Firm and smooth
Caciocavallo Kaskaval Cashkavallo	Italy Rumania and Bulgaria Syria	Slightly salty with faintly nutty aftertaste	Firm
Edam	Netherlands	Mellow, full flavor; very like Gouda	Semisoft to firm; small holes; lower milkfat content than Gouda
Gouda	Netherlands	Mellow, full flavor; very like Edam	Semisoft to firm; small holes; higher milkfat content than Edam
Gruyère	Switzerland and France	Delicate, with a slight sweetness	Semisoft with tiny holes
Jack	United States	Mild to sharp	Firm and smooth
Nokkelost	Norway	Mellow, full flavor with caraway seed	Firm and smooth
Provolone	Italy	Mellow to sharp, smoky, salty	Firm and smooth
Swiss or Emmenthaler	Switzerland	Sweet, delicate	Firm, smooth with large round eyes which should glisten if the cheese is properly ripe
Vermont Sage	United States	Mellow with distinct sage flavor	Firm and smooth

Color	How Bought	Uses
Pale yellow to bright orange	Circular loaves and cuts therefrom by the pound	Appetizers, sandwiches, sauces, in hot dishes, for grating, with apple pie
White	By the pound, cut to order from a wheel	Appetizers, in cooking, for dessert with crackers
Yellow to orange; red wax coating	Cannonball shape. Sometimes in a crock with wine	For breakfast, as appetizer, for dessert with crackers
Yellow to orange; red wax coating	Round with flattened top and bottom	For breakfast, as appetizer, for dessert with crackers
White	Wheels	Appetizers, sandwiches, in cooked dishes such as Quiche Lorraine, for dessert with crackers
Pale yellow	By the pound from round loaves	Appetizers, cooking, for dessert with crackers
Orange	By the pound from rounds, flattened top and bottom	For breakfast, appetizers, for dessert with crackers
Creamy yellow interior, brown outside	Pear-shaped, long like sausage	Appetizers, in cooking, for dessert with crackers
Pale yellow	By the pound from big wheels	Sandwiches, in cooking (as for fondue), in sauces
Pale yellow with flecks of green	By the pound from round loaves	Appetizers, for dessert with crackers

216. What are the semisoft, ripened natural cheeses?

Name of Cheese	Place of Origin	Flavor	Consistency
Bel Paese	Italy	Domestic very mild; imported (much better) fairly robust	Medium firm, creamy
Brick	United States	Mild to strong	Semisoft to medium firm
Münster	Germany	Mild to strong, depending upon age and amount of caraway or anise which is sometimes added	Semisoft with many small holes
Oka	Canada	Aromatic; made by Trappist monks from secret method of the order which originated in France	Medium soft
Port du Salut	France	Superb mellow flavor; this is the original Trappist cheese	Soft, creamy, rather like the consistency of butter
Pont l'Évêque	France	Medium strong	Semisoft

217. What are the soft, ripened natural cheeses?

Name of Cheese	Place of Origin	Flavor	Consistency
Brie	France	Mild; very distinctive	Soft, smooth, slightly runny when exactly ripe
Camembert	France	Mild; distinctive flavor quite different from Brie	Soft, smooth, slightly runny when exactly ripe
Hablé Crème Chantilly	Sweden	Delicate, fresh, rich, unique	Soft, butter-like
Limburger	Belgium	Very strong and pungent; strong, unpleasant (to many) odor	Soft, smooth with small, irregular openings
Liederkranz	United States	Strong flavor and fairly strong odor, but not unpleasant	Soft, smooth

Color	How Bought	Uses
Creamy yellow interior; slightly gray or brownish surface, sometimes coated with yellow wax	Small wheel, foil wrapped, in a cardboard box	Appetizers; especially good with pears or other fruit for dessert
Creamy yellow	Brick-shaped loaf or cuts therefrom	Appetizers, sandwiches
Yellow interior; brick red surface	Circular cake or block	Appetizers, sandwiches, or in cooked dishes
Creamy yellow	Round wheel	Appetizers or dessert with crackers or fruit
Creamy yellow	Wheels and wedges	Appetizers or dessert with crackers or fruit
Golden	In box about 5″ square	Definitely a dessert cheese

Color	How Bought	Uses
Creamy yellow, edible thin brown and white crust	Round, about 1 inch thick, wrapped in transparent plastic	With crackers or fruit, as appetizer or dessert
Creamy pale yellow interior; edible thin white or gray-white crust	Either round, like Brie, or in small triangular wedges, foil-wrapped, six to a box	With crackers or fruit, as appetizer or dessert; also makes very rich soufflé
White	In wedge-shaped boxes of thin wood	With crackers, French bread, or toast, usually as dessert
Creamy white interior, reddish yellow surface	Rectangular package	With crackers or dark bread; especially good with beer
Creamy yellow interior; pale orange edible crust	Rectangular package	With crackers, French bread or toast, usually as dessert

218. What are the soft and firm unripened varieties of natural cheeses?

Name of Cheese	Place of Origin	Flavor	Consistency
Cottage, plain or creamed (also called pot or farmer cheese)	Unknown	Bland	Soft; large or small curd
Cream	United States	Bland	Soft and smooth
Neufchatel	France	Mild	Soft, smooth; has less milkfat than cream cheese
Feta	Greece	Slightly salty, a little sharp; made from sheep's milk	Soft; curd like cottage cheese
Ricotta	Italy	Bland	Soft; moist or dry; like cottage cheese
Gjetost	Norway	Sweet, like caramel; made from goat's milk	Firm, but not hard
Mozzarella	Italy	Mild	Slightly firm, plastic

219. What are the very hard ripened natural cheeses?

Name of Cheese	Place of Origin	Flavor	Consistency
Parmesan	Italy	When young, slightly sweet; when hard, a bit sharper	When young, soft enough to break; when hard, very dry
Romano	Italy	Sharp and tangy	When well aged, brittle
Sap Sago	Switzerland	Sharp, pungent with distinct flavor of clover	Hard

Color	How Bought	Uses
White to creamy	In round cardboard or plastic containers with lids	In salads, with fruits or vegetables, in sandwiches, dips, cheesecake, coeur à la crème, hot dishes with noodles, pastry
White	In 3- and 8-ounce packages, foil-wrapped	In salads, sandwiches, dips, cheesecake; with crackers and guava or other jelly
White	In 4- and 8-ounce packages	In salads, sandwiches, dips, cheesecake
White	By the pound or in cans	In appetizers, salads, cheese pie, omelets, for fried cheese
White	In pint and quart cardboard or plastic containers	In salads, appetizers, omelets, Italian pasta dishes, desserts
Brown	In paper-wrapped rectangles	Best with dark bread; should be cut paper-thin
Creamy white	Small, round, wrapped in transparent paper or plastic, sealed with metal clip	In hot sandwiches, pizzas, Italian pasta dishes, and casseroles

Color	How Bought	Uses
Creamy white with black rind	By the pound from a wheel	When young, with bread; when aged, grated and used in many hot dishes or sprinkled over soup
Yellowish-white with greenish-black rind	By the pound from rounds, flattened top and bottom	Grated in cooked dishes and as topping for soups
Light green	Small, truncated cone wrapped in paper	Grated; to be used with great discretion or it will overwhelm any cooked dish; often mixed with butter to make a spread

220. What are the blue-vein mold ripened natural cheeses?

Name of Cheese	Place of Origin	Flavor	Consistency
Blue or Bleu	France (Denmark also makes very fine Bleu)	Tangy, peppery	Semisoft; sometimes crumbly
Gorgonzola	Italy	Tangy, peppery	Semisoft; sometimes crumbly; lower moisture than Blue
Roquefort	France (Imported only; name may not be used for cheese made outside France)	Tangy, with very slightly sweet undertone	Semisoft; sometimes crumbly
Stilton	England	Piquant; milder than Gorgonzola or Roquefort	Semisoft, flaky; slightly more crumbly than Blue

221. Should cheese be kept in the refrigerator?   Yes, since few of us have places to keep cheese at 60° F., which is best for the moldy cheeses, such as Blue, Roquefort and Gorgonzola. However, any cheese should be removed from the refrigerator and brought to room temperature at least an hour before it is to be served, in order that it may return to the full flavor which refrigeration dulls.

222. Should cheese be kept in a container when refrigerated? Cheese stored in the refrigerator should be tightly wrapped to keep out air (Saran Wrap is especially good for this). Most ripened cheeses will keep several weeks thus. Hard cheese will keep indefinitely. Cheeses with strong odor, such as Limburger, should be stored tightly covered. Soft cheeses, such as cottage, cream, and Camembert, should be stored, tightly covered, in the coldest part of the refrigerator and used within five days of purchase.

223. Must cheese which has mold on the surface be thrown away? No, just scrape the mold off and use as you would ordinarily.

224. Will hard cheeses keep in grated form?   You will get much more and truer flavor if you grate cheese just before using it. How-

Color	How Bought	Uses
White, marbled with veins of blue mold	Large cylinders or cuts thereof, usually foil-wrapped	Appetizers, dips, salad dressings, sandwiches, for dessert with crackers
Creamy white, streaked with veins of blue-green mold	Cylinders or cuts thereof	Appetizers, dips, salad dressings, sandwiches, for dessert with crackers
White or creamy white, marbled with veins of blue mold	Large cylinders or cuts thereof, foil-wrapped	Appetizers, dips, salad dressings, spread on steaks, for dessert with crackers
Creamy white, marbled with veins of blue-green mold	Cylinders or cuts thereof; in crocks with wine or brandy	Appetizers, with salads, for dessert with crackers

ever, if you find you have grated too much, store it in a tightly covered glass jar in the refrigerator, and use it as soon as you can, for best flavor.

225. How much grated cheese does one pound make? Four to four and one-half cups.

226. Can you grate cheese in a blender? Yes. Put cubed cheese into blender, about ½ cup at a time. It will be "grated" in a few seconds.

227. Can cheese be cooked at a high heat? It should not be, since either high temperature or overcooking toughens cheese. Most cheese dishes should be cooked at low temperature over hot water or, if part of a casserole, in a low to moderate oven.

228. What is a Cheese Fondue? This Swiss dish, often called Fondue Neufchateloise, is made of Swiss cheese (preferably imported) melted in dry white wine and flavored with kirsch. It is kept bubbling hot over an alcohol flame, and is eaten by dipping into it small cubes of French bread impaled upon forks.

There is also an American cheese fondue, totally different in character. It is really a sort of cheese pudding, made with cubes of bread, grated Cheddar cheese, eggs, and seasonings and baked in the oven.

229. What are Cheese Blintzes? Thin pancakes, much like French crêpes, rolled around seasoned cottage cheese, then fried in butter until golden. They are usually served with sour cream to place on top and sugar to sprinkle over.

230. What is Fried Cheese? In Eastern Europe, slices of Swiss Emmenthaler cheese are cut about ¼ inch thick, dipped into a batter of egg, milk, flour, and seasonings and fried in butter over brisk heat so that they will brown before the cheese melts. This is a wonderful luncheon dish, served with a simple green salad.

231. What is a Welsh Rarebit? Often now (and I think wrongly) called a "rabbit," probably because of frequent mispronunciation, a Welsh rarebit is a mixture of melted Cheddar cheese, stale ale or beer, egg, and seasonings, stirred until smooth over hot, not boiling, water and served over buttered toast.

232. What type of cheese is best in a soufflé? This is a matter of taste. Some people prefer a good, sharp Cheddar, others like grated Swiss or a combination of Swiss and Parmesan. You can also make a lovely soufflé out of Rumanian Kaskaval—or, for that matter, any gratable cheese which suits your fancy.

The same variety of choice holds true for cheese omelets. (See Questions 257, 261, 262.)

233. Should cheese for a soufflé be diced or grated? It does not really matter, since it melts in the hot basic sauce. However, if you elect to dice it, it should be diced fine to avoid any possible lumping.

234. What is Coeur à la Crème? Well-whipped cottage cheese, mixed with heavy cream and a little sugar, is placed in a cheesecloth-lined, heart-shaped basket and left in the refrigerator over night so that the whey will drain off. The heart is unmolded onto a serving dish and served with fresh fruit and French bread as a dessert.

235. What is Liptauer Cheese? A mixture of cream cheese, sweet butter, chopped capers, anchovy paste, minced onion, sour cream, and seasonings, served chilled with crackers.

236. What are the egg grades? Grade AA, A, B, and C.

Grade AA, when broken, covers a small area. The yolk is firm and stands high. The thick white is large in quantity and stands high and firm around the yolk. There is a small amount of thin white. Especially desirable for cooking in the shell, poaching, frying, and scrambling.

Grade A, when broken, covers a moderate area. The yolk is round and stands high. The thick white is large in quantity and stands fairly well around the yolk. The thin white is small in amount. Especially desirable for cooking in the shell, poaching, frying, and scrambling.

Grade B, when broken, covers a wide area. The yolk is somewhat flattened. The thick white is medium in quantity and flattened. The thin white is medium in amount. Good for use in baking and general cooking with other ingredients.

Grade C, when broken, covers a very wide area. The yolk is very flat and breaks easily. There is very little thick white and a large amount of thin, watery white. Good for use in baking and general cooking with other ingredients.

237. Is it possible to buy eggs by weight? Unfortunately not, as a rule. Our recipes could be much more accurate if we could give egg quantities by weight, rather than by the egg. However, the following chart, which gives the Federal government standards for minimum weight of eggs per dozen in the various egg sizes, gives you a rough idea of what the eggs you buy will weigh.

Minimum Weight Per Dozen

Jumbo	30 ounces, or 1 pound, 14 ounces
Extra Large	27 ounces, or 1 pound, 11 ounces
Large	24 ounces, or 1 pound, 8 ounces
Medium	21 ounces, or 1 pound, 5 ounces
Small	18 ounces, or 1 pound, 2 ounces
Peewee	15 ounces

238. Have large eggs more food value than small ones? No. Weight for weight, the nutritive value and cooking performance of small eggs are equal to those of large eggs of the same quality grade. But because of their smaller size, the price per dozen is less than the price for the larger eggs.

For the same weight of eggs of the same grade:

Small eggs are as economical as Large ones when they cost no more than three-fourths as much as the Large ones.

Medium eggs are more economical than Large ones if they cost no more than seven-eights as much as the Large ones.

Extra Large eggs are cheaper than Large eggs when they cost no more than one-eighth more than the Large ones.

239. Is there any difference in the food value of brown and white eggs? Some breeds of poultry produce eggs with brown shells; others with white. Nutritive value and cooking performance of white and brown eggs of the same grade are identical.

240. Do blood spots in eggs make them unfit for use? Ordinarily the candling of eggs for quality eliminates those with blood spots, but if very small spots of this sort escape detection, they in no way affect the desirability of the egg for cooking.

241. Is there anything special about a double-yolked egg? Only that they are rather unusual. They come ordinarily from pullets coming into their laying period. If they cost more in your market, it is only because they are something of a curiosity.

242. Should eggs be refrigerated? Yes. They are refrigerated from farm to store and in retail stores. Thus, they should be refrigerated at once when they arrive in your kitchen. Since they should be lightly covered, the egg box makes a good refrigerator container. Or place them in the egg-keeper if your refrigerator contains one.

243. How long do eggs have to be out of the refrigerator to achieve room temperature, such as they should have for omelets? Remove the eggs from the refrigerator an hour or so ahead of using them so that they may achieve room temperature.

244. Can one freeze egg whites or yolks in the home freezer? Yes, they freeze beautifully and are most useful, the yolks for making Hollandaise or other sauces, the whites to add as that extra needed for making a good soufflé. For the latter, if the whites from separated eggs are at room temperature, you can throw in the frozen egg white, and as soon as it is defrosted it whips perfectly with the other whites. Many cooks freeze egg whites in the little plastic containers intended for ice cubes. Each holds an average egg white.

245. Are frozen eggs used like fresh eggs in cooking? Frozen eggs can be measured after thawing and used in place of fresh eggs, thus:
  3 tablespoons thawed frozen whole egg—1 whole fresh egg
  2 tablespoons thawed frozen egg white—1 fresh egg white
  ⅓ tablespoon thawed frozen egg yolk—1 fresh egg yolk

246. What is the best way to break an egg? Hold the egg firmly between the thumb and fingers. Tap the egg sharply at the center, midway between the large and small ends, to break through the shell. Tap on the edge of a bowl or other utensil, or tap it with a knife blade. Hold egg in both hands over bowl or cup, with thumbs on each side of the crack. Turn egg so that cracked side is toward you. Pull thumbs away from each other, spreading the break in the shell so that it breaks into halves. At the same time turn the shell halves open-side down carefully and let the egg slip into the utensil.

247. How do you separate an egg? Have ready a bowl for the whites and one for the yolks. Follow directions for breaking an egg (see Question 246) up to the point of pulling the egg shell apart. As the halves separate, rock the yolk into one half and let the white begin to pour into the bowl. Keep rocking the yolk back and forth, using the edge of whichever half is empty to help cut the white away from the shell in which the yolk is reposing, until all of the white is in the bowl. Drop yolk into second bowl.

248. What do you do if some of the yolk gets into the whites when you are separating eggs? Carefully remove the yolk, either with a teaspoon or with the edge of an egg shell. Egg whites will not whip properly if there is any yolk in them.

249. How many eggs, egg yolks, or egg whites make a cup?

To Fill a Standard 1-cup Measure (8 fluid ounces)

	Extra Large	Large	Medium	Small
Whole eggs	4	5	6	7
Egg yolks	12	12–14	14–16	15–19
Egg whites	6	7–8	8–9	9–10

250. How do you add beaten egg yolks to a hot sauce?   Add about a cup of the sauce to the egg yolks, a spoonful at a time, beating constantly with a wire whisk. Return this mixture to the sauce and stir well to incorporate. *Never* let a sauce come to the boil after the egg yolks have been added.

251. What is the best way to boil eggs?   The best way is *not to boil them.* You may have noticed that most recipes today refer to soft-*cooked* or hard-*cooked* eggs. The eggs should be placed in cold water to cover them, brought to the boil, removed from the heat, covered tightly, and allowed to stay in the water for the time it takes to get them to the consistency you like. As an approximate guide: the consistency of the old 3-minute "soft-boiled" egg is achieved by letting the egg stay in the water for 3½ to 4 minutes after removing from the heat. Hard-cooked eggs done by the same method are left in the water for 20 minutes, then placed under running, cold water to cool quickly. This way of cooking is also known as "coddling." It does not toughen the whites as boiling does.

252. What is poaching eggs?   Cooking in or over simmering water until they achieve the degree of doneness you like. The best way to keep them symmetrical *in* boiling water is to place metal rings (sometimes known as "muffin rings") in a skillet with enough salted water to cover the whites of the eggs. Break fresh eggs, one by one, into a cup and slip each one carefully into one of the rings. Be sure that the water is simmering gently—never boiling. (If you cannot find muffin rings, take both top and bottom from deviled ham cans and use the rings thus made.)

Eggs may also be poached in a "poacher." This consists of a good-sized pan with a rack into which several small round pans are fitted. Water is brought to the simmer in the larger pan. A bit of butter is melted in each little pan to prevent sticking, then an egg is slipped into each. The poacher is covered and the eggs cooked to the desired doneness. This method glazes the yolks over with steam, so that they are not as handsome as those poached directly in water.

253. How should eggs be fried? This is largely a matter of taste. They should be broken, one by one, into a cup and slid gently into a skillet containing about half a tablespoonful of fat (usually butter or bacon fat) per egg. They are then cooked over gentle heat, basted occasionally with the fat or not, as preferred, until they are done to taste. If served at this point they are "sunny side up." If desired, the eggs may be turned over carefully and fried on the second side for whatever time suits your taste.

254. What is the best way to scramble eggs? There are various ways to scramble eggs. The one you choose will depend entirely upon your individual taste.

1. The simplest way to scramble eggs is to break them into a skillet in which there is about a teaspoonful of melted butter per egg. They are then stirred constantly with a fork over low heat until done to the consistency you like, which if you really care about eggs at all, will be soft and creamy. Season and serve at once.

2. Though many people regard it as a desecration and as the ruination of the eggs, sometimes they are broken into a bowl, beaten briefly, then mixed with about a teaspoonful of milk or cream per egg, seasoned and scrambled in butter. I happen to like Method 1 best, but these are good, too.

3. Eggs can also be scrambled in a double boiler. This is perhaps of especial interest to persons who can not have butter. The eggs are beaten lightly and seasoned, then put into the top of a double boiler over gently bubbling water. They need only to be stirred occasionally until they reach the desired consistency. The addition of a bit of butter makes this dish taste even better, but is not necessary.

255. What is a shirred egg? An egg (or two) broken into melted butter in an individual shallow baking dish (which the French call a "plat"), seasoned, and cooked for a minute over low heat on top of the range. A little melted butter is then poured over each egg and the cooking is finished in a moderate oven. Sometimes a couple of

cooked sausages or chicken livers or some crisp bacon are added to
the plate before it goes into the oven. Shirred eggs can also be started
as above in a little butter, then have a little cream or sauce added,
then be put into the oven.

256. What is a baked egg? Baked eggs are very much like shirred
eggs, except that their entire cooking is done in the oven, in sauces,
in hollowed-out tomato or sweet pepper shells, in nests of vegetables
or rice—either in individual ramekins or in a large, shallow baking
dish. One must be careful not to overcook them, and remember that
they go on cooking for a moment after they are removed from the
oven.

257. What are the essentials for making a good French omelet?
1. The eggs must be *fresh.*
2. The eggs should be at room temperature.
3. An omelet should be made with two or three eggs, never more.
A three-egg omelet will serve one as an entrée or two as a first course.
If you want to serve more people, simply make more omelets.
4. The eggs should be beaten with a fork, *lightly.*
5. The pan should be heated over medium heat to the degree that
a drop of water thrown on it bobs around and disappears fast. If
the pan smokes it is too hot. Cool it slightly by waving it in the air.
6. Put in one tablespoon of salted butter and spread it over the
bottom and sides of the pan with the back of a fork, being careful
not to scratch the pan. The heat should be kept at medium.
7. Instantly add your egg mixture and stir with fast circular mo-
tions, again with the *back* of a fork held in the right hand. Hold the
handle of your omelet pan with the left hand and shake the pan back
and forth as you stir. This is to make layers.
8. Spread the egg evenly over the pan, and let it stand a few seconds to set. Add filling, if any, tilt the pan, and roll the omelet up
with a fork, working gently and lightly.
9. During the rolling process, hold the handle of the omelet pan
with the palm of the left hand *up,* just the reverse of the way you
usually hold it. This makes it much easier to roll the omelet neatly
out of the tilted pan onto a plate.
10. The whole process of cooking the omelet should not take

more than a minute and a quarter. If it takes longer, you will not have made a good omelet.

11. Serve *at once!*

258. Should a French omelet be browned on the outside?   This is a matter of taste. French chefs, however, seldom allow these delicate omelets to brown at all. When finished they are golden yellow.

259. Should a proper French omelet be well cooked through?   It is usually soft in the middle and thus much more tender and delicate.

260. Should one use just salt and pepper to season an omelet?   Use salt and Tabasco, *not* pepper, which toughens the omelet. Mix the salt and Tabasco with the required amount of water (1½ teaspoons per egg) before adding to the beaten eggs.

261. What is used to fill an omelet?   Almost anything which strikes your fancy: vegetables, meat, seafood (all chopped fine), caviar, fresh herbs, grated cheese, all make delicious fillings. Whatever you use should be placed in a thin row on the third of the omelet farthest from the handle of the pan and thus covered by the last roll of the omelet before it goes onto the plate. If you want to add any kind of food in a sauce to an omelet, serve it on the side or over the omelet, not rolled inside.

262. Is it all right to add cheese, herbs, or other ingredients to the beaten eggs before making an omelet?   Certain ingredients, such as herbs or finely minced ham or spinach in very small quantity, may be put into the pan with the butter for a few seconds and sautéed lightly before the eggs are added to the pan. The rapid stirring incorporates these ingredients into the omelet itself. Cheese may then be sprinkled over the omelet before rolling. (See Question 232.)

263. Can any skillet be used to make an omelet?   No. You should have a special pan which is used for making omelets, *only*. It should have gently rounded sides with no line of demarcation between the sides and bottom. It may be made of cast iron, cast aluminum, or stainless steel.

264. How do you "season" an omelet pan? Heat a tablespoon of oil or butter in the pan slowly. Sprinkle in a little salt, and rub the pan well with a paper towel. If you have a brand new cast aluminum pan, first polish the inside of it with a soap-filled steel wool pad until the pan shines. Dry the pan and treat it with oil, or butter, and salt, as instructed above. Never wash it again.

265. Is it true that one should never wash an omelet pan? Yes. An omelet pan should be wiped out with paper toweling and *not washed*.

266. What makes an omelet stick to the pan? It will stick if you do not get the pan hot enough before adding your butter. It will also stick if you have washed the pan instead of wiping it out with paper toweling.

267. What is a soufflé omelet? It is an omelet in the preparation of which yolks and whites of eggs are separated. Yolks are beaten with seasonings, stiffly beaten whites then folded in. The omelet is cooked slowly on top of the range until puffed and browned on the bottom. It is then finished in the oven at 375° (until dry to the touch). This type of omelet is often made in an "omelet pan" which folds in the middle. It is frequently called a puffy or a fluffy omelet.

268. Is there more than one type of soufflé? Yes, there are two. First, there is the type which is made by folding beaten egg whites into a thick yolk mixture, to which may be added cheese, meat, vegetables, chocolate, liqueurs, what you will. This takes 35 to 40 minutes to bake in a 375° oven and is fairly solid all through. Second, there is the French dessert soufflé type which is made by combining egg yolks with sugar and flavoring (usually a liqueur), then folding in the beaten egg whites and baking in a 500° oven 12 to 15 minutes. This type is definitely wet in the center and feather light.

269. How can one be sure that a soufflé will rise properly?
1. Have the eggs at room temperature.
2. Add an extra egg white to all soufflés.
3. Beat egg whites until stiff but not dry.
4. Cool the yolk mixture at least slightly before folding in the whites.

5. Be sure to preheat the oven so that it has attained the right temperature before you are ready to put the soufflé in.
6. *Fold* the egg whites in gently. Never beat them into the yolk mixture. They should be pretty well incorporated, but it is not necessary, in fact not good, to mix them *thoroughly* with the yolk mixture.

270. What is a "collar" for a soufflé? A strip of brown paper or waxed paper placed around the top of a soufflé dish and rising about 2 inches above it. This is buttered. The soufflé mixture is then poured into the dish, coming just about to the top, and placed in the oven. Be sure the dish is small enough so the mixture will come to the top. When the soufflé rises, the collar keeps the top in shape. It is removed before serving the dish, and the results are spectacular. If you do not wish to bother about the collar, however, simply use a bigger dish in which your mixture comes not more than a quarter of an inch below the rim.

271. Does opening the oven door cause a soufflé to fall? No! That is an old superstition, and if you want to peek at a soufflé while it is cooking, go ahead. Do not leave the door open long and do not *slam* it shut.

272. What are Eggs Mollet? Eggs simmered in the shell in water just under the boiling point for six minutes, quickly cooled in cold water, and shelled. The white is set and the yolk runny. Eggs mollet are used in much the same way as poached eggs: in eggs Florentine, covered with a sauce or an aspic, et cetera.

273. What are Eggs Florentine? Raw eggs set in a shallow dish on a bed of chopped spinach, covered with a little Mornay sauce (see Question 723), and baked in a moderate oven for about 10 minutes. They are then removed, sprinkled with grated cheese and run under the broiler briefly to brown. If you make this dish with eggs mollet (see Question 272), simply eliminate the baking.

274. What is a Scotch Woodcock? Scrambled eggs flavored with sherry are served on pieces of toast spread with anchovy paste.

275. What are Eggs Benedict? A toasted half of English muffin is covered with a thin slice of ham, topped with a poached egg, and covered with Hollandaise sauce. Sometimes a slice of black truffle is placed on top, but this is not essential. Though invented, one understands, by a Mr. Benedict who, awaking with an awful hangover, instructed the chef of the old Waldorf Hotel in New York to combine in some fashion the only foods which appealed to him at the moment, and hence served at breakfast, eggs Benedict are usually served at luncheon or supper.

276. What makes a baked custard watery? Baked custards will "weep" if they are cooked too long or at too high temperature. Almost any baked custard served warm will "weep," but a good cold baked custard will be firm and smooth. Custard baked in a large dish should be done in a 350° oven for 30 to 40 minutes. Individual custards take less time. The best way to test for doneness is to insert a flat knife in the center of the custard. If it comes out clean, the custard is done.

277. What is a Quiche Lorraine? A cheese custard, with bits of bacon or ham in it, baked in a Pâte à Brisée crust (see Question 921). Fish, vegetables, whatever suits your fancy may be substituted for the ham or bacon.

V. MEATS

278. How can you tell good cuts of meat?   First, the USDA inspection stamp indicates that the meat comes from healthy animals and was slaughtered under exacting sanitary conditions. Second, the USDA grade stamps, in the shape of a shield, are a guide to quality.

Inspection stamp   Grade stamp

279. Is ground meat inspected?   Yes, and ground meat prepared in federal-government inspected establishments comes from wholesome carcasses and is prepared in a sanitary way.

280. How should meat be stored?   Cured and smoked meats may be stored in their original packages. Fresh meats should be in the coldest part of the refrigerator, loosely wrapped so that the meat may benefit from some circulation of air in the refrigerator. Ground meat should be used within one or two days of purchase. Roasts, chops, steaks, and cold cuts may be held three to five days. Leftover cooked meats and meat dishes should be used within one or two days.

281. How long will leftover gravy and broth keep in the refrigerator?   They are very perishable and should be kept, covered, in the refrigerator for not more than one or two days.

282. Should meat be washed before it is cooked?   Not as a rule. It is preferable to wipe meat with a damp cloth before cooking.

283. Should one use a meat thermometer?   It is unquestionably the surest way to check whether your meat has reached the degree of doneness you desire. Always be careful to insert it as near the center of the roast as possible, and *never* let its tip rest on bone, fat, or gristle.

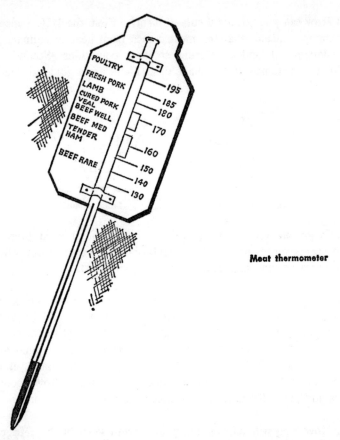

Meat thermometer

284. What is the object of a rack in a roasting pan?   It is to keep the meat up out of the drippings while roasting. Meat is easier to baste when held up by a rack. The best kind is a stainless steel one which can be adjusted to hold almost any size roast.

285. Should a roast be carved immediately upon being removed from the oven?   No. It should be allowed to stand outside the oven for at least 15 minutes to let the juices settle.

286. What goes into a meat loaf? Any ground meat or combination thereof which strikes your fancy. Many meat loaves combine beef and pork, sometimes with the addition of ground veal. Ground ham is delicious in a meat loaf. Most meat loaves add fresh bread crumbs, many use milk, some add an egg or eggs. Seasonings vary tremendously. I happen to think that a meat loaf cooked half way, then covered with more tomato ketchup than you would think possible, and the cooking finished, is the greatest of all.

287. What is a Cassoulet? It is a French dish consisting of dried beans and meats. It is made in many ways in different parts of France. The beans are usually white, and the meats may be any combination of pork, lamb, game, and sausages—or the whole lot. The ingredients are cooked, then put into a casserole, covered with crumbs, and baked.

288. What are the USDA grades for beef? Prime, Choice, Good, Standard, Commercial, and Utility. Prime and Choice are likely to contain more fat and to have better flavor than the other grades. The meat itself is well marbled with fat (streaks of it going through the lean, red meat).

289. Is Prime beef the best? Yes, but you are not likely to find it in many butcher shops. Most of it is bought up by hotels, clubs, and restaurants. So the best grade of beef most of us can buy is Choice, which is excellent meat. As a matter of fact, some people like it best, as it has not as much fat as prime beef has.

290. Why is fat in beef sometimes yellow and sometimes white? The color depends on the feed the animal has consumed. Cattle which eat a large proportion of grass get carotene in their fat, which gives it a yellow color. Cattle fed on grain have whiter fat. Their meat is of better quality.

291. How much beef should one buy per person to be served? One-third to one-half pound of boneless beef, ½ to ⅔ pound of beef with a small amount of bone, and 1 pound of beef with a lot of bone.

292. Should beef be removed from the refrigerator just before cooking? No. It should be brought to room temperature before cooking and should thus be removed from the refrigerator at least an hour before it is to be cooked.

293. What are the kinds of beek steak?   Porterhouse, rib, T-bone, filet mignon or tournedos, sirloin, pin-bone, and shell.

294. How thick should a steak be cut?   Never less than 2 inches and preferably 3 inches or more.

295. What is a filet mignon?   It is an individual slice of filet of beef, usually 2 to 2½ inches thick, which is broiled or sautéed. Although it is the most tender cut of beef, many do not think it has as much flavor as sirloin or porterhouse.

296. What are tournedos?   Exactly the same thing as filet mignon (see Question 295), though they are often cut not quite so thick as the latter.

297. What are Tournedos Rossini?   Sautéed tournedos are placed each on a hot artichoke bottom. On top of each is laid a warm slice of foie gras, topped with a slice of truffle. Over all is poured a sauce made from the juices of foie gras and truffle, with a little Madeira wine.

298. What is New York cut steak?   This is a designation used only in the Middle West and West. It is a porterhouse without the fillet. In New York it is called strip steak—*never* New York cut.

299. What is club steak?   It is a boneless cut from the end of the loin, or it can be cut from the rib, in which case the bone is left in.

300. What is Delmonico steak?   A boneless cut from the end of the loin. The same as club steak.

301. What is a minute steak?   It is a steak cut from the rib without bone, usually not more than an inch thick, but far easier to cook well if it is thicker—about 2 inches.

302. What is a planked steak?   A large steak is cooked as usual to

Beef Chart

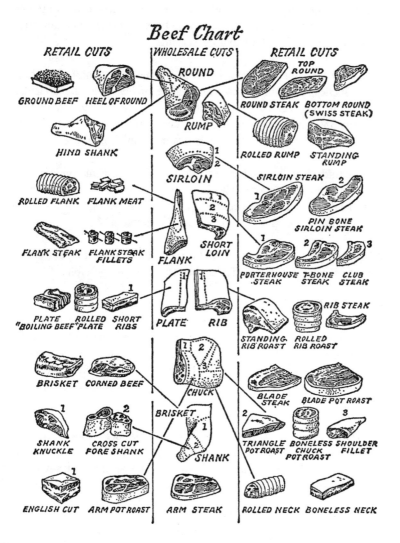

RETAIL CUTS — **WHOLESALE CUTS** — **RETAIL CUTS**

GROUND BEEF HEEL OF ROUND

ROUND

TOP ROUND ROUND STEAK BOTTOM ROUND (SWISS STEAK)

HIND SHANK

RUMP

ROLLED RUMP STANDING RUMP

ROLLED FLANK FLANK MEAT

SIRLOIN

1
2

SIRLOIN STEAK

2
1

PIN BONE SIRLOIN STEAK

FLANK STEAK FLANK STEAK FILLETS

FLANK

1
2
3

SHORT LOIN

1
2
3

PORTERHOUSE STEAK T-BONE STEAK CLUB STEAK

PLATE "BOILING BEEF" ROLLED PLATE SHORT RIBS

1

PLATE RIB

1
1

RIB STEAK

STANDING RIB ROAST ROLLED RIB ROAST

BRISKET CORNED BEEF

CHUCK

1
2
3

BLADE STEAK BLADE POT ROAST

SHANK KNUCKLE
1

CROSS CUT FORE SHANK
2

BRISKET

1
2

SHANK

2

3

TRIANGLE POT ROAST BONELESS CHUCK POT ROAST SHOULDER FILLET

ENGLISH CUT
1

ARM POT ROAST ARM STEAK

ROLLED NECK BONELESS NECK

the desired degree of doneness, then placed on a well-greased, heated plank and surrounded with rosettes of Duchesse potatoes. (See Question 619.) The whole is run under the broiler to brown the potatoes, then other vegetables, in as good a variety of colors as you can think of, are added to the plank before serving.

303. How far should a steak be from the heat for broiling? Three to five inches, depending upon the degree of heat and the doneness you wish to achieve. Sear on both sides at high heat, then reduce heat to about 350° and finish cooking. If done on an outdoor grill, sear close to coals, then move the coals lower to finish cooking.

304. Should steak be cooked well done? This is a matter of taste, but in my opinion anyone who cooks steak well done has no taste. It need not be blue in the center, but it should be rare—a condition of which there are many degrees. (See Question 414.)

305. How do you test to see whether a steak is done to your taste? Cut into it with a sharp knife as near the bone as possible.

306. What steaks are good for sautéing? Any steak that will fit into a skillet can be cooked this way—club, T-bone, porterhouse, rib, filet mignon, small sirloin. The French often use this method, melting a little butter or beef fat very hot, searing the steak on both sides, cooking it on each side for 3 or 4 minutes. With this method you lose none of the steak's juices. Steaks cooked this way should not be more than 1½ inches thick.

307. What sauces are good to serve with steak? Béarnaise, red or white wine sauce, a sauce of mushrooms with Madeira wine. But please, please, *never* tomato ketchup—and, if you can restrain yourself, not most of the bottled so-called steak sauces. (See Question 720.)

308. What is Steak Diane? Minute steak, pounded thin, and quickly sautéed, served with a sauce containing shallots, Worcestershire, mustard, stock, and other seasonings. It can be flambéed with cognac just before serving, if desired.

309. What is Steak Au Poivre? It is steak into which crushed pep-percorns in considerable quantity have been pressed before cooking. It is usually sautéed, but can be broiled.

310. What is Steak Bouquetière? It is a well-cooked steak, usually porterhouse or sirloin, surrounded by bouquets of vegetables in as many different but blending colors as possible.

311. What is Steak Roquefort? Butter and Roquefort cheese are mixed together and seasoned to taste. The steak is browned on one side, turned and spread on the brown side with the butter-cheese mixture, which melts into it as the second side browns. Blue cheese may be substituted for the Roquefort. It is, in my opinion, a sad thing to gild a perfectly good steak in this fashion, but many people love it.

312. What is Fondue Bourguignonne? The best filet of beef is cut into inch-square cubes and cooked in a mixture of bubbling hot oil and butter by each guest to suit his own taste. Several sauces are also presented for dipping the cooked bits of steak.

313. What is Beef Stroganoff? This dish should be made of fine filet of beef, cut into thin strips and cooked very quickly in butter, to which is added sour cream, seasonings, and, depending upon which school you join, tomato paste. There are those who consider the lat-ter a desecration. My recipe, which I obtained from a Russian years ago, calls for the tomato paste, and I like the result. The dish is cooked only long enough to warm the sauce through, and is served sprinkled with minced parsley.

314. What is London Broil? Flank steak broiled rare (3 to 4 min-utes on each side) and sliced on a very long diagonal. The meat must be of the best quality to be tender when cooked this way, and the proper slicing is of great importance.

315. What cut is used for Swiss Steak? Lean round or chuck. It is likely to be tough, so needs long slow cooking—usually braising.

316. What cuts of beef are good for roasting? A standing rib roast, a rolled rib roast, a sirloin roast, or a whole filet of beef. It is also possible to roast rolled rump if it is Prime or Choice meat, but it will not be as tender as the others. (See Question 413.)

317. If one has only two people to serve, is it all right to buy a one-rib roast?   It is not recommended. Small roasts are inclined to dry out. To get the best flavor buy at least a three-rib roast. If this is too much meat for your purpose, roast a filet of beef, or a part thereof.

318. What is Filet of Beef Wellington?   It is a filet of beef roasted very rare, spread with pâté de foie gras, covered with pastry, and baked in a hot oven until the pastry is done. It is usually served with a Sauce Perigourdine. (See Question 721.)

319. Can I roast a round of beef?   You can, but it is not recommended. It contains a considerable amount of connective tissue and is therefore not likely to be tender. It is better to braise this cut, as in stew or pot roast. (See Question 415.)

320. How do you tell a blade roast from a chuck roast of beef?   A blade roast comes from the rib end of the chuck. It contains a section of the shoulder blade and portions of rib bones. There is also an arm roast which comes from the lower part of the chuck. It is distinguished by the cross section of round shank bone which appears in it.

321. What is the best cut to buy for boiled beef?   Rump, brisket, or round. Many people prefer the brisket because it has a good deal of fat, which gives added flavor and can be cut off before serving.

322. What cuts of beef are best for braising?   Chuck, top or bottom round, rump, heel of the round, brisket, short ribs, flank steak, and plate are all good for braising and are best cooked that way. (See Question 415.)

323. What is Boeuf à la Mode?   It is a pot roast of beef rump or chuck, marinated in red wine, browned, then cooked in the reduced marinade with veal bone, calf's foot, and beef stock. This dish is customarily served garnished with cooked carrots and onions. Boeuf à la Mode is also often served cold and is particularly good, as the sauce jells when cold.

324. What is a Yankee Pot Roast? In the part of the United States where "Yankees" live it is called Pot Roast with Vegetables. Carrots, potatoes, turnips, and onions are added toward the end of cooking a pot roast and are served surrounding the meat.

325. What is Sauerbraten? A German pot roast of chuck, marinated for two or three days in vinegar, sugar, and spices, then cooked like any other pot roast, using the marinade as part of the liquid.

326. What is a Carbonnade of Beef? It is a dish made of slices of browned chuck, alternating with slightly browned onions, cooked long and slow in beer.

327. What are Beef Birds? Thin, well-pounded slices of beef are covered with a well-seasoned meat stuffing, rolled and secured with string or toothpicks. They are then browned and cooked long and slow with wine, stock, seasonings, and sometimes vegetables.

328. What is Boeuf Bourguignonne? It is a stew made from good-sized chunks of chuck, cooked in red Burgundy wine with vegetables. (See Question 415.)

329. What is Hungarian Goulash? It is a stew of many, many variations. Usually made of beef, it also sometimes contains pork. Often, but not always, it has sour cream added at the end of the cooking. Occasionally it contains sauerkraut or other vegetables. (See Question 415.)

330. What is Stifaido? A Greek stew of beef round cut into chunks, cooked with onions, garlic, tomatoes, and white wine. (See Question 415.)

331. What is Hotchpotch? It is a Netherlands dish, to be found almost everywhere in the country, but particularly famous in Leyden, where it is always served to celebrate the lifting of the siege of Leyden, at which time it was given to the starving populace. Hotchpotch consists of flank steak, carrots, onions, and potatoes. At the end of the cooking, the vegetables are mashed and served on top of the meat with the cooking liquor as a sauce—not very exciting, but substantial.

332. What is the best cut for ground beef?   Round or chuck, and have it ground when you order it.

333. What cut goes into the hamburger you buy ready-ground?   You have absolutely no way of telling, and while the law says there can be only 30 per cent of fat in ready-ground hamburger, you can be sure of one thing: there will be too much and thus a lot of waste, as the fat simply cooks out, shrinking the hamburger greatly.

334. What are Swedish Meatballs like?   They are made from ground beef and pork, mixed with onions, soft bread crumbs, milk, and eggs, chilled, then made into small balls. These are browned on all sides and cooked all the way through. They are usually served with a brown gravy which sometimes has cream incorporated into it. The Swedish name for them is Köttbullar.

335. What is Chili Con Carne?   A combination of kidney beans and chopped beef in a sauce based largely on tomatoes and flavored with chili powder.

336. What is Pasticha?   A dish of Greek origin made of elbow macaroni, ground beef, eggs, milk, and seasonings which include a great deal of garlic, baked in the oven with a topping of grated Parmesan cheese.

337. What is a Cornish Pasty?   Chopped round of beef, chopped potatoes, salt, and pepper are mixed together and baked in pastry. The pasties (like little round pies) are served hot or cold.

338. What are Empanadas?   Little South American pies filled with chopped beef, highly seasoned and mixed with chopped black olives, chopped hard-cooked egg, and white raisins. In miniature size they make fine canapés.

339. What is corned beef? Beef which has been preserved or pickled in a salt solution.

340. What is a New England boiled dinner? It consists of boiled corned beef with cabbage, carrots, onions, turnips, and potatoes added. It is one of the dullest of the few dishes which this country has contributed to the cuisine of the world!

341. What is Red Flannel Hash? It is a New England mixture of chopped corned beef, chopped cooked potatoes, chopped beets, and seasonings, browned and served with a poached egg on each portion.

342. What are the USDA grades for veal? Prime, Choice, Good, Standard, Utility, and Cull. The nearer the color of the meat is to white, the better it will be. The redder it is, the less fine and the tougher it will be.

343. How much veal should one buy per person? One-third to one-half pound of boneless veal, and ¾ pound of veal with bone in, is the usual allowance per person.

344. Why is veal in Europe so much better than ours? It is more delicate and whiter in color because it is milk-fed, and milk-fed veal is very hard to come by here. Also, Europeans slaughter their calves at a younger age than we do, which means our veal has less flavor and is less tender than theirs.

345. Is it true that veal should not be cooked rapidly over high heat? It is true except in the case of veal scallops, which are so thin that they can take this kind of treatment. Veal lacks fat and has a good deal of connective tissue. Thus it needs long, slow cooking, as in braising or stewing. It is especially good with fine sauces to enhance flavor.

346. What cuts of veal are good for roasting? Rib, leg (shank half), loin, sirloin, shoulder, rump (standing or boneless), and breast. The rib is always roasted, but the other cuts are equally good, and in some instances better, if they are braised. (See Question 413.)

347. What are veal scallops? Very thin slices of cutlet, without bone, are pounded almost paper-thin. They can then be cut into pieces of any size desired for the dish you want to make. Though they are sometimes referred to as scallops, most of our butchers understand better what you want if you ask for "veal cut for scaloppine." In France, veal cut this way is referred to as "escalopes." A good butcher shop gives you veal scallops separated each from the other by sheets of thin paper.

348. Why is it difficult to brown veal scallops, as so many recipes require? They will not brown well unless they are thoroughly dried with absorbent paper. Also, any transparent filaments, skin, or fat must be removed or the meat will curl and thus not brown evenly. Sometimes you can get a better brown on veal scallops if you flour them lightly before browning. They should be browned in butter (and/or olive oil) over moderately high heat for 4 to 5 minutes on each side. They are now not only browned but cooked, but may be reheated at a simmer in sauce, if they are to be served in one. However, they are excellent served at once, decorated with parsley and perhaps a few capers and with a lemon wedge to squeeze over them.

349. What is Wiener Schnitzel? Veal cutlet, breaded and sautéed in butter.

350. What is Schnitzel à la Holstein? A sautéed veal cutlet (not breaded), topped with a fried egg.

351. What is the best way to cook a veal chop? Veal chops can be broiled (see Question 414) or panfried, but they are best braised, thus keeping them moist and presenting them with a sauce or gravy, to which veal takes so kindly.

352. What is "city chicken"? Cubes of boneless veal on a skewer. They are braised or panfried.

353. What are mock chicken legs? Ground veal is molded into the shape of chicken legs, around a wooden skewer, which sticks out at the end to represent a leg bone. They are braised or panfried.

Veal Chart

RETAIL CUTS   **WHOLESALE CUTS**   **RETAIL CUTS**

STANDING RUMP ROAST

ROLLED RUMP ROAST

LEG (ROUND)

HEEL OF ROUND

HIND SHANK

LOIN CHOP

SIRLOIN STEAK

KIDNEY CHOP

ROUND STEAK

LEG (ROUND) CENTER-CUT ROAST

LOIN

CROWN ROAST

RIB ROAST

RIB CHOP

SCALLOPS

ROSETTES

BREAST

BREAST

BLADE ROAST

ARM ROAST

RIB

BLADE STEAK

ARM STEAK

SHOULDER

MOCK CHICKEN LEGS

LOAF

RIBLETS

STEW MEAT

ROLLED SHOULDER ROAST

CITY CHICKEN

SHANK

FORE SHANK

PATTIES

354. What is Blanquette de Veau? It is a marvelous French veal stew, fit to serve to the grandest company. It is best made with breast of veal, in which case you should allow a pound per person, as it is very bony. If you prefer to use boneless veal, allow ⅓ to ½ pound per person. In this case, add a veal bone to the stew while it is cooking. The veal is cooked long and slow in a good white stock or chicken broth and is served with tiny onions and mushrooms in a sauce made from the liquid in which the veal was cooked, with plenty of lemon juice added, thickened with egg yolks and heavy cream. (See Question 415.)

355. What is Osso Buco? It is a hearty Italian dish made from veal shanks with plenty of meat on them, braised and cooked in wine with seasonings which always include lemon rind.

356. What is Vitello Tonnato? A famous cold Italian dish of veal with a sauce of tuna fish, seasoned with anchovies.

357. What are the USDA grades for lamb? Prime, Choice, Good, Utility, and Cull. The higher grades are more tender and juicy and have a smaller percentage of bone than the lower grades.

358. How much lamb should one buy per person? One-third to one-half pound with bone in; ¼ to ⅓ pound boned.

359. Is there anything to do with lamb to make it interesting? There are many things, but the most important is not to overcook it. By and large, Americans are inclined to overcook lamb. Europeans, especially the French, serve lamb pink, and thus succulent and flavorsome. The reason many Americans find it dull is that they overcook it, as the English are inclined to do, so that it becomes stringy and gray and loses much of its basically delicate flavor. (See Questions 413, 414, 415.)

360. Are all lamb chops best broiled? Yes, and broiled only long enough to make them brown on the outside and pink in the middle. (See Question 414.) It is also possible to panbroil or panfry them, if desired.

Lamb Chart

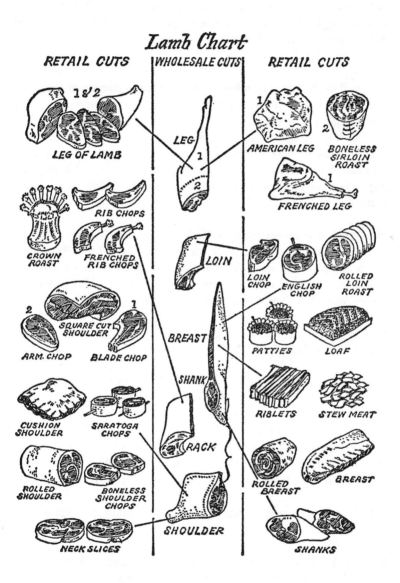

RETAIL CUTS   **WHOLESALE CUTS**   **RETAIL CUTS**

1 & 2

LEG OF LAMB

LEG

1

2

AMERICAN LEG

BONELESS SIRLOIN ROAST

2

FRENCHED LEG

1

CROWN ROAST

RIB CHOPS

FRENCHED RIB CHOPS

LOIN

LOIN CHOP

ENGLISH CHOP

ROLLED LOIN ROAST

2

SQUARE CUT SHOULDER

1

ARM. CHOP

BLADE CHOP

BREAST

PATTIES

LOAF

CUSHION SHOULDER

SARATOGA CHOPS

SHANK

RIBLETS

STEW MEAT

ROLLED SHOULDER

BONELESS SHOULDER CHOPS

RACK

ROLLED BREAST

BREAST

NECK SLICES

SHOULDER

SHANKS

361. What cuts of lamb should be roasted? Leg: loin (with bone, or boned and rolled); boneless sirloin; shoulder (with bone, or boned and rolled); crown (see Lamb Chart, page 93) and rib roast (or rack). (See Question 413.)

362. Is it correct to sear a leg of lamb at the beginning of roasting? The French always do it that way. In this country searing any roast is now regarded as old-fashioned, and there is much talk about how meat shrinks in such a process. For my part, I think that the very small amount of weight thus lost is more than compensated for by the much better flavor achieved. Despite advice to the contrary, all good roast cooks sear meat before roasting it, in this way adding flavor and sealing in the juices.

363. What is a crown roast of lamb? It is a rack, with meat removed from the rib ends, then two or more sections of the ribs shaped into a "crown" and tied. The meat is then roasted, and frequently served with a filling in the center of the crown, of either potato or puréed vegetable. (See Lamb Chart, page 93.)

364. What cuts of lamb are good for stewing? Breast, neck, or shoulder. (See Question 415.)

365. What is an Irish stew? It is a stew of lamb with vegetables, and as made in Ireland, it could scarcely be duller, since the meat is not browned and the sauce is therefore a dull gray color. Moreover, it is likely to contain overcooked meat and vegetables and thus have little texture. The French, on the other hand, brown the lamb first and cook the stew in stock instead of water. Also, they do not overcook the vegetables, which helps a lot.

366. What is a Navarin Printanier? A French lamb stew with spring vegetables.

367. What is a Shish Kebab? Cubes of meat (usually lamb) strung on a skewer, alternating with mushrooms, onions, pieces of tomato, and whatever else suits your fancy, and broiled. Often the meat is marinated in wine with seasonings before being placed on the skewers.

Similar dishes are served all over the world. This is the Middle Eastern name.

368. What is Shashlik?   Exactly the same thing as Shish Kebab. This is the Russian name for it.

369. What are the USDA grades for pork?   No federal-government graded pork is available to consumers at present.

370. How much pork should one buy per person?   Three to four ounces without bone, 6 to 8 ounces with bone should be adequate for most appetites, though only you can know whether your family or guests will eat more or less. However, for roasts, do not buy less than 3 pounds, as less will not cook well.

371. How should one store pork—and for how long?   Pork should be stored, loosely wrapped, in the refrigerator and for not more than a few days. Ground pork is perishable and should be eaten promptly, as should sausage. Uncooked cured pork may be stored longer than fresh pork, but the fat will become rancid if the meat is held too long. Cooked pork should be stored in the refrigerator and used promptly.

372. Why must pork be cooked until well done?   Because in rare or underdone pork there is danger of trichinosis, a very serious disease. Thorough cooking kills the parasites.

373. Is it possible to overcook pork?   Yes. Pork is done when all trace of pink color has disappeared. If you cook it too long, pork will get dry and lose flavor.

374. What is a fresh ham?   It is the uncured leg of the pig. It will weigh from 5 pounds up. It is sold whole, by the half, or as steaks, butt end, and shank end.

375. What are the best cuts of pork for roasting?   The loin (center cut or blade); the sirloin roast; Boston butt; fresh ham; crown roast. (See Question 413.)

376. What is the best method of roasting pork?   It should be roasted, fat side up, in a shallow pan on a rack, uncovered. Arranged thus, it is self-basting. It will become well done, with brown, crisp fat, in a 325° oven. (See Question 413.)

377. What is a crown roast of pork? It is made from the rib sections of the loin, cut so as to expose the ends of the rib bones, and shaped into a circle for roasting. The center is not filled, as is usually the case with crown roast of lamb, because this would considerably lengthen the cooking time. (See Pork Chart, page 97.)

378. What is the best way to cook pork chops? They can be pan-fried, but in my opinion they are best braised—that is, browned without additional fat, then covered with stock or water and cooked long and slow at a simmer. Gravy can be made from the liquid remaining in the pan.

379. What are pig's knuckles and how are they cooked? Pig's knuckles (or hocks) are cut from the shoulder (front leg) of the hog. They are simmered long and slow in water, then sauerkraut or cabbage is usually added, cooked until just done, and served with the knuckles. Pig's feet are cooked in the same way.

380. From what animal do spareribs come? The pig—and they are usually fresh, but can sometimes be obtained cured and smoked.

381. What is the best way to cook spareribs? You can roast them, using any basting material you like. They can also be braised or boiled. Sometimes spareribs are boiled for a time, drained, patted dry, then broiled or roasted.

382. Which keeps better, bacon in the slab, or the kind which is packaged sliced? The slab kind keeps longer, which is a worthwhile consideration if you do not mind the slight bother of slicing it as you wish to use it.

383. What is Canadian bacon? It is made by curing and smoking the lean muscle portion of boneless loins of pork.

384. What are chitterlings? Portions of the large intestine of the hog which have been emptied and thoroughly rinsed.

Pork Chart

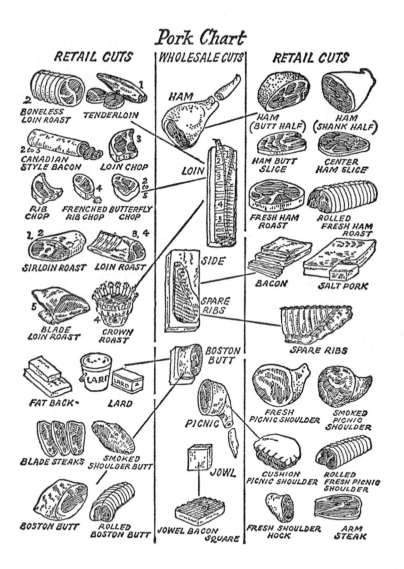

RETAIL CUTS   WHOLESALE CUTS   RETAIL CUTS

HAM

2 — BONELESS LOIN ROAST   1 — TENDERLOIN

HAM (BUTT HALF)   HAM (SHANK HALF)

2 to 5 — CANADIAN STYLE BACON   3 — LOIN CHOP

HAM BUTT SLICE   CENTER HAM SLICE

LOIN

RIB CHOP   4 — FRENCHED RIB CHOP   2 to 5 — BUTTERFLY CHOP

FRESH HAM ROAST   ROLLED FRESH HAM ROAST

1, 2 — SIRLOIN ROAST   3, 4 — LOIN ROAST

SIDE

5 — BLADE LOIN ROAST   4 — CROWN ROAST

SPARE RIBS

BACON   SALT PORK

SPARE RIBS

BOSTON BUTT

FAT BACK   LARD

FRESH PICNIC SHOULDER   SMOKED PICNIC SHOULDER

PICNIC

BLADE STEAKS   SMOKED SHOULDER BUTT

JOWL

CUSHION PICNIC SHOULDER   ROLLED FRESH PICNIC SHOULDER

BOSTON BUTT   ROLLED BOSTON BUTT

JOWL BACON SQUARE

FRESH SHOULDER HOCK   ARM STEAK

385. What are cracklings? The little bits of crisp meat left from "trying out" (frying) fat salt pork.

386. What is fat back? It is pure fat from the back of the pig and most of it is rendered into lard, but some is cured and sold on the retail market. It is used in the South in cooking many vegetables, but elsewhere in the country it is not liked in this manner. It appears also in canned pork and beans.

387. What is a frankfurter? It is a sausage, usually made of a mixture of beef, pork, and dry milk solids, stuffed into a casing, smoked, and cooked. There are also all-beef frankfurters, sometimes flavored with garlic.

388. Is sausage always made of pork? No. There is usually some pork in it, but sometimes none at all. Beef, veal, and lamb all go into sausage meat at times.

389. What is scrapple? It is a mixture of cooked pork and cornmeal, well seasoned, formed into a loaf. To serve, it is sliced off and fried brown and crisp. It is usually served for breakfast.

390. From what part of the pig does a ham come? It is cut from the upper part of the hind leg.

391. What is the difference, if any, between hams designated as "fully cooked" and "ready to eat"? Fully cooked ham is just what it says it is and may be eaten "as is" or reheated, if preferred. Ready-to-eat ham is perhaps safe to eat as is, but it will be far more palatable if you treat it as you would an uncooked ham, that is, boil it, then bake it. (See Question 413.)

392. What is the best way to cook a ham slice? Either in the oven, almost covered with milk, or braised in a skillet, using any liquid you like after browning—fruit juice, stock, wine, or milk—and simmering long and slow, covered.

393. What is Smithfield ham? It is a long-cured ham of very characteristic (and excellent) flavor, which must be prepared in Smithfield, Virginia, to carry the name. The hams are dry-cured and aged for about 18 months. Such long-cured hams can be kept for a considerable length of time without refrigeration.

394. What is Prosciutto? It is an Italian ham of unusual and delicious flavor, usually served in paper-thin slices with melon or other fruit (with fresh figs it is especially wonderful). It is also used in Italy in cooked dishes. The prosciutto hams prepared in this country are federal-government inspected and are safe to eat without cooking.

395. What is a picnic ham? It comes from the front leg, or shoulder, of the hog. It is cured and smoked (the picnic cut can also be obtained in fresh pork). These hams contain a higher percentage of bone, skin, and connective tissue than other ham and are less expensive.

396. Are canned hams fully cooked? Yes, but they may be reheated or glazed if desired. Observe the label carefully to see whether your canned ham should be refrigerated.

397. What are variety meats? Liver, heart, tongue, kidneys, tripe, sweetbreads, and brains. They are known in Britain by the (to us) unappetizing title of offal.

398. Is calf liver the only kind which sautés well? No. Steer liver can be treated in exactly the same way and will produce an excellent dish, provided it is not overcooked, which will toughen it. It is far less expensive than calf liver.

399. Does liver need any preparation for sautéing or broiling? Yes. If your butcher has not removed the filament from the liver, peel it off or the meat will curl up as it cooks. Otherwise, just add salt and pepper to it and dredge it lightly with flour. Sauté thinly sliced liver quickly in butter which is hot but not burning. For broiling, have the liver cut thick—about 1½ inches. Broil 4 to 5 inches from heat. Cooked either way, the juices should run pale pink when liver is pricked with a fork.

400. How many kidneys should one buy per person? One veal kidney and two or three lamb kidneys, depending upon size, will serve one person well. One beef kidney will make sufficient stew for four.

401. How do you cook veal kidneys? In my opinion, they are best split (not all the way through), broiled, and served with either a butter or a deviled sauce (plenty of mustard). They can also be sliced and sautéed and served in a brown sauce.

402. How do you cook lamb kidneys? Just as you do veal kidneys: broil or sauté them.

403. What is the best way to cook beef kidney? Since beef kidney is inclined to be tough, the best way to cook it is long and slow in water to cover; then cut it up to make a stew or a beef and kidney pie.

404. Do pork liver and pork kidneys make good eating? If you can get them almost immediately after the pig is slaughtered, they are delicious, but after only a day or two their flavor becomes too strong for most tastes.

405. Are sweetbreads and brains very much alike? Yes, but brains are more delicate. Both are handled in much the same way. They are soaked and sometimes blanched before cooking. Either brains or sweetbreads can be sautéed, broiled, braised, or cooked in liquid and served with a sauce.

406. What are Brains au Beurre Noire? Brains sautéed to a delicate brown, then dressed with a sauce of butter which has been cooked to a golden brown with vinegar or lemon juice and capers added.

407. How does one cook heart? Hearts, whether beef, veal, pork, or lamb, are best cooked by braising or simmering long and slow in liquid. They are also very good stuffed and baked long and slow in the oven.

408. How is oxtail best cooked? It is best braised with herbs and other seasonings, vegetables, and sometimes wine to make a stew. With more liquid, it makes a fine soup.

409. What kind of tongue is best? You might say a civil one, but for the purposes of this book let us say that either beef, veal, lamb, or pork tongue makes good eating. However, beef is the most commonly used. It may be smoked or fresh, though the latter is harder to find in most markets.

410. What is the best way to cook tongue? Cook it in water to cover, with an onion stuck with cloves and any other seasoning which suits your fancy, long and slow in a covered kettle. When it is done, let it cool in the liquid in which it was cooked. There are many delectable sauces with which tongue can be served. It is excellent hot or cold. Slivers of tongue add greatly to a chef's salad.

411. What is tripe? It is part of the stomach of an ox. Plain tripe is taken from the walls of the rumen, or first stomach, and honeycomb tripe is taken from the second stomach, the walls of which have a net-like lining.

412. What is the best way to cook tripe? That is a matter of taste, and there are many wonderful tripe dishes, their delectability depending largely upon the sauce in which they are served. Tripe must be cooked long and slow in liquid, usually 3 to 4 hours. Sometimes it is cooked in the sauce in which it will be served, sometimes the sauce is added after the tripe is done. Tripe à la Mode de Caen is one of the most famous French dishes. In it the tripe is served in a sauce containing vegetables, wine, and sometimes brandy, varying with the chef who concocts it. One of the best tripe dishes I ever ate was in Buenos Aires. It was cooked in champagne, with cognac added, and was superb. The Irish like tripe in cream sauce. In truth, it takes kindly to almost any sauce at all.

413. How long do you roast the various meats?

	Constant Oven Temperature	Degree of Doneness	Meat Thermometer Reading	Minutes Per Pound
Beef (tender cuts)	325°–350°	Rare	140°	18–20
		Medium	160°	22–25
		Well done	180°	30–35
Veal	300°–350°	Well done	165°	20–30
Lamb and Mutton	300°–350°	Medium rare	150°	10–12
		Well done	160°	25–30
Pork	325°–350°	Well done	185°	25–30
Ham	275°–300°	Well done	160°	25–30

414. How long do you broil the various meats?

		Degree of Doneness	Total Broiling Time
Beef steaks	(1 inch thick)	Rare Medium	8–9 minutes 12–15 minutes
	(1½ inches thick)	Rare Medium	9–12 minutes 15–18 minutes
	(2 inches thick)	Rare Medium	15–25 minutes 25–35 minutes
	(2½ inches thick)	Rare Medium	25–35 minutes 35–40 minutes
	(3 inches or more thick)	Rare Medium	25–30 minutes 35–40 minutes
Veal chops	(1 inch thick) (moderate heat)	Well done	15–20 minutes
Lamb chops	(1 inch thick) (moderate heat)	Medium rare	10–12 minutes
	(2 inches thick) (moderate heat)	Medium rare	15–20 minutes

415. How long do you braise the various meats?

	Cooking Time
Beef (4 pounds, whole)	3 hours
(Stew, in chunks)	2 hours
Veal (3–5 pounds, whole)	2¼–2¾ hours
(Stew, in chunks)	2–2½ hours
Lamb stew	2–2½ hours
Ham	25–30 minutes per pound

VI. POULTRY AND GAME

416. How long should the various kinds of poultry be cooked?

Poultry	Thermometer	Oven Temperature	Minutes Per Pound
Turkey	185°	325°	20–25
Chicken	175°–180°	325°	18–30
Duck	175°–180°	325°	20–25
Goose	175°–180°	325°	20–25
Squab		325°	45–60
Cornish Rock Hen		325°	45–60

Note: If you prefer the searing method, to achieve especially crisp skin, start bird in a 425° oven and cook 15 to 20 minutes, basting frequently, until it begins to brown nicely. Then reduce oven heat to 325° and proceed as above, counting the searing time in the total. The larger a bird is, the less time it takes, relatively, to roast.

417. Is poultry graded by the Department of Agriculture? Yes.
There are three grades: A, B, and C. All are safe, wholesome food, but the quality differs. Grade A is full-fleshed and meaty, with a good layer of fat. The skin is smooth and almost without tears, discolorations, or pinfeathers. There are no crooked or broken bones. Grade B may not be perfect in any of these respects. Grade C may have poor flesh on breast and legs. It may have no fat. It may have misshapen or broken bones and pinfeathers, cuts, tears, or discolorations of the skin.

Inspection stamp for poultry

Grade stamp

418. How much chicken should one buy per person? Broilers: allow ¼ to ½ bird per person. Roasting chickens and fryers: ⅔ to ¾ pound per person. Stewing chickens: ½ to ⅔ pound per person.

419. Is it better to buy a ready-to-cook or a dressed chicken? A ready-to-cook chicken is just what it purports to be. A dressed chicken has been plucked, but its head and feet are still on and the viscera still in it. The butcher will "draw" it for you (remove viscera, head, and feet), but you usually have still to clean it up before you cook it. The ready-to-cook chicken is more expensive, but remember you are paying for waste when you buy a dressed bird, so it may be a questionable bargain.

420. How long may uncooked poultry be held in the refrigerator? One or two days.

421. Should poultry be washed before cooking? Many people wash poultry under cold running water before cooking it. I am inclined to go along with the French theory that this destroys flavor. Since our ready-to-cook poultry is usually beautifully clean, the washing hardly seems necessary, but if you do it, be sure to pat the poultry thoroughly dry with paper toweling, or it will not brown well.

422. How do you singe a bird? Most of our poultry is so well cleaned that it rarely requires singeing. However, if you see signs of hairs or pinfeathers on a bird, hold it over an open gas flame, turning it about quickly to sear off any hairs or feathers.

423. How do you prepare poultry for roasting? Remove the giblets which you will usually find in a bag inside the carcass. Remove all pinfeathers (an eyebrow puller is good for this chore). Singe off hairs. Feel inside the bird along the ribs to remove bits of lung. Remove the oil sac above the tail. Wash the bird inside and out with cold running water, if necessary. Pat dry with paper towels and place in the refrigerator until ready to cook.

424. Should birds be seasoned before stuffing? Yes. Season them lightly, inside and out, with salt and pepper.

425. Can poultry be stuffed the day before roasting? It is not a good idea to stuff a bird and store it in the refrigerator or freezer because it takes so long for the heat to permeate the cold stuffing that the bird may be overcooked in the process. Stuff it just before roasting.

426. What is the best way to close the cavity after a bird is stuffed? You can sew it up, if you like, but the easiest way is to place several short skewers across the opening and then lace around them with heavy white string.

427. How do you truss a bird? Fold the wings back and press the tips against the back. Tie the ends of the legs together with white string and carry the string down around the tailpiece. Turn the bird over on its breast and bring each end of string forward over the front and tip of one of the wings and across the back to the other wing. Tie ends together in the middle of the back. Fold loose neck skin toward back and fasten with poultry pins.

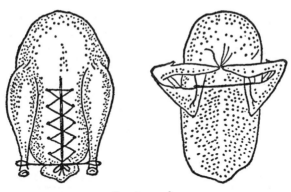

Trussing poultry

428. What is the best method for roasting poultry? The old-fashioned method is to sear the bird in a very hot oven 25 to 30 minutes, basting often, so that you get a crisp brown skin, then reduce the heat to 300°–325° and continue roasting until done, basting at least every 20 minutes. The second method is to roast the bird from the start in a 325° oven. There is not as much shrinkage in this method, but since the loss is relatively small anyhow, you may think it worth while in order to get a crisper skin. Basting is of great importance in either method. (See Question 416.)

429. What do you do if a bird becomes too brown on breast or thighs before it is done?   Place a piece of bread or cheesecloth soaked in melted butter over the too-brown part to protect it from further heat.

430. Should poultry be cooked in a covered roaster?   Never! If you do that you are simply steaming the bird. All birds should be roasted, breast side up, on a rack in a shallow roasting pan.

431. How do you know when a roasted bird is done?   A meat thermometer placed in the center of the inside thigh muscle or the thickest part of the breast muscle should register approximately 185°. If the bird is stuffed, the stuffing should register 165°. A less sure, but good, test is to press the thickest part of the drumstick with protected fingers. If it feels very soft, the bird is done. Also, the leg joints move easily when the bird is done.

432. Should roasted poultry be served at once when taken from the oven?   No. It should stand out of the oven 20 to 30 minutes, which gives you plenty of time to make the gravy. The meat thus has a chance to absorb the juices. It is also easier to carve.

433. How should one garnish the platter upon which a roasted bird is served?   If you have the carver's best interests and comfort in mind, the answer is not at all. Garnishes, such as one sees in pretty color pictures, simply get in the way when the bird is being carved. The platter should be ample in size, and you should provide an extra warmed plate upon which the carver can put slices as he carves them.

434. What is the best method for making giblet gravy?   In the first place, the giblets should be cooked as soon as the bird is brought home. Put gizzard, heart, and neck into a pan and cover with water, adding salt, pepper, and a little minced onion. Bring to the boil, then simmer about 1 hour. Add the liver and simmer 20 minutes longer. Discard neck and chop gizzard, heart, and liver. If the gravy is not to be made at once, refrigerate in the remaining liquid, well covered. After the bird is cooked, remove to a hot platter. Discard most of the fat in the roasting pan. Place pan over low heat. Add flour and stir to blend well, scraping up all the good brown solids from the pan. Add giblets and broth, plus water, and stir until thickened.

435. How soon should one remove the stuffing from a roasted bird? As soon after the bird has been served as possible. Cool as quickly as you can, place in a covered container, and refrigerate. Eat within a day or two, thoroughly heated before serving.

436. Is all poultry good in curry sauce? Yes, though chicken is perhaps the best of all.

437. What should be served with a curry? Rice is the perfect accompaniment for curry, and if you dress it up by making it into a pulao as the Indians do, it is even more fun to eat. Put a few slivered almonds and white raisins into your cooked rice and add some spices if you like. Serve Major Grey's (a variety, not a brand) chutney with the curry and, if possible, popadams or poories (Indian breads). Popadams can be bought in tins and fried or baked. If a first course is desired, make it a light tossed salad or a clear consommé. For dessert serve something light and cooling, such as fresh pineapple or a fruit juice. And, by the way, the proper beverage to serve with curry is beer. Any curried dish is too strong for wines, the sturdiest of which is overcome by it.

438. What is a Salmis? The meat of cooked (usually roasted) poultry or game is carved into pieces and served in a sauce, which sometimes is based on red or white wine, sometimes on a variety of other ingredients.

439. Is a capon better for roasting than an ordinary chicken? It is, indeed, because these birds are usually especially fattened and are very tender. In fact, there is nothing better for making chicken salad and such dishes than a boiled capon. It is, of course, more expensive, but many consider it worth the price.

440. Is it possible to roast chicken in a casserole? Yes. The French do this. A whole chicken is trussed, then browned well on all sides in butter and oil in a casserole. Herbs and seasonings are added, the casserole covered, and cooked either in a 325° oven or at a simmer on top of the range.

441. What is the difference between a "broiler" and a "fryer"? It used to be that a broiler was a smaller, younger, and lighter bird, but nowadays there is no difference, though you may find chickens in the market marked either "broiler," "fryer," or "frying." All these can be either fried or broiled with equal success.

442. What is the best way to broil chicken? Probably on a grill over an open fire, being sure that the coals are in exactly the right condition to cook the chicken well and not burn it, and brushing it with garlic-flavored olive oil. Otherwise, the best "broiled" chicken I know is done in the oven! Season the broiler-fryer with salt and pepper, dredge with flour, and dot liberally with butter. Put on a rack in a shallow roasting pan and put a little water into the pan. Cook 45 to 55 minutes in a 400° oven, basting frequently.

443. What is Chicken Sauté? Broiler-fryers, cut up, browned in butter and oil, then cooked entirely at a simmer without the addition of any liquid. Sautéed chicken may be served with many sauces, which are usually made in the pan after the cooked chicken has been removed to a hot platter.

444. What is Chicken Chasseur? It is sautéed chicken in a tomato and mushroom sauce.

445. What is Chicken Cacciatore? It is sautéed chicken which, after browning, is cooked with tomatoes, onion, green peppers, and sometimes other vegetables in small quantity, plus seasonings.

446. How do you cook chicken on an outdoor grill? In my opinion, the best way is to broil the broiler-fryer type, basted well with garlic-flavored olive oil. Whole chickens can also be spit-roasted, with delectable results.

447. How is chicken sold "in parts"? Usually it is packaged as wings, drumsticks, thighs, and breasts. You buy whichever of these suits your pocketbook and your recipe.

448. Is it economical to buy chicken in pieces? Chicken wings, legs, and thighs are relatively less expensive than whole broiler-fryers, so if you have recipes requiring any of those three, it is definitely economical to buy them in pieces. If you want to make dishes out of chicken breasts only and do not wish to go to the bother of cutting off and freezing the remaining parts of the chickens, then buy the breasts, which will cost more, relatively speaking, than buying the whole birds.

449. When you order a chicken breast from the market, what should you expect to receive? This can really be quite confusing. To some, a chicken breast means one side of the chicken's breast, to others it means both sides. If the latter is what you want, be sure to specify a *full* chicken breast. If you order a *half* chicken breast, it should be clear to anyone that you do not want both sides. If you buy frozen chicken breasts, the package should specify how many "pieces" there are in it—and a "piece" means half of the full breast.

450. What is Suprême de Volaille? Skinned and boned breast of chicken. It may be cooked in many ways and takes kindly to an infinite number of sauces. A suprême takes only 8 minutes to cook in butter, after which one removes the suprême to keep warm and proceeds with the sauce to go over it.

451. What is Chicken Kiev? Boned breasts of chickens are rolled around very hard pieces of sweet butter in such a way that they completely enclose the butter. The rolled pieces are then dipped in egg and bread crumbs and fried in deep fat. Care should be taken in breaking into each piece, as the butter, which melts inside, is likely to spurt out.

452. What is Chicken Jeannette? Cold breast of chicken, covered with white chaud-froid sauce, set on a slice of pâté de foie gras, then covered with aspic and decorated with tarragon leaves and/or truffle.

453. What is a fowl? This is the old terminology for what is now called a stewing chicken. These are older birds and require long, slow cooking in liquid.

454. What is Chicken Fricassee? To most Americans it is a stewing chicken cut into pieces and cooked long and slow in broth or water with seasonings. When it is done the sauce is thickened. I have found that the dish is infinitely tastier, however, if the chicken pieces are first browned in butter or chicken fat, then stewed.

455. What is a French Chicken Fricassee? The French use broiler-fryers for a fricassee. The chicken is cut into pieces, browned in butter, then simmered for half an hour in a relatively small amount of liquid. The liquid may be chicken stock, wine, clam juice, or tomato juice—what you will. Cream, with or without the addition of egg yolk, may be added at the end of the cooking. Mushrooms, onions, and other vegetables are sometimes added. In place of these, herbs are sometimes added, such as tarragon to make Chicken Tarragon.

456. What is the best way to make chicken hash? That is a matter of opinion, so I will give my own. I like chicken (or turkey) hash the way it was made in the old Ritz in New York: the chicken ground fine and stirred into a rich cream sauce, put into an individual shallow casserole, piped with a border of puréed peas, then run under the broiler to brown the top of the hash lightly. Some people like chicken hash made of cubed chicken and served over toast. It is good, but not as beautiful as the Chicken Hash St. Germain described above.

457. What is Chicken à la King? Diced cooked chicken in a rich cream sauce, with diced mushrooms, green pepper, and pimiento added. It is usually served on toast or in patty shells.

458. What is Chicken Tetrazzini? Diced cooked chicken in a rich cream sauce with sherry in it, poured over cooked spaghetti in a casserole, covered with bread crumbs mixed with grated Parmesan cheese, and browned in the broiler.

459. What goes into a chicken pie? Cooked chicken (usually the stewing variety) cut into good-sized chunks, a rich sauce made from chicken stock and cream, carrots, tiny onions, peas, mushrooms—any or all of these and seasonings to taste. The pie may be topped with biscuit dough or with rich pastry.

460. What is Chicken Paprika? A Hungarian dish made in a variety of ways, but always with enough paprika to give the sauce a pink color and always with either sour or sweet cream involved in the sauce.

461. What is a Paella? It is a Spanish dish containing saffron rice, browned pieces of chicken (with bone in), seafood (clams, mussels, shrimp, et cetera), and sometimes bits of vegetable and pimiento, all cooked together in broth. In Spain paella is made in individual flat metal dishes with handles on the sides, with all the ingredients tastefully and neatly arrayed in an attractive pattern. The dish is quite dry by the time the cooking is finished.

462. What is Arroz con Pollo? Chicken, sectioned, sautéed, then cooked with rice, saffron, tomatoes, green peppers, and seasonings.

463. What is Chicken Maryland? Chicken pieces, well breaded, either fried or cooked in a casserole and basted with butter. Served brown and crisp on the outside, moist and tender inside, with a cream gravy.

464. What is Chicken Marengo? Chicken pieces are browned, then cooked in a casserole with wine, tomatoes, mushrooms, and seasonings.

465. What is Coq au Vin? It is chicken cooked in either white or red wine, but usually in France it is done in red, with mushrooms and onions, and accompanied by parsleyed potatoes.

466. What is Chicken Mole? This is a South American dish of chicken in a sauce containing hot chili peppers and other seasonings, tomato, and chocolate. Strange as it sounds, it is very good.

467. What is the best Chicken Salad you know? Cold cooked chicken, cut in good-sized chunks, mixed with homemade mayonnaise and served on crisp lettuce with a garnish of capers, or slivered almonds if you prefer. The addition of lots of celery to a chicken salad makes it seem like just what it is—extended beyond the real and delectable point!

468. What is the best way to cook chicken livers? Chicken livers are marvelous grilled on skewers, either alternating with mushrooms and other vegetables or not. They are also excellent sautéed in butter. If you cook them that way, you may add wine and/or cream for a sauce after they are almost done. Whatever way you cook chicken livers, be careful not to overcook, which dries them out.

469. How much turkey should one allow per person? If you are buying a turkey under 12 pounds, allow ¾ to 1 pound per person. If the turkey weighs 12 pounds or over, allow ½ to ¾ pound per person.

470. Is it more economical to buy a big turkey rather than a small one? Yes, it is, especially since leftover turkey makes many fine dishes. On the other hand, if you are a very small family, you may never be able to figure out how to use up a big turkey, in which case you will pay the penalty and spend more, relatively speaking, for a smaller bird.

471. Is it possible to buy turkey in parts? Yes. Turkey is sold in halves, in quarters, or by the piece: legs, thighs, wings, and breasts.

472. What is the fastest way to thaw a frozen turkey? Put it into a gas oven set at 155°, or into an electric oven at the Warm designation. An 8-pound bird will thaw in 3 hours and a 20-pound bird in 5 hours. It takes about 3 days to thaw a 20-pound bird in the refrigerator.

473. How much stuffing will a turkey hold? Allow a scant cup of stuffing for each pound of turkey in birds under 20 pounds. The body cavity of very large birds does not vary much, so allow 18 to 20 cups of stuffing for birds over 20 pounds. Place stuffing lightly into the neck and body of the bird. Stuffing expands in cooking, so be careful not to overpack.

474. Is it possible to roast a large turkey partly one day and finish cooking it the next? The United States Department of Agriculture says that this is not a good idea because the roasting process should not be interrupted until a temperature of 195° for an unstuffed or 165° for a stuffed bird is reached, at which point it is done.

475. Is it a good idea to cook turkey in aluminum foil? It shortens the cooking time and prevents the oven from being splattered, which are advantages. However, a turkey cooked in foil does not turn out exactly like one roasted in an open pan on a rack. Therefore, whether or not to cook in foil becomes a matter of taste. Some people feel that one never gets a properly crisp brown skin, even though the foil is folded back at the end of the cooking for browning purposes. Others, who prefer the method, think you cannot get a turkey as succulently moist by the ordinary method.

476. What is the best way to cook half a turkey? Season it with salt and pepper, inside and out. Mound stuffing into the cut side of the half-turkey, cover stuffing with aluminum foil, and tie strings around the meat and foil to hold in the stuffing—also to hold down the wing. Dredge skin with flour and dot with butter. Place, foil side down, on a rack and roast as you would a whole turkey. (See Question 416.)

477. What is a Turkey Roll? Boneless turkey meat, made into a thick roll. It is cooked like roast turkey, but in a 350° oven until it registers 170° to 175° on a meat thermometer.

478. How is smoked turkey served? Smoked turkey is, of course, already cooked. It is usually served cold, sliced, on a buffet table or as a canapé, in which case you can either cube it and impale it on toothpicks or have crackers or hot buttered toast triangles handy to eat it on. Smoked turkey is a very rich meat, so a little goes a long way. It can be used in cooked dishes, but remember its richness in planning a sauce for it.

479. What is the average weight of a duck? Ducks weigh from about three to six pounds. The smallest are hard to find in many markets, but can be picked up in any Chinatown. However, larger ducks, while they contain more fat, also contain proportionately more meat, which is usually of the best quality.

480. How many people are served by a five- to six-pound duck? Not more than four, and it is often quite possible for three to consume such a bird. There is not a great deal of meat on a duck, but the crisp skin is so good and so rich that it helps to stretch the servings.

481. Is a duck ever boiled? It certainly is, and while one thus loses that lovely crisp skin, a beautiful dish results. The Danes serve boiled duck, for instance, skinning it before carving and serving it with melted butter to pour over and frozen cream horseradish sauce to accompany it. Delectable!

482. Can a duck be cooked on the outdoor grill? Yes. It can be split and broiled, or roasted whole on a spit. It takes a long time to cook, depending somewhat, of course, on the heat of your fire. But the duck really needs long, slow cooking and a 5- to 6-pound one will take about 2 hours to cook well.

483. What is Canard à la Presse? Duck, roasted for a very short time, then carved. The bones are crushed in a duck press and the resultant blood made into a sauce to go over the duck. This is the great speciality of the Tour d'Argent restaurant in Paris and is known to many Americans as "Bloody Duck."

484. What is Caneton à l'Orange? Roast duck with an orange sauce which is sometimes made separately and served with the duck, sometimes cooked with it. One of the best I know comes from South America and is cooked with orange marmalade spread over the duck and made into a sauce when the roasting is finished. This duck dish is also known as Caneton à la Bigarade.

485. Is a goose hard to cook well? Though for some reason it is so regarded by many, it is not difficult at all. A goose is a very fat bird. For that reason, the skin should be well pricked before the bird goes into the oven, to let the fat run out during the cooking. Otherwise, a goose is roasted like any other poultry, allowing 20 to 25 minutes a pound for the total roasting. Also, one should allow 1¼ pounds per serving. A goose has relatively little meat on it, even compared to a duck, but it is a delicious thing to eat. Because it is so fat, a goose need not be basted.

486. What is a squab? A pigeon about five weeks old, usually weighing less than a pound.

487. How do you roast a squab? Stuff the bird or not, as you please. Tie its legs and place pieces of bacon or fat salt pork over its breast. Roast in 325° oven from 45 to 60 minutes, or until well done, basting frequently. Remove the bacon or pork for the last 15 minutes of cooking so that the skin will brown.

488. Is there any way to cook squab besides roasting? Yes. Squab can be braised, either whole or cut up, and cooked in a casserole with a variety of sauces, including wine ones.

489. What is a Cornish Rock Hen? A small domestic bird which is a cross between two others, but the man who achieved the cross will not tell which two. A little larger than a squab, this is a relatively uninteresting bird to eat.

490. Is there any easy way to get a wild duck plucked? Yes. Take it to your butcher and pay him whatever he asks to do it! He will also draw it for you, though the hunter should eviscerate any bird or animal in the field. Plucking a wild duck, as the wife of any hunter knows, is a perfectly fiendish job and should not be attempted except by an old hand at the business.

491. How long should a wild duck be hung? At least a week at 40° F.

492. Is there any way to reduce the gamey flavor of wild duck? Yes. Soak it in buttermilk for a couple of hours.

493. How many people are served by a wild duck? Usually two, unless the duck is very small or the diners very hungry.

494. What is the best way to cook wild duck? They can be roasted, braised, or broiled, with good results.

495. Should wild duck be cooked well done? That is a matter of taste, and mine says they should be rare but not blue. The red juice should run free and the meat should not be cooked thoroughly. However, if you like your wild duck well done and intend to roast it, you should stuff it. Rare wild duck is not stuffed, though you may put an onion, an apple, or some herbs in the cavity if you like.

496. How long do you roast a wild duck to make it rare?   About 15 minutes to the pound in a 500° oven, basting constantly with butter.

497. How do you broil wild duck?   Small, young ducks are best for broiling. Split, rub well with butter, and broil in a 350° broiler 10 to 20 minutes, depending upon the degree of doneness desired, turning occasionally.

498. What should one serve with wild duck?   Wild rice or hominy grits, currant or grape jelly, and a green vegetable. A Burgundy wine goes beautifully with it, too.

499. What kind of quail do we eat?   There are many kinds of quail in the United States, but the most commonly eaten is the bobwhite, which is called partridge in the South.

500. Should quail be hung?   Not more than a day or two. It should be eaten quite fresh.

501. How many quail should one serve per person?   One or more, depending upon appetites.

502. How do you cook quail?   They can be roasted, sautéed, broiled, or braised. They are dry, like most game birds, and must therefore be well larded, or cooked in plenty of butter.

503. Should partridge be hung?   Yes, or it will be pretty dull eating. Hang for at least 48 hours at 40° F.

504. How many are served by a partridge?   Two people, as a rule.

505. How do you cook partridge?   Either roast it, well larded, in a 400° oven for 20 to 25 minutes, or broil it, well coated with melted butter and basted frequently, in a 350° broiler for 15 to 20 minutes.

506. Does pheasant need to be hung?   Yes. For at least several days at 40° F.

507. How many are served by a pheasant?   Two to four, depending upon size.

508. What is the best way to cook pheasant?   Most people like pheasant best roasted. Since pheasant are inclined to be dry, they need to be well larded with fat salt pork or bacon over the breast. They may be stuffed or not, as you choose. Roast in 350° oven for about an hour.

509. How can pheasant be cooked other than roasting?   Pheasant is very good braised, particularly with sauerkraut or cabbage. It is also excellent sautéed, for which purpose it is cut into serving pieces. It is delectable cooked in a casserole with wine or fruit juice, and with sour cream added just long enough before the end of cooking to warm through.

510. What do you serve with pheasant?   Currant jelly and bread sauce. (See Question 718.) Fried hominy is also excellent with pheasant; or try German potato pancakes. Vegetables of the cabbage family —brussels sprouts, red cabbage, or cauliflower—have an affinity for pheasant, too.

511. How are doves cooked?   Like most small birds, they can be roasted (very briefly and basted often with melted butter) or browned in fat and cooked in a casserole with wine, turtle soup, milk, or cream. In the South, where they are plentiful, doves are always served with hominy grits.

512. How many doves should one allow per person?   Depending on the size, from one to three.

513. Must venison be hung?   Emphatically, yes. Fresh venison meat is not tasty and is inclined to be tough, no matter what the cut or the age of the animal. The meat should be hung for eight to ten days at 40° F. If you have a full carcass, take it to your butcher for hanging.

514. Should one marinate all venison?   Some people do, and one might say it does no harm, and often does considerable good. However, the tender cuts from a young animal—the tenderloin, saddle, and filet—need no marinating and should be roasted or broiled rare. If the meat has been properly hung, they will be tender and delicious.

515. What is a good marinade for venison?   Red wine to cover, plus vinegar, salt, cloves, and a stick of cinnamon. From there you are on your own. You may add garlic, onion, peppercorns, juniper berries, bay leaves, thyme, carrots, celery—any or all of these. The venison should remain in this marinade for at least two days. If you are then going on to make a stew or pot roast with it, use the strained marinade as part of the liquid for cooking. Venison may also be marinated in beer, with seasonings.

516. What cuts of venison are roasted?   The tenderloin, saddle, or leg. The first two can be cooked without marinating, but should be well larded. The leg is best marinated before roasting. (Follow timetable for roasting beef. Question 413.)

517. What cuts of venison can be broiled?   Loin chops, filet, and tenderloin, cut into mignons. (Follow timetable for broiling beefsteak. Question 414.)

518. What cuts does one use for venison stew?   Shoulder, shank, and breast, well marinated.

519. What is good to serve with broiled or roast venison?   Puréed chestnuts and a tart jelly are almost indispensable. Otherwise, noodles or potatoes in any form you like, plus a green vegetable, are fine with venison.

520. Is hare the same thing as jack rabbit?   Yes. Hare is called jack rabbit in the South.

521. Has hare a strong flavor?   It can have one, too strong for most tastes. If you have a hare which has a strong odor, marinate it for several days before cooking and discard the marinade.

522. How do you cook hare? It can be cut into pieces and sautéed, fried, or stewed, after marinating in wine or beer and spices.

523. What is Jugged Hare? Hare, cut into serving pieces, is marinated in red wine and spices for several days, then stewed in the marinade with vegetables. A sauce is made from the stock, plus the liver, heart, and blood (now congealed) of the hare. The blood is most important in making this dish right, so if you have the butcher prepare your hare, be sure that he saves it for you. Garnish the cooked hare with crisp bacon, mushrooms, and croutons, and serve currant jelly with it.

524. How do you cook rabbit? It may be broiled, fried, baked, or stewed. Rabbit is much more tender than hare and thus does not require marinating except for flavoring purposes, if desired.

525. What is Hassenpfeffer? A German dish in which one hare or two small rabbits, cut up, are marinated for two or three days in vinegar, water, and spices, then patted dry, floured or crumbed, and fried to a nice brown. Some of the marinating liquid is added and the rabbit gently stewed until done. Sometimes beer is added to the marinade.

526. What is a Civet de Lapin? It is a French rabbit stew in which the rabbit is marinated in red wine, spices, and vegetables overnight, then cooked and thickened at the end with the blood, which is exceedingly important in achieving the right flavor.

527. Is squirrel good eating? Yes. If it is young, it is delicate and tender, rather reminiscent of chicken meat.

528. How do you cook squirrel? It can be broiled, roasted, fried, or stewed, and an average one will serve 1 or 2.

529. What is a Brunswick stew? It is a Southern concoction of squirrel, vegetables, and seasonings. Nowadays it is often made with chicken, but squirrel was the original base.

VII. FISH AND SHELLFISH

530. Why do so many Americans dislike fish? The chief reason is that they are inclined to overcook it, which dries it out and detracts from the flavor.

531. How much fish should one buy per person? When buying a whole fish, allow 1 pound per person. Of dressed fish (eviscerated, scaled, with head, tail, and fins removed), steaks, and fillets, buy ⅓ to ½ pound per person.

532. How can you tell whether fish is fresh? There should be no strong, fishy odor. The eyes should be bright and bulging, the skin and scales should be shiny. The gills should be red. The flesh should be firm and springy to the touch.

533. How does one prepare a just-caught fish? Fishermen ought at least to eviscerate fish before presenting them to family or friends. But you must also scale the fish and take off the head, tail, and fins —in addition to slitting it down the belly and eviscerating it, if that has not been done.

534. Is there any way to get the fishy smell off one's hands? Squeeze a little lemon juice on them.

535. How can you tell when fish is done? When the meat flakes easily with a fork, the fish is done.

536. What are the various ways of cooking fish? Broiling, baking, poaching, sautéing, and deep-fat frying.

537. What fish are best for broiling? Bluefish, flounder, haddock fillets or whole, halibut fillets or steaks, mackerel, porgies, salmon steaks, scrod, shad, striped bass, fresh-water bass, pike whole, steaks, or fillet, whitefish whole or fillets, perch fillets (ocean or yellow). Any whole fish which is broiled is first split. It should be seasoned and liberally dotted with butter before it is placed under the broiler, and basted occasionally as it cooks to keep it moist and flavorful.

538. Should fish be turned while broiling?   Not if it is a whole, split fish. It should be placed in a greased pan, skin-side down, seasoned and dotted with butter and cooked until done, *without turning.*

539. What fish are best for baking?   Bluefish, mackerel, halibut steaks, pompano, salmon steaks, swordfish steaks, shad, pike, whitefish.

540. Must the head be left on a whole fish when it is baked?   It should be, as this is the traditional way to bake fish. Furthermore, the head adds a lot to the flavor. But if you are a sissy, have the head removed.

541. Is baked fish always stuffed?   No. Bluefish, mackerel, and shad are very good stuffed, though they may be baked unstuffed if preferred.

542. What fish are best for poaching and how is this done?   It is usually the large fish, such as salmon, cod, haddock, and halibut, that are poached. However, carp, catfish, pike, trout, and whitefish can also be poached to good advantage. The fish are poached (cooked) in a barely simmering court bouillon, which is a combination of water or wine with vegetables and seasonings. Sometimes fish heads and bones are added to the court bouillon, and the whole cooked before the fish itself is put in.

543. What are Quenelles?   Ground fish, bread soaked in milk, eggs, and seasonings are shaped into small cylinders and poached. They are usually served with a Sauce Nantua (see Question 723).

544. What fish are best for sautéing?   Trout, sole, flounder fillets, butterfish, porgies, smelts, catfish, whitefish, perch fillets (ocean or yellow).

545. What fish are best for deep-fat frying?   Butterfish, sea bass, halibut or haddock (cut into chunks), flounder fillets, catfish, perch fillets (ocean or yellow). Any fish which is deep-fat fried should be dipped in flour, beaten egg, and crumbs and fried in 375° fat until nicely browned—*not too long.*

546. What is Kedgeree?   It is a combination of flaked cooked fish, rice, chopped hard-cooked eggs, butter, and seasonings, heated together and usually served for breakfast or lunch.

547. What is the best way to cook trout?   In my opinion, it is the way you would do them outdoors. Dip the whole, cleaned trout, well seasoned, in flour or (preferably) cornmeal, then fry them quickly in bacon fat to a nice crisp brown. They are also lovely sautéed in butter with slivered almonds.

548. What is Trout Doria?   Trout sautéed and served with oval-shaped pieces of cooked cucumber. Any fish dish served with cooked cucumber is called "Doria." For instance, shad roe is sometimes presented in this fashion. The combination is felicitous.

549. What is Truite au Bleu?   The trout must be alive until almost the moment when it is cooked. It is given a blow on the head to kill it, quickly eviscerated, and plunged, whole, into a court bouillon (see Question 543), one fourth of which is vinegar, and cooked until just done (about 5 minutes). The vinegar causes the fish to turn a bright blue color. These trout may be served hot with melted butter or cold with mayonnaise.

550. What is Gravad Lax?   It is Swedish salmon and got its name originally from the fact that it was buried in the ground. Nowadays it is not necessary to do that to achieve success. The salmon is marinated in the refrigerator in salt, sugar, white pepper, and dill, with a weight on top of it. It is turned a couple of times a day. It is sliced thin and sometimes served with a mustard sauce as a first course. At the Stallmästaregården in Stockholm it is cut thick and grilled so that it is browned on the outside and cold in the middle, topped with dill-flavored butter pats, and served with a mustard sauce.

551. Is smoked salmon ever cooked?   Yes. It is sometimes used in place of other fish in a kedgeree. (See Question 546.) It is also browned with rice, put into pastry for a canapé, in fact used in any way your imagination dictates. And in the end, in my opinion, smoked salmon is much better cold and not used in cooked dishes. On toast points, with lemon to squeeze over, it is a fine canapé. Served in thin slices and accompanied by a wedge of lemon and freshly ground pepper, it makes a lovely first course at dinner. An especially delectable first course served at the Imperial Hotel in Copenhagen is cold white European asparagus with thinly sliced smoked salmon on top and a cold cream horseradish sauce to accompany it.

552. What are Kippers? They are smoked herring and constitute a well-known English breakfast dish. They may be heated in the oven with butter ("oven-broiled") or served, broken up, in a cream sauce with hard-cooked eggs.

553. What is Finnan Haddie? It is smoked haddock, which comes whole or in fillets. It is best broiled or poached in milk.

554. What is a Norwegian Fish Pudding? Carefully skinned and boned codfish and haddock are put through the meat grinder, with egg white added, six times. Seasonings are added and the mixture is then beaten in an electric mixer for half an hour while milk and cream are gradually added. This is then baked in a loaf pan in a 350° oven for an hour, or until it is like a solid custard, dry enough to slice. It is served with a lobster or shrimp sauce.

555. What is Seviche? A South American dish of fish fillets (or sometimes scallops), marinated in lime juice for 8 hours or so, until they are "cooked" in the process. They are often served in South America with paper-thin onion slices sprinkled over them. A very similar dish is served in the South Pacific.

556. How many types of lobster are native to the United States? Two. First there are lobsters with claws which come from Maine and other parts of the New England coast, known in France as "homard." Then there are the clawless lobsters, which the French call "langouste," and which come from California and Florida. The type with claws has always been preferred, though the meat of a langouste is delicious.

557. What are the green and pink substances inside a lobster? The green is the liver, sometimes called the tomalley. It is delicious and should never be removed for serving. The pink is roe, known as the coral. It is also marvelous eating and should be left in the lobster when it is served.

558. From what sort of lobster do South African rock lobster tails come? They come from a member of the crayfish family, without claws, like the langouste type. (See Question 556.)

559. What is a collop or scallop of lobster meat? A slice of tail meat.

560. How do you boil lobster? Have water or fish stock (best of all, sea water) at a rolling boil in a big kettle. Plunge the live lobsters in, cover and cook for the required time (4 to 5 minutes to the pound). Remove from water. If the lobster is to be served hot, split in half, starting at the head. Remove stomach and intestinal vein. Serve with melted butter. If it is to be served cold, cool, then chill in the refrigerator. Split and clean just before serving.

561. How do you make Lobster Newburg? Sauté chunks of cooked lobster meat in butter until they turn pink (about 3 minutes). Flambé with cognac, then mix with a sauce made of heavy cream and egg yolks, flavored with sherry.

562. What is Lobster Thermidor? It is one of the richest and, if well done, the most delicious of French lobster dishes. The lobster is cooked, its meat carefully removed and diced, then put into a rich sauce involving cream and egg yolks, well seasoned. This mixture is piled back into the shells (claws removed, of course), sprinkled with Parmesan cheese, and browned in the oven or under the broiler.

563. What is Lobster à l'Américaine? It is a French dish of lobster, cut in pieces (including the shell) and served in a sauce which includes tomatoes, dry white wine, and seasonings, amongst which there must be garlic. There is a good deal of controversy over the name of this dish. There seems to be little doubt that it came originally from Provence, home of tomato and garlicky sauces, but some people think that in its present form it came from Armorique and was originally called Lobster Armoricaine, the present name being a corruption. It is also possible that it was renamed in honor of some American patron in a French restaurant. In any case, it is one of the most famous of lobster dishes.

564. What is Lobster Fra Diavolo?   It is the Italian version of Lobster à l'Américaine (see Question 563), almost exactly the same, except that the lobsters are only split, not cut up.

565. Are big shrimp of better quality than small ones?   Size has nothing to do with quality, but it has a lot to do with price. The big ones are likely to be much more expensive than the small.

566. Is it better to shell shrimp before or after they are cooked? It is much better to shell and devein them first, though they may be done either way. However, they keep their shape better if shelled before cooking. Save the shells to make shrimp butter. (See Question 208.)

567. How long should shrimp be boiled?   They should be plunged into boiling water and *simmered* 3 to 5 minutes, depending upon size. They should then be drained instantly.

568. What are Butterfly Shrimp?   They are a Chinese dish. First you shell the shrimp, leaving the tails on, and devein them. Then split them, but *not all the way through,* and flatten them. Dip them into a batter and fry in deep fat. Sometimes a piece of bacon is pressed onto the shrimp before it is dipped into the batter. Sometimes the shrimp is simply coated with egg white to which a little cornstarch has been added, then fried. They look like butterflies when done.

569. What is Shrimp Toast?   A Chinese dish, which makes a fine appetizer for us. Raw shrimp is minced very fine and mixed with minute quantities of ginger, wine, other seasonings, and egg white, then spread on pieces of bread and deep-fat fried.

570. What is Tempura?   It is a Japanese dish in which all sorts of fish and vegetables are dipped into a simple egg batter and deep-fat fried. We are inclined here to think of it as shrimp alone done in this manner, because in most Japanese restaurants in America shrimp is the only tempura dish served. Various sauces are provided for dipping the tempura, among them soy sauce with slivered ginger in it.

571. What is Jambalaya? It is a New Orleans dish involving always rice and ham (jambon) and usually tomatoes, shrimp or other shellfish, together with seasonings, all cooked together in a fish stock until the liquid is absorbed.

572. What is the best way to make Oyster Stew? Sauté the oysters in butter with Worcestershire sauce and celery salt until their edges curl. Add milk, cream, and oyster liquor and bring just to the boiling point. Serve with generous pats of butter floating on top.

573. What are Oysters Rockefeller? Oysters on the half shell are placed on beds of rock salt in tin pie plates. They are then covered with a sauce composed of creamed butter, finely chopped cooked spinach, onion, parsley and other herbs, plus anisette, if you can get it. If not, use a bit of anise seed. The pans are then placed in a 450° oven for 5 to 8 minutes, until lightly browned on top, and served at once in their tin plates.

574. What are Angels on Horseback? Oysters, seasoned and sprinkled with chopped parsley, rolled in strips of bacon, and broiled until the bacon is crisp (about 6 minutes). They are served on buttered toast with lemon wedges on the side.

575. What is a New Orleans Oyster Loaf? First, oysters are sautéed in butter, then stuffed into a hollowed-out loaf of French bread (which has been cut almost in half, but with a hinge left at the back). The loaf is closed and wrapped tightly in a piece of cheesecloth dipped in milk. The loaf is then baked for about a half hour in a 350° oven.

576. What are Clams or Oysters Casino? Clams or oysters on the half shell, sprinkled with chopped green pepper, chopped onion or shallots, topped with small pieces of "tried-out" bacon, are placed in tin plates half filled with rock salt, and run under the broiler until

the bacon is crisp (3 to 5 minutes). They can also be baked in a 450°
oven, which will take about 10 minutes.

577. How do you tell whether clams are fresh?   If any of the shells
are open, tap them sharply. If the clam is fresh, it will close up
tightly. Discard any which do not close.

578. How can you be sure to get mussels and soft-shell clams clean?
Scrub them well with a stiff brush and cold water. Use several wa-
ters and keep at it until you can see no more sand in the bottom of
the pan. Then let them stand for an hour or so, covered with cold
water. Discard any which do not float. Now they should be clean
and ready to cook.

579. How long do you steam mussels and soft-shell clams?   Put
them into a pot with about an inch of salted water in it. Cover the
kettle tightly and steam until the shells open (about 6 minutes). Discard any which do not open. Serve with melted butter and cups of
the broth.

580. How do you serve mussels?   They can be served in almost
any way you might serve soft-shell clams. They are particularly good
cold with a Ravigote Sauce (see Question 725) and as Moules
Marinière (steamed in well-scrubbed shells until they open, then
served in the shells in a sauce of white wine, mussel liquor, shallots,
butter, fine white bread crumbs, and parsley).

**581. What is the difference between deep sea scallops and bay scal-
lops?**   The deep sea scallops are much larger and less tender than
bay scallops. Also, the latter are more delicately and deliciously
flavored, and much more expensive.

582. How many people are served by a pound of scallops?   Two
or three.

583. What is the best way to cook scallops?   The most delicious
way is to sauté them in butter, with a dash of lemon juice and a
sprinkling of parsley added before serving. They must first be washed
and thoroughly dried with paper toweling (else they will not brown).

They may also be breaded and deep-fat fried, or broiled on skewers with or without bacon. Scallops also take kindly to sauces, which should not be so strongly flavored as to top their own delicate flavor. Scallops make a delicious stew.

584. Can scallops be eaten raw?   Yes, and they make a good appetizer that way, with a squeeze of lemon over them.

585. What are Coquilles St. Jacques?   The French name for scallops, which we are likely to think of as scallops in a rich sauce, browned in the oven in scallop shells. They make a delicious first course, and can be prepared with a variety of sauces, usually named in France for the restaurant in which they are served. For example, "Coquilles St. Jacques à la Façon du Restaurant Jacques-Coeur"!

VIII. VEGETABLES

586. How many servings are there in a pound of each of the following vegetables?

	Servings per Pound		Servings per Pound
Beans, green or wax	4	Peas	2 or 3
Broccoli	3	Squash, winter	2 or 3
Carrots	3 or 4	Tomatoes	3 or 4
Greens, salad, raw	8	Other vegetables	3 or 4
Greens, cooked	2 or 3		

587. Is it a good idea to cook vegetables in chicken stock? Most vegetables which are not going to be peeled later are improved by being cooked in chicken stock because they take on delicate flavor from it. Sometimes sturdily flavored vegetables (like carrots) are cooked in beef stock.

588. What is Ratatouille? It is a Mediterranean vegetable stew, using eggplant, tomatoes, zucchini, onions, green peppers, and garlic —and additions of your own, if you like. Sometimes the sliced vegetables are layered in a casserole with olive oil in the bottom, seasoned as the layering goes on, then cooked either on top of the range or in the oven, covered until the last few minutes, when the cover is removed so the sauce can thicken. Sometimes the vegetables are fried separately in olive oil, then mixed together. Ratatouille is good hot or cold.

589. What is a globe artichoke? It is the bud of a plant which is related to the thistle (hence its "choke"), with tightly clinging leaves surrounding it. A fresh one yields slightly to pressure and is of a good green color.

590. How do you prepare globe artichokes? Trim off any tough outer leaves and, with scissors, cut the pointed tips off all remaining outer leaves. Cut off the stem to within a half inch of the artichoke. Plunge into boiling salted water, into which you have put a peeled clove of garlic and a little olive oil. Simmer until a fork can easily be stuck into the bottom (about 45 minutes). Drain well, upside down. Serve with drawn butter or Hollandaise sauce. (See Question 709.) Or chill and serve with a vinaigrette sauce (see Question 661) as a first course.

591. How do you serve canned artichoke bottoms? Stew them gently in butter to heat through without browning. Then, if you like, serve them filled with a mound of puréed peas (see Question 611), or with chopped sautéed mushrooms. They can also be stuffed with creamed ham, chicken, or shellfish, sprinkled with grated cheese, and browned in the oven or under the broiler. Sometimes they are quartered and served in a rich cream sauce.

592. What is a Jerusalem artichoke? It is a tuber which grows underground and produces a type of plant related to the sunflower. It is usually boiled and served in place of potatoes.

593. Should one peel the stalks of asparagus? Not unless they are very tough. Cut the bottom ends of the stalks so that each is even in length with the rest. Tie them together with white string and stand in boiling, salted water to the depth of three inches. Cover the pot (with another pot turned upside down to give extra height if necessary) and cook 15 to 20 minutes until done to taste. Serve hot with melted butter or Hollandaise sauce (see Question 709) or cold with vinaigrette sauce. (See Question 661.)

594. What is Asparagus Milanese? For each serving: four stalks of cooked and drained asparagus topped by a lightly fried or poached egg, sprinkled with grated Parmesan cheese and melted butter, and run under the broiler very briefly to turn the cheese golden brown.

595. What can be added to green beans for a change of pace? Slivered, sautéed almonds, thinly sliced water chestnuts, sliced mushrooms, slivers of pimiento, or a sour cream sauce flavored with herbs.

596. What are Harvard beets? Sliced beets glazed with a sauce of sugar, vinegar, and cornstarch, with butter added.

597. Is there a more interesting way to serve Brussels sprouts than just buttered? A lot of contrast and character is added by serving them mixed either with cooked chestnuts, broken up, or with warmed seedless white grapes.

598. Is it all right to husk corn and put the ears into cold water until one is ready to cook it? No! Corn should be husked just as near the time it is to go into the pot as is possible. It loses greatly in flavor and freshness if it is husked too early.

599. How long should you boil fresh corn? From the time the water comes back to the boil after putting the ears in, *not more than 3 minutes* if the corn is really fresh.

600. How do you cook corn outdoors in an open fire? Pull the husks down to the end of the ear, but do not tear them off. Remove the silk and soak the corn in cold salted water about 30 minutes. Drain and brush the kernels with butter. Sprinkle with salt and pepper. Pull the husks up around the ear again. Wrap each ear in heavy-duty aluminum foil and close the ends tightly. Roast the corn in hot coals, turning frequently, for about 25 minutes, or until done to your taste.

601. What is the best way to make corn fritters? Grate corn from the ears. Mix with egg yolks, milk, a bit of melted butter, and a *very small* amount of flour and baking powder. Last, fold in beaten egg whites. The batter should be about the consistency of heavy cream, quite thin. Fry in butter or fat until brown and crisp on both sides. These come out thin and lacy and absolutely delicious, bearing no relation to the puffed-up corn fritters (more fritter than corn) sometimes served.

602. What goes into a New England Corn Pudding? If you want to be a purist about it, use kernels of corn scraped from the cob, eggs, milk and/or cream, and seasonings. If you want to add a little fun to it, put in some chopped green pepper, chopped pimiento, and minced onion, also a little mustard in the seasoning. However you do it, the pudding is then baked in a 375° oven until brown and bubbling.

603. Can cucumbers be cooked?   Yes, they are very good cooked. They can be stuffed and baked or poached in chicken broth, to which, after they are done, you add lemon juice, butter, and an egg yolk to make a sort of cucumber Hollandaise.

604. What is Eggplant Caviar?   It is a dish of Middle Eastern origin in which peeled and cooked eggplant is mixed with onion, garlic, tomatoes, seasonings, and sesame oil. Olive oil may be used if preferred. The mixture is chilled and served as a first course.

605. Is Belgian endive ever cooked?   Indeed it is, and it is very good. I find that I do mine backwards according to the French and Belgians, but it comes out very well. First, in order that the leaves will not spread all over the pan, I tie each head with white string. Then I brown them in butter to a nice golden color on all sides. Then I put in a bit of chicken broth (not too much—it is better to add more if necessary than to drown them), cover the pan, and cook them until they are tender, which takes about 15 to 20 minutes.

606. How do you cook leeks?   They are generally braised (in chicken stock is best) and sometimes browned in the broiler, covered with cheese or a cheese sauce. Or they can be boiled, drained, and chilled and served with a sauce vinaigrette (see Question 661) as a first course. Be sure to get leeks *clean,* as they are inclined to be gritty. Soaking in cold water will usually do the trick.

607. Which is a better buy—canned or fresh mushrooms?   If the price of a 4-ounce can is one-third that of a pound of fresh mushrooms, they are equally good buys, based on the premise that a pound of fresh mushrooms gives six servings and a 4-ounce can gives two servings.

608. Are raw mushrooms edible?   Yes. Edible and delicious. They are especially good chopped and mixed with a bit of mayonnaise, then spread on a sautéed bread round to make a canapé.

609. How do you serve hearts of palm?   Well drained, cut into 1-inch pieces, and warmed (not browned) in butter. Or cut in half, lengthwise and served in a salad.

610. Which is cheaper—canned or frozen peas? You must compare prices at the time you wish to buy to determine this. A 1-pound, 4-ounce can of peas, for instance, yields about 2½ cups, and a 10-ounce frozen package yields 1½ cups. Taking half a cup as a serving, the can will then yield five servings and the frozen package three. Divide the price of the can and the package by the number of servings it will give you to see which is cheaper. Sometimes it will be one, sometimes the other, depending usually upon the season.

611. How do you make a purée of peas? The easiest way is to make it in the blender, using as much of the water in which the peas were cooked as you need to get the consistency you like. A food mill is harder, but is a good way also to make a purée. This goes not only for peas but for any cooked vegetable.

612. What are peas in the French style? Peas braised with lettuce, onions, butter, and seasonings.

613. What are snow peas? Small pods in which the peas do not mature. They are primarily a Chinese vegetable, but are raised all over the world. They are cooked very briefly in hot oil (about 1 minute with constant stirring) and are crisp, sweet, and delicious to eat. They now come frozen, but these are not nearly as good as the fresh.

614. How do you keep raw, pared potatoes from turning dark? Place them in cold water for a short time. Do not pare them so far ahead that they must soak in water for a long period.

615. Is there any way to hasten the baking of potatoes? Yes. There are metal rods, the pointed ends of which you force into the potatoes. These rods conduct the oven heat straight into the center of the potatoes, and they bake in about half the usual time.

616. Is it best to boil potatoes with their skins on? Yes, because cooked in this way they retain vitamins and flavor. It is also a good idea to serve them with the skins on, because once people get accustomed to eating them they will find the skins have more flavor than the potato.

617. What makes potatoes waxy?   The fact that they have a low content of starch and a high content of water. This is more likely to be true of new potatoes, which are harvested before they are fully mature, than of mature potatoes, which are mealy when cooked.

618. What is the best way to cook pan-browned potatoes?   Of course, the name of this dish means that whole boiled potatoes are browned in the oven with the meat. However, I have found that they are infinitely better to look at and to eat if you brown them in butter in a skillet, turning until all sides are golden and crisp.

619. What are Duchesse Potatoes?   Boiled potatoes, mashed and mixed with eggs and egg yolks and seasonings, then piped through a pastry tube to make the border of a dish, or piped onto a cookie sheet in any shape you like, and browned in the oven or under the broiler.

620. What are Potatoes Anna?   White potatoes are sliced into thin rounds, then put into a well-buttered baking dish in overlapping layers, each layer seasoned with salt and pepper and well dotted with butter. The dish is then baked in a 400° oven for 40 minutes or until the potatoes are done and crisply brown on the bottom. They are inverted onto a hot plate or platter to serve. When the potatoes are layered with partially cooked carrots, this dish is known as Potatoes Crécy.

621. What is a Gratin Dauphinoise?   Thinly sliced white potatoes are mixed with scalded milk, beaten eggs, seasonings and grated Gruyère cheese, then put into a shallow baking dish, sprinkled with more cheese and baked 50 to 60 minutes in a 350° oven.

622. What is the best way to make potato pancakes?   As the Germans do, grating the raw potatoes, squeezing all possible liquid out of them, then mixing them with eggs, seasonings, and a rather small amount of flour. They are fried to a good brown on both sides and turn out to be crisp and lacy.

623. Is it hard to make soufflé potatoes?   It is hard, but not impossible. First, you must cut your potatoes in uniform pieces, about

2 inches long and 1 inch thick. Soak them at least a half hour in ice water. Pat them thoroughly dry. Then put them into 275° deep fat for 4 to 5 minutes. Drain with frying basket, then on absorbent paper, and refrigerate until ready to finish. Put them, a few at a time, into 400° deep fat. When they are well puffed and brown (be careful not to burn), drain, sprinkle with salt, and serve.

624. What are shallots? Small members of the onion family, with reddish brown skins which have a sharper flavor than scallions, with a faint garlic flavor, in some people's opinion.

625. What is salsify and how do you cook it? It is the root of a member of the chicory family, also known as oyster plant because some people think it has something of the flavor of oysters. Boil and mash it and mix with egg and a little flour, salt, and melted butter to make a thick batter which can be formed into patties. Roll these in bread crumbs and fry in butter until golden brown. Or boil and serve with melted butter and seasonings, or a well-flavored cream sauce. Another way to use salsify is to boil it whole, cut into halves lengthwise, dredge with flour, and fry in butter or bacon fat until golden brown.

626. Is it necessary to cook canned sauerkraut? No. Just heat it up, adding butter, a bit of onion, caraway seeds, what you will.

627. How long should sauerkraut bought by the pound be cooked? Half an hour. Ever cook it in champagne, by the way?

628. Should you add any water to spinach for cooking? No, simply use the water which clings to the leaves after washing. There is a lot of water in spinach, which will be drawn out in the cooking, so no more is needed.

629. What can be added to spinach to vary the flavor? Finely chopped spinach is excellent in a cream sauce. Mushrooms are very good with spinach, either in a cream sauce in the center of a spinach ring or sautéed and mixed with the spinach. And, believe it or not, spinach is very good finely minced, with a bit of onion, garlic, and seasonings and chopped clams with their liquor stirred in!

IX. PASTA AND RICE

631. What is pasta?   Pasta is a mixture of flour and water, sometimes with eggs added, which is made into many forms and shapes.

632. What are some of the forms of pasta?
1. The string types: spaghetti, spaghettini, vermicelli.
2. The tubular type with a hole through the middle: macaroni.
3. The flat types: lasagna (broad), linguine, and fettucine (very narrow).
4. The filled types: ravioli, manicotti, cannelloni.
5. The fancy shapes: stars, shells, wheels, et cetera, usually known as pastina.

There are many, many more names and shapes and an infinite variety of sizes.

633. Is it worth while to make your own pasta?   The difference in taste and delicacy between homemade pasta and that which comes in a box is infinite. Making it takes time, but once you have done it you will never be quite happy with the commercially made variety again. If you have a pasta rolling and cutting machine, the task is greatly eased. After making and cutting the pasta you should hang it up to dry a bit, and in a small apartment the best place for this is over clean tea towels on the shower curtain rod.

634. What is pasta verdi?   Pasta colored and flavored with spinach juice.

635. Is pasta confined to Italy?   No. Marco Polo probably brought it back to Italy from China (ravioli and won ton are very similar). The Russian piroshki is a good deal like fried won ton or ravioli. Middle European countries make many similar foods (such as spätzle and tarhonya noodles).

636. How much spaghetti or fettucine or similar pastas serves one person?   A fourth of a pound serves one Italian and two or three Americans!

637. How is pasta cooked "al dente"?   It is cooked briefly, compared to what most of us are accustomed to, and thus one can get the teeth into it because it is not soft or mushy. For pasta like fettucine, for instance, this means cooking it 8 to 9 minutes. Homemade pasta takes far less time than the store-bought variety (fettucine about 6 minutes).

638. How can you keep pasta from sticking together when boiled?
Put a little olive oil into the cooking water.

639. Is pasta always served in place of potatoes?   It is not served in the same meal with potatoes, but neither does it always accompany meat. One of the best first courses ever invented is either green noodles or fettucine tossed with butter and grated Parmesan cheese (and sometimes a bit of cream). After that, one serves meat and a vegetable or salad with no accompanying starchy food.

640. Can macaroni and cheese be used as a main dish?   It frequently is, and is particularly good for this purpose if you put cubed ham into it before baking.

641. What is spaghetti with clam sauce?   One of the most popular spaghetti dishes. The sauce may be either red or white, well seasoned, and mixed well with the spaghetti. (See Question 724.)

642. What is Cannelloni?   Rectangles of pasta dough, cooked, filled with meat or any other kind of filling in a sauce, rolled up, placed in a baking dish, sometimes covered with a sauce, always sprinkled with Parmesan cheese, and browned under the broiler. In some elegant restaurants in Rome, cannelloni are made with French crêpes (see Question 752) instead of pasta, but this is not authentic.

643. What is Manicotti?   Pasta dough, cut into rectangles, cooked, filled with ricotta cheese, rolled up, and placed in a baking dish. It is then covered with tomato sauce and baked.

644. What are Ravioli?   Two sheets of pasta dough are rolled out and a filling of meat, chicken, brains, or whatever you like, is placed at intervals on one sheet, covered with the second sheet and the dough then cut into squares or rounds, pinched well together, and cooked in boiling water. When well drained, the ravioli are usually served with a sauce of some sort over them, sometimes put into a baking dish, covered with sauce, and browned on top.

645. What is Lasagna Verdi al Forno? One of the most distinguished Italian pasta dishes. Broad strips of spinach lasagna, cooked "al dente," are layered with Ragù Bolognese (see Question 724), Béchamel sauce (see Question 708), and grated Parmesan cheese and baked. The result is superb.

646. What are Gnocchi? There are two kinds, the one made from potato being really a sort of pasta dumpling and the one made from semolina mush quite different—usually cut into rounds, sprinkled with butter and grated Parmesan and broiled, or served with a rich mushroom sauce.

647. How much rice serves one person? This depends upon whether the rice dish is the main one of the meal or a side dish. It also depends upon whether one comes from a rice-eating country. For most Americans ¼ cup of uncooked rice (which makes ½ cup, cooked), served as a side dish is a great sufficiency. Italians, Far Eastern peoples, and Middle Easterners would serve at least twice that. If the dish contains meat and other ingredients which are filling and thus becomes the main course, ⅓ cup of uncooked rice would be plenty for Americans, but not for real rice-eaters.

648. Should rice be washed before cooking? The packaged rice you buy in this country is perfectly clean and not only does not need washing but loses food value if you wash it. However, if you buy rice by the pound in Chinese or other foreign food stores, you had best wash it before cooking.

649. How long should rice be boiled? Long grain rice about 14 minutes. Converted rice takes longer and you should follow package directions.

650. What kind of rice is best? Either long grain or converted rice, but the latter has more food value.

651. Does instant rice save time? In my opinion, the fact that it may be ready a couple of minutes sooner than long grain rice, for instance, does not compensate for the fact that it has not as much flavor. However, many people love it.

652. What is wild rice? Just what the name implies. It grows wild in water in a few parts of this country and must be harvested by hand, which makes it exceedingly expensive. It has, however, great flavor and texture and is a delicious accompaniment to many dishes, if you can afford it. It must be cooked longer than other rice (35 to 40 minutes).

653. What is brown rice? It is the whole grain of rice with only the husk removed. It has more flavor and nutritional value than white rice.

654. What is a Pilaf? It is the name usually given to rice dishes in the Middle East and is made in many ways. It may contain meat, chicken livers, vegetables, raisins, and nuts. It is usually cooked in chicken broth, sometimes in the oven.

655. What is Fried Rice? It is a Chinese dish. Cold cooked rice is fried briefly in oil (not to brown it) with meats, seasonings, and all sorts of additions to suit the fancy of the cook or the area in which it is being served. It was originally invented in Yang Chow.

656. What is a Pulao? It is an Indian dish of cooked rice, mixed with thinly sliced onion, raisins, nuts, spices, tomatoes, or other vegetables—any or all of these. Sometimes rice and spices are mixed with chicken or meat to make a main dish.

657. What is a Risotto? It is an Italian rice dish, cooked in many ways in the various northern cities of Italy. A Risotto Milanese (which I think is the best) is rice cooked in chicken broth with saffron and a little onion, tossed when done with butter and grated Parmesan cheese, and served with grated or slivered white truffle over it as a first course. Around Venice, the risottos usually contain fish and/or shellfish, which makes them meals in a dish. In Florence they serve a Risotto alla Sherry, which is rice cooked in beef stock with onion and sweet red peppers. It is tossed before serving, with grated Parmesan cheese and a little sherry wine.

658. What is Spanish Rice?   Cooked rice, mixed with chopped green pepper, chopped tomato, chopped onions, and seasonings, sometimes served with grated Parmesan cheese.

659. What is a Rijsttafel?   It is the Dutch name for a fascinating Indonesian meal. Many servants, each carrying one dish, serve the guests. Everyone has rice and then whatever he wants from the other dishes, meats, vegetables, and egg dishes—some in hot sauces, some quite dry—all eaten with the rice and many chutneys.

X. SALADS

660. What is French Dressing? To the purist it is a mixture of olive oil, vinegar, salt, and pepper—*period.* However, in this country we sometimes make additions of one or more of the following: mustard, garlic, paprika, curry powder, celery salt, grated onion, cheese, chives, chopped parsley, chopped shallots, sugar, and sometimes even ketchup (of the last two I do not approve). Also, we substitute wine vinegar, herbed wine vinegar, or lemon juice for plain cider vinegar at times, as well as other oils for the olive oil.

661. What is a Vinaigrette Dressing? This term is frequently used in France as interchangeable with our French dressing. (See Question 660.) It is also used here and in France for a dressing which is used on cold cooked vegetables (especially artichokes and asparagus), cold meats, fish, or greens, and in this case consists of a plain French dressing with chopped capers, parsley, onion, hard-cooked egg, gherkins, and sometimes other herbs added.

662. Should olive and other salad oils be refrigerated? If you use these oils frequently and therefore use them up in fairly short time, there is no reason why they must be refrigerated, though the advice is generally that you should do so. Some oils become cloudy and solidify in the refrigerator, but if left at room temperature for a sufficient time they liquify and become clear.

663. What are the important points in making good mayonnaise?
1. All ingredients should be at room temperature. (If egg yolks are cold, warm the mixing bowl in hot water to take off the chill.)
2. Beat yolks briefly before starting to add other ingredients.
3. The olive oil must be added *by the drop* until one fourth to one third of the oil has been absorbed, and the beating must be constant during the process of adding the oil. (This is most easily done with an electric beater at medium speed.) After that, the oil may be added by the tablespoonful.

664. What is the proper proportion of egg yolks to olive oil in making mayonnaise? Use ½ to ¾ cup of olive oil to one large egg yolk—*not more*. If this is exceeded, the mayonnaise will almost certainly curdle.

665. What is the proportion of vinegar or lemon juice in good mayonnaise? Two to three tablespoons to two egg yolks, depending largely upon taste. If the mayonnaise becomes too thick, thin it with vinegar or lemon juice, added by the drop.

666. Can you make good mayonnaise in a blender? Yes. It makes a fluffier, less rich-seeming dressing than that which you make by hand or with an electric mixer, particularly if you make it with whole eggs, which is possible with this method.

667. How should mayonnaise be stored? Tightly covered in the refrigerator if it is homemade. Commercially made mayonnaise may be stored on the shelf until it is opened. After that it should be refrigerated.

668. How can one insure against mayonnaise cracking? By observing the rules given in Question 663 and by adding a little boiling water (1 to 2 tablespoons, depending upon the quantity of mayonnaise) at the end.

669. If mayonnaise curdles (or cracks), is there any way to rescue it? Yes, there are two ways. First, in a warmed bowl place a teaspoonful of prepared mustard. Add a tablespoonful of the cracked mayonnaise and beat with a wire whisk until they are smoothly combined. Add the rest of the mayonnaise, a teaspoonful at a time, until all is incorporated smoothly. The second method is to place an egg yolk in a warmed bowl, beat it briefly, then beat in the cracked mayonnaise very gradually until it thickens and is smooth again.

670. What is Mayonnaise Chaud-Froid? Mayonnaise to which gelatin has been added. It is then mixed with chopped cooked vegetables or meat, or used to coat fish fillets and the like, and refrigerated until well chilled and jelled.

671. What is Green Mayonnaise?   Spinach leaves, watercress leaves, parsley, and any desired herbs are blanched briefly, dried, and either whirled in the blender or pressed through a fine sieve, then stirred into mayonnaise, which they flavor and color green. Especially handsome to serve with cold salmon or other fish.

672. What is Thousand Island Dressing?   Mayonnaise with chili sauce, Worcestershire, chopped pimiento, chopped green pepper, and minced chives added.

673. What is Russian Dressing?   Mayonnaise with chili sauce, chopped pimiento, and minced chives added.

674. What is Lorenzo Dressing?   Chili sauce mixed with French dressing (see Question 660) in the proportion of one part to four, and with chopped water cress added.

675. Should a wooden salad bowl be washed?   Preferably not. Wipe such a bowl out well with paper towels when the salad is finished. Store covered with Saran, which will cling and keep the bowl clean. If treated thus, the salad bowl will always be treated and ready to receive the next salad. It will also be beautiful to look upon, as the rubbing with paper towels when there is some oil left in the bowl deepens the color of the wood and brings out the pattern of its grain.

676. What is the best way to store greens?   They should first be thoroughly washed and drained. The French wire salad baskets offer the best method of draining greens well. When well drained, greens should be placed in plastic bags or wrapped in a tea towel and stored in the refrigerator crisper.

677. What goes into a tossed green salad?   A variety of greens chosen from what is available in the markets, usually at least two kinds, tossed with a simple French dressing. (See Question 660.) See Check List for Salads (Question 65).

678. Should greens be cut up for salad?   Never! They should be *torn* into whatever size pieces you prefer.

679. What vegetables other than greens may be put into a green salad?   Green or sweet red pepper, avocado, carrots, radishes, tomatoes, onions, cucumbers, celery, scallions, and fresh herbs, all raw, and sliced or chopped.

680. What is a wilted green salad?   Lettuce or, preferably, dandelion greens are shredded. Diced bacon is fried until crisp, then sugar, seasonings, and vinegar added to it. When the sugar is dissolved, this hot mixture is poured over the greens and they are tossed.

681. How is a Chef's Salad made?   Julienne strips of chicken, tongue, ham, and Swiss cheese, in equal proportions, are mixed with water cress or other greens and served with French dressing.

682. What is Salad Mimosa?   It is a tossed green salad, flavored with garlic if desired, with chopped hard-cooked egg sprinkled over it. The latter is what makes it "Mimosa."

683. What is a Caesar Salad?   Greens are torn into a salad bowl, mixed with lemon juice, olive oil, seasonings, and grated Parmesan and crumbled blue cheese. A raw egg is broken into the salad and it is tossed thoroughly, so that the egg clings to every leaf and causes the cheese to stick to the leaves. At the end, garlic-flavored croutons are added and tossed lightly. It has sometimes seemed to me that every chef in California claims to have invented Caesar salad. In any event, it is Californian.

684. What are wilted cucumbers?   Cucumbers are pared and sliced paper-thin, then sprinkled with salt and mixed well, with the hands, in a bowl. Next, a plate is pressed down firmly on the cucumbers, and they are left to stand for an hour, then are drained, and dressed with vinegar, sugar, dill, and seasonings.

685. What is a Greek Salad?   It is made of lettuce, sliced cucumber, cubed tomatoes, Greek Feta cheese, pitted Greek black olives, sliced onion, cubed beets, chopped anchovy filets, capers, and oregano. These are tossed gently with a French dressing (see Question 660) made with a dash of mustard.

686. What is Salade Niçoise?   It is composed of one or more greens, quartered tomatoes, chopped green and/or sweet red pepper, thinly sliced onion and radishes, finely chopped white and red cabbage, white-meat tuna, anchovies, black olives, fresh basil, and sliced hard-cooked egg, tossed with a French dressing (see Question 660) made with wine vinegar.

687. What makes a salad a "chiffonade"?   The addition of cold cooked beets (usually in julienne slices, but diced, if desired) to greens before tossing.

688. What is Beetroot Salad?   Chilled cooked or canned beets are cut into julienne strips or thin slices, covered with very thin slices of onion, and marinated in French dressing (see Question 660) for a couple of hours before serving, and decorated with minced parsley.

689. What is Coleslaw?   Shredded red and/or white, new or old cabbage, mixed with mayonnaise, French dressing (usually strong of vinegar), sour cream dressing, or whatever other kind of dressing is preferred. The addition of celery salt to coleslaw is a pleasant one, and some people like caraway seed in it. One may also add grated onion, carrot, and/or green or sweet red pepper to the mixture.

690. What is Céleri Rémoulade?   Celery root, cut in julienne slices (sometimes used raw, sometimes parboiled, always chilled), served in a mustard mayonnaise. This may be served as a first course or in place of salad.

691. What is a Salade Macédoine?   It is a mixture of cooked vegetables, chilled and mixed with mayonnaise.

692. What is Italian Salad?   It is a mixture of chilled cooked vegetables, diced and mixed with mayonnaise. They are then arranged in a dome shape and garnished with strips of anchovy, sliced Italian ham or salami, tomato wedges, olives, and capers—any or all, but the anchovy is never omitted.

693. What is Salade Parisienne?   It is a mixture of chilled, cooked vegetables cut up small, with slivers of truffle, lobster, or crabmeat, and mayonnaise added. It is sometimes arranged in a mold lined with clear aspic and mixed with mayonnaise chaud-froid (see Question 670), then unmolded as a beautiful buffet dish.

694. What is Russian Salad? Sometimes listed as Salade Russe, this is a mixture of cooked, chilled, and cubed vegetables, mixed with cubed ham or tongue, a few shreds of truffle, and mayonnaise.

695. What is the best way to make Potato Salad? I like to marinate potatoes first in French dressing (see Question 660) with onions, green peppers, or any other additions I choose to make—perhaps none!—in the refrigerator for an hour or so at least. Then at the last I mix in mayonnaise to taste.

696. Should you cook potatoes for Potato Salad until they are very soft? No. You should cook them until they are just barely done. They will hold their shape much better.

697. Should potatoes be sliced or diced for Potato Salad? This is a matter of preference. One point in deciding which you will do is to remember that diced potatoes are not as likely to break up as sliced ones when mixed with dressing.

698. What garnish should be used on Potato Salad? You may garnish a potato salad with hard-cooked eggs, parsley, pimiento strips, crumbled bacon, or with nothing at all.

699. What fruits should go into a Fruit Salad? Any fruits you wish to use, well drained if they are juicy—and fresh ones, please, insofar as possible.

700. What is a Waldorf Salad? A salad made of apples, walnuts, celery, and mayonnaise, served on a bed of lettuce.

701. What is Guacamole? A salad or appetizer made of mashed avocado mixed with mayonnaise, garlic, chili powder, and if you like, finely chopped, well-drained tomato. French dressing may be substituted for the mayonnaise if desired. This is served as a first course on lettuce leaves or as a canapé with corn chips for "dunking."

702. Can you make a Tomato Aspic with tomato juice as the base?
You can, but a tomato aspic is infinitely more interesting if you make it of stewed or canned tomatoes, seeds and all (no skins, of course).

703. Is rice ever used in salad?   Yes, indeed, and one of the best rice salads is made by seasoning rice well with curry powder as it cooks, so that it becomes a beautiful yellow color and well flavored with curry. Drain, chill well, and serve either just as is, mixed with cooked, chilled green peas, or with crabmeat or lobster. French dressing (see Question 660) may be added if desired.

XI. SAUCES

704. How do you make cream sauce? Melt butter, stir in flour smoothly, add milk and/or cream, and stir until thickened, then season to taste. Proportions for cream sauce are as follows:

Thin	1 tablespoon butter	1 tablespoon flour	1 cup liquid
Medium	2 tablespoons butter	2 tablespoons flour	1 cup liquid
Thick	3 tablespoons butter	3 tablespoons flour	1 cup liquid

705. How do you prevent lumps in cream sauce? First, by stirring the flour into the melted butter smoothly until there is not one lump left. For some people it is easiest to accomplish this off the heat. Also, some find it easier to keep the sauce smooth if the milk is scalded first. Next, you must stir the mixture *absolutely constantly* after you put the liquid in, until the sauce is thickened. If you leave it on the heat without stirring even for a few seconds, it will tend to lump. If, however, you get lumps anyway, whirl the sauce in the blender or force it through a sieve, then reheat it without boiling.

706. What do you do if your cream sauce is too thin? Either reduce it over fairly high heat, stirring constantly, or add beurre manié. (See Question 207.)

707. What do you do if your cream sauce is too thick? Beat in more milk or cream, a tablespoonful at a time.

708. What is Béchamel Sauce? In my opinion, this is a matter of controversy. Even among the French, whence the sauce obviously came, there are a variety of definitions. To some, it is a basic cream sauce. (See Question 704.) I was first taught to make it like a cream sauce, but using chicken stock instead of milk, cooking it at a simmer for 10 minutes with minced onion in it, then adding a few tablespoons of cream. Finally it is strained before using. Other French recipes recommend making Béchamel with veal stock and milk.

709. How do you make Hollandaise Sauce? In the proportion of 1 egg yolk to 1½ teaspoons lemon juice and ½ stick butter (may be doubled or tripled successfully), proceed as follows: Melt butter. Blend egg yolk and lemon juice in top of double boiler over hot, *not boiling,* water. Add butter gradually to the egg yolk, beating constantly with a wire whisk. Continue beating until sauce has reached the consistency you like. The more you beat, the thicker it will get. Remove from heat and season with salt and cayenne.

710. Can anything be done to correct cracked Hollandaise? Yes. Beat in hot water, a little bit at a time until the sauce comes together again.

711. Can a too-thin Hollandaise be fixed? Yes. Put a teaspoonful of lemon juice and a tablespoonful of the sauce into a warm bowl and beat with a wire whisk until it thickens. Then beat in the rest of the sauce, a very little at a time, beating with each addition until it thickens again.

712. Why does Hollandaise sometimes fail to thicken? Probably because you added your butter too fast.

713. What do you do if your Hollandaise is too thick? Beat in a couple of tablespoons of hot water.

714. How do you keep Hollandaise warm? It can be kept warm by setting the pan in which it was cooked in a pan of lukewarm water. It is not supposed to be served *hot.*

715. What is Glace de Viand? It is a highly concentrated brown meat jelly, which is used in many sauces. Making it is something which no one but a skilled chef would, or should, undertake. It can be bought in jars and is usually called meat glaze or meat extract.

716. What is Sauce Espagnole? It is a very important basic sauce which originated in France and is also sometimes called Brown Sauce. There are many recipes for making it, but it is basically a matter of browning chopped carrot and onion in fat (sometimes with bits of ham, which makes it very tasty), stirring in flour, then adding good strong beef stock and cooking the whole until it reduces and thickens. Tomato paste or fresh tomato is added at the end. It is cooked anywhere from ¾ hour to 1½ hours. At the end it is strained and can be frozen or kept in the refrigerator. It is used as the base of many sauces and gives them wonderful, strong flavor.

717. What is Brown Sauce? Sauce Espagnole. (See Question 716.)

718. What is Bread Sauce? It is a sauce often served with game, particularly pheasant and grouse. It is made by cooking milk and fine dry bread crumbs with an onion stuck with cloves, in the top of a double boiler. Coarse bread crumbs are fried in butter and stirred into the original mixture with seasonings to taste.

719. Is there any point in saving small amounts of leftover sauces? Yes. They are marvelous to incorporate into new sauces and gravies you may make. A dab of leftover Hollandaise improves nearly any other sauce. A bit of curry sauce adds tantalizing flavor to a meat gravy. Any leftover sauce at all gives life and character to a cream sauce, provided that whatever you add marries well with the food you are saucing.

720. What sauces go well with meat?
1. *Béarnaise:* See Question 723. Particularly good with beefsteak.
2. *Bordelaise:* A red wine sauce with beef marrow in it.
3. *Barbecue:* There are probably hundreds of versions of this sauce, but it is usually based on tomatoes and contains any or all of the following: wine (usually red), onions, garlic, herbs, mustard, brown sugar, and other seasonings. Used to marinate, baste, and serve with meats grilled outdoors or broiled indoors, mostly with beef.
4. *Caper:* Add capers to cream sauce (see Question 704) and serve with boiled mutton.
5. *Chasseur:* Espagnole (see Question 716) with tomatoes, garlic, and herbs. Very good with veal.
6. *Cumberland:* Port wine and melted currant jelly, with orange peel, shallots, orange juice, and other seasonings added. Served hot or cold, but usually cold with cold meat, especially game.
7. *Curry:* A proper Indian curry sauce is made by first grinding spices, either in the blender or with mortar and pestle, frying

them for about five minutes, usually with onion and garlic, then adding flour or cornstarch, stirring until blended, and last stirring in stock and/or yoghurt (in place of Indian curd). Spices used vary greatly, but always include hot (chili) peppers and turmeric (which makes the curry yellow). Other possibilities for the mixture are listed in Question 938. Green chilis are also often added. Burmese and Thai curries are usually made with coconut milk as the liquid. Fish, shellfish, eggs, vegetables, and poultry are also served in curry sauce.

8. *Horseradish:* Horseradish sauce can be made with sour cream, with whipped sweet cream, or with applesauce, with grated fresh horseradish added. It is served usually with either hot boiled beef or cold beef of any description.

9. *Madeira:* Espagnole (see Question 716) with Madeira wine. Very good with ham.

10. *Mint:* Made of vinegar, a little sugar, and chopped mint leaves. Served hot with lamb or mutton.

11. *Mustard:* The easiest way to make this is to add prepared mustard to cream sauce (see Question 704) according to your taste. It is usually served with ham or tongue.

12. *Perigueux:* Espagnole with Madeira wine and truffles. With fillet of beef, ham, veal, and egg dishes.

13. *Raisin:* A thickened sauce made with stock, vinegar, brown sugar, and seasonings to taste, with raisins in it. Served hot with ham or tongue.

14. *Robert:* Espagnole (see Question 716) with mustard in it.

15. *Smitane:* Sour cream sauce, seasoned with onion, a little white wine, and lemon juice if desired. Very good on veal. Also used a good deal with poultry.

16. *Soubise:* See Question 723. Often used with veal, also lamb.

17. *Sweet and Sour:* A Chinese sauce which involves stock, vinegar, and sugar, and which is made in many ways, sometimes requiring pineapple, green pepper, carrot, ginger, and other seasonings. It is thickened with cornstarch. We in the West think of it as being served with pork, but it is also used with fish and with other meats and sometimes with vegetables.

18. *Tomato:* Made at home with either fresh or canned tomatoes and good seasonings, this is a very different sauce from that you buy in a can. Try making it, and if you still like the canned

variety, or using canned soup as a sauce, go ahead! Especially good on hamburgers, but used with many meats, pastas, fish, and other dishes.

721. What sauces go well with chicken?

1. *Curry:* See Question 720.
2. *Cream:* See Question 704.
3. *Mornay:* See Question 723.
4. *Poulette:* See Question 723.
5. *Velouté:* See Question 725.
6. *Paprika:* This can be a Suprême with good Hungarian paprika added. It can also be a cream sauce (see Question 704) made with half milk, half sweet cream, or with sour cream. Chicken Paprika is a Hungarian dish.
7. *Ivoire:* Chicken is cooked in champagne with rich chicken stock and sour cream added half way through the cooking. When done, the chicken is removed and the sauce reduced, with mushrooms added, until it bubbles fiercely and takes on an ivory color. The chicken is then returned to the sauce and served at once.
8. *Perigourdine:* Reduce Espagnole (see Question 716) until it is half the original quantity, then add Madeira wine and truffles. Very like Sauce Perigueux. (See Question 720.)
9. *Sauce Supreme:* Made like a cream sauce (see Question 704), but substituting chicken broth for milk.

722. What sauces go well with duck?

1. *Black Cherry:* The juice of black cherries is seasoned to taste, a little Espagnole (see Question 716) added, the whole thickened with cornstarch, and the pitted cherries heated in it.
2. *Olive:* Espagnole (see Question 716), with white wine and whole pitted green olives in it.
3. *Orange:* Espagnole (see Question 716), with wine, orange juice, seasonings, and slivered orange rind. When the duck has been roasted, add the pure juice from the pan, with fat removed.
4. *Red Currant:* Stock thickened with a roux, with red currant jelly melted in it. May be flavored with dry sherry, if desired.

723. What sauces go well with fish?

1. *Aioli:* A garlic mayonnaise, much used in the Provence area of France. Garlic cloves in *quantity* are crushed, mixed with egg yolk, vinegar, and seasonings, then olive oil is added slowly while the mixture is beaten, as in making mayonnaise. (See Question 663.)

2. *Béarnaise:* Is made just as Hollandaise is made (see Question 709), except that in place of lemon juice, vinegar and wine, boiled down with shallots and tarragon, is strained and beaten into the egg yolks before the butter.

3. *Colbert:* Béarnaise sauce (see Question 723) with a little dissolved meat glaze stirred into it. Used for steak, chicken, and eggs, as well as for fish.

4. *Egg:* Cream sauce (see Question 704) with chopped or sliced hard-cooked eggs added; a dash of Worcestershire is a good seasoning, also some minced parsley. Served usually with poached or steamed fish.

5. *Horseradish Cream:* Cold, salted whipped cream, mixed with freshly grated horseradish to taste. Very good with cold salmon.

6. *Lamaze:* Mayonnaise mixed with an equal quantity of chili sauce and India Relish, plus mustard, Worcestershire, horseradish, chopped hard-cooked egg, chopped pimiento and chives, Tabasco, and other seasonings. Good with shellfish or cold fish of any kind—also on cold hard-cooked eggs.

7. *Matelote:* Red wine sauce in which fish has been poached, is cooked down to thicken it a bit and reduce it, then finished off with seasonings and butter.

8. *Meunière:* Brown butter (not black), mixed with lemon juice and chopped parsley.

9. *Mornay:* White sauce with grated cheese (usually Gruyère and/or Parmesan) blended well into it. It is usually poured over fish or eggs and the dish run under the broiler to brown.

10. *Nantua:* Heavy cream, shrimp butter (see Question 208), and chopped shrimp added to Béchamel. (See Question 708.) Crayfish or lobster butter may be substituted for shrimp. This sauce is often served with Quenelles de Brochet (Question 543).

11. *Newburg:* Make a thin roux of butter and flour, add cream and seasonings, including cayenne, and beat in egg yolks. Flavor with dry sherry. *Do not boil.*

12. *Poulette:* Minced shallots and mushrooms, sautéed in butter and added to a basic rich cream sauce with egg yolks beaten into it. Lemon juice and minced parsley are added at the end. This sauce is also used with poultry.

13. *Rémoulade:* Mayonnaise with anchovies, pickles, capers, herbs, and sometimes chopped hard-cooked egg added.

14. *Soubise:* To a cup of chopped onions, sautéed in butter until soft but not brown, add two cups basic cream sauce (see Question 704) and cook gently for 15 minutes. Purée in blender or press through a sieve, then add cream to taste. Correct seasoning. The basic cream sauce may be made from fish stock, if desired. This sauce is also used with lamb, veal, vegetables, and poultry.

15. *Tartare:* Mayonnaise made with hard-cooked, instead of raw, egg yolks and with minced pickles, capers, olives, and parsley added. It is generally served with fried fish and shellfish.

16. *White Wine:* White wine fish stock (court bouillon) is boiled down until it is a fumet (about 3 tablespoons left from a cup of stock). It is then substituted for the lemon juice in Hollandaise sauce. (Question 709.)

724. What sauces go well with pasta?

1. *Bacon:* Diced bacon is cooked in lard until crisp, a good lot of freshly ground pepper is added, and the sauce is then poured over spaghetti.

2. *Bagna Cauda:* This means a "hot bath sauce." It is made of butter, olive oil, garlic, anchovy fillets, and truffle.

3. *Clam:* This can be red or white. For the red, heat olive oil with garlic, put in clams in their shells, tomatoes, and water. Cook until clam shells open, then take the clams out and return them to the sauce, discarding shells. Add parsley, salt, and pepper and pour over pasta. For the white, clams in their shells are steamed in a little white wine until they open. They are then removed from the shells and chopped. The broth is strained and boiled until it is reduced by half. Garlic and parsley are simmered in olive oil, then seasoned with salt and freshly ground pepper. The reduced broth and clams are added and heated through and the whole mixed with spaghetti, or noodles if you prefer.

4. *Green:* Anchovy filets, chopped parsley, water cress, capers, pickles, onion, and garlic, beaten with olive oil and either vinegar or lemon juice. The sauce should be creamy.

5. *Marinara:* A sauce of tomato, seasoned with onion, garlic, and oregano, and hot pepper if you like.

6. *Meat:* A mixture of chopped beef, tomatoes, tomato paste, red wine, onion, garlic, and other seasonings, cooked down to a good thick consistency. Used mostly over spaghetti or noodles.

7. *Pesto:* This is a green sauce from Genoa, made by mixing 2 cups of blanched basil leaves with a cup of grated Parmesan cheese, a mashed clove of garlic, and ¼ cup of pine nuts, then gradually adding olive oil, beating constantly with a fork, until the desired degree of thickness is reached. Then a dash of milk is added and the sauce served over spaghetti or noodles.

8. *Ragù Bolognese:* This is a meat sauce for which there are many recipes. The best I know has chopped beef, veal, and salt pork, onion, carrot, and celery, browned with a clove. Stock is then added and the whole cooked until the stock evaporates, at which point tomato paste and seasonings are added and the mixture simmered for an hour. Next, chopped mushrooms and chicken livers are added and cooked. Last of all, heavy cream is stirred in. This sauce is used to fill ravioli, with lasagna, and in many other Italian dishes. It is superb.

9. *Tomato:* See Question 720. Used over spaghetti, and with cannelloni and manicotti.

10. *Tomato and Mushroom:* Sliced or button mushrooms in a tomato sauce, flavored with garlic and onion.

725. What sauces are good with vegetables?

1. *Aioli:* See Question 723.

2. *Cream Sauce:* See Question 704.

3. *Hollandaise:* See Question 709. Especially good with asparagus and artichokes.

4. *Lemon Butter:* Four tablespoons lemon juice reduced by boiling it down to one, then beaten with a stick of butter, which melts in the process, over low heat until thick and creamy. Just before serving add a couple of teaspoons of vegetable water. Also served with fish, in which case add fish stock.

5. *Mousseline:* Equal quantities of Hollandaise (see Question 709) and whipped cream, heated but not boiled. Served also with fish.

6. *Mushroom Sauce:* Chopped or sliced mushrooms, sautéed in butter, then flour added and blended well. Next add cream and/or milk and stir until thickened. Season to taste. Especially good with spinach or green beans.

7. *Ravigote:* French dressing (see Question 660) mixed with herbs, capers, and onions. Served also on cold fish.

8. *Velouté:* Made like cream sauce (see Question 704), but substituting chicken stock for milk and adding a little mushroom liquor and a little cream. Used also on fish.

726. What sauces are good with eggs?

1. *Aurore:* Tomato paste or tomato sauce is added to cream sauce (see Question 704) or Mornay. (See Question 723.)

2. *Colbert:* See Question 723.

3. *Cream:* See Question 704.

4. *Creole:* Based on tomatoes, with green pepper, onion, celery, garlic and other seasonings. Also good for fish and seafood.

5. *Curry:* See Question 720.

6. *Hollandaise:* See Question 709. Especially to make Eggs Benedict (see Question 275).

7. *Lamaze:* See Question 723. On cold, hard-cooked eggs.

8. *Mornay:* See Question 723. On poached or sliced hard-cooked eggs.

9. *Mushroom:* See Question 725. Especially on hard-cooked eggs.

10. *Nantua:* See Question 723.

727. What are the most popular dessert sauces?

1. *Butterscotch:* Brown sugar, mixed with a little flour, is cooked with boiling water and constantly stirred until thick. Then butter and cream are added. The sauce is usually served hot.

2. *Chocolate:* Probably the most popular dessert sauce of all. Best made by melting semi-sweet chocolate with a little unsweetened chocolate in a little coffee, then adding cream and stirring until smooth.

3. *Custard:* This is simply a boiled custard which is poured over cakes, puddings, and the like.

4. *Foamy:* Butter, sugar, egg yolks, and flavoring (cognac or vanilla or wine) are beaten over hot water until heated through.
   Very good with plum pudding, flavored with cognac.
5. *Fruit:* Made either from puréed fresh fruit mixed with sugar
   syrup or from jams or jellies, melted in water. May be flavored
   with liqueurs.
6. *Hard:* Mix softened butter with granulated sugar, using the
   back of a spoon, until you achieve the consistency you like.
   Flavor with vanilla, rum, brandy, or other liqueurs if you like,
   and if whatever you use fits the dessert with which the sauce
   will be served. (Can also be made with brown sugar.)
7. *Lemon Mousseline:* Sugar, water, and cornstarch are cooked together until thick, then grated lemon rind and lemon juice are
   added. Cool and fold in whipped cream.
8. *Zabaglione:* Egg yolks, sugar, and Marsala wine are cooked
   over hot water, with constant stirring, until thick and creamy.
   May be served either cold or hot.

XII. DESSERTS AND FRUIT

728. What is Indian Pudding? It is a New England dessert made of corn meal, milk, molasses, brown sugar, and spices, baked long and slow. It is usually served hot with vanilla ice cream.

729. Is it hard to make Jelly Roll? No. First, it is a help to have a jelly roll pan because of the size and shape. You line this pan with buttered wax paper. Then you put in your batter and bake it. While this is going on, put a sheet of aluminum foil or a clean tea towel on a cooling rack and sprinkle it with sugar. When the cake is done, invert it onto the foil or towel and peel off the waxed paper. Roll the cake up while it is warm. Cool. Unroll and spread with jelly or whipped cream or whatever you like. Roll again and ice or sprinkle with sugar.

730. What is Zabaglione? A mixture of eggs, sugar, and Marsala wine, beaten over hot water until thick and foamy. It is an Italian dessert which is served warm. It is also a dessert sauce. (See Question 727.)

731. What is Salzurger Nockerl? It is a beautifully light Austrian soufflé, made by baking a stiffly beaten egg-white mixture in a shallow layer of flavored milk.

732. What is a Cold Soufflé? It is a name often erroneously given to a Bavarian cream. (See Question 747.) A real cold soufflé is baked like a hot one, then refrigerated, which causes it to sink and to shrink from the mold. It is then unmolded and served with a custard sauce.

733. What is an English Trifle? Sponge cake well soaked with sherry, served with a boiled custard poured over it. We call it Tipsy Pudding.

734. What is Zuppa Inglese? An Italian dessert (created for Lady Hamilton, Nelson's mistress) which is very similar to an English Trifle. (See Question 733.) It is made from lady fingers, rum, and

Crème Pâtissière (see Question 735), chilled in the refrigerator until set and topped with whipped cream for serving.

735. What is Crème Pâtissière?   A rich vanilla custard used to fill cream puffs, Napoleons, and the like.

736. What is Crème Brulée?   A very rich baked custard (all cream, no milk), which is thoroughly chilled, then covered with well-sieved light-brown sugar and run under the broiler to caramelize the top. It must be watched constantly to see that it does not burn. The dessert is then chilled again.

737. What is a Floating Island?   Poached egg-white meringue floating in boiled custard, sometimes with fruit in it. The French call this Oeufs à la Neige. Their Île Flottante is more elaborate. A meringue is baked in a mold, chilled, unmolded, and served with custard sauce around it.

738. What is the best way to freeze ice cream?   This is a matter of opinion, and those who are devoted to the old hand freezer will never admit that there is a better way than theirs. As a matter of fact, it does make wonderful ice cream if properly done. But many people cannot or will not take the time to turn the handle, so they freeze ice cream in the freezing compartments of their refrigerators and achieve good results. There are also quite expensive electric ice cream freezers, which are fine to have if you have a large, always-eating-ice-cream family!

739. How do you freeze ice cream with a hand freezer?   Fill the container three-quarters full and place the lid on securely. Pack the freezer with four to six parts chopped ice and one part rock salt. Turn the handle slowly and constantly until it becomes difficult to turn it. Take out the dasher and pack the ice cream down solidly in the container. Put the lid on securely and repack the freezer with ice and salt. Let stand for several hours so that the ice cream will mellow.

740. How do you freeze ice cream in the freezer compartment?   The first very important matter is your mixture. It should be very rich and creamy. Make a custard of eggs and milk. The eggs act as a stabilizer, in addition to providing richness. Add whipped cream, which helps keep the ice crystals small. If desired, stir the ice cream up, or beat it with a rotary beater when it has frozen enough so that there is a thick mush around the edge of the pan. This is not always necessary, however. Freeze at the coldest setting.

741. What is a sherbet? It is an ice (usually fruit-flavored) made with milk.

742. What is a Bombe? It is a mold of ice cream and/or sherbet, the outer lining being different from the inner filling. For instance, the outside might be orange sherbet, the inside vanilla or coffee ice cream. All sorts of combinations are possible, but when you plan one be sure that the flavors are compatible. Use about half the capacity of the mold for the lining, half for the center filling. Put the mold into the freezer before you start to work. Then quickly line it with whatever you have chosen, and return it to the freezer to make it very firm. Fill the center, cover, and freeze at least 4 hours, preferably over night.

743. What is a Parfait? In this country it is ice cream (sometimes more than one flavor) put into a tall, thin parfait glass with sauce poured over so that it trickles down through the ice cream in an irregular pattern. The European version is made from scratch with heavy cream, whole eggs or egg yolks, and seasonings and frozen in the parfait glass. It is more creamy than ice cream.

744. What is a Baked Alaska? A mold or brick of very hard ice cream is placed on a piece of sponge cake which extends an inch wider than the ice cream all round. This is put on a board. The whole is covered with a meringue and baked in a hot (500°) oven until the meringue browns delicately (this takes about 5 minutes). Serve at once, sliced.

745. What are Profiteroles? Small cream puffs, Pâte à Chou (see Question 919), filled with ice cream and served covered with a sauce, usually chocolate.

746. What is Biscuit Tortoni? An Italian dessert in which whipped cream is flavored sometimes with rum, sometimes with other flavorings, combined with macaroon crumbs, put into little paper cups, sprinkled with more macaroon crumbs or with ground almonds, and frozen.

747. What is Bavarian Cream? It is a custard with gelatin, beaten egg whites, whipped cream, and flavoring incorporated into it. It can be flavored with fruit, chocolate, coffee, liqueurs—almost anything which suits your fancy.

748. What is Spanish Cream? A dessert made with gelatin, milk, eggs, sugar, and vanilla. Not as rich as Bavarian cream, it is otherwise similar. It is usually served with whipped cream.

749. What is the best way to make Bread Pudding? Soak half-slices of bread (crust removed) in melted butter and sauté until golden brown. Pile into a baking dish, pour over it a mixture of milk, beaten egg, sugar, vanilla, and a dash of salt. Bake in a 350° oven until nicely browned on top (45 to 50 minutes). You may put raisins into this if you like. It is also exceedingly good—even elegant—flavored with melted chocolate.

750. What is a Charlotte? The French version is a mold lined with bread slices which have been soaked in melted butter, filled with a fruit purée and baked, then turned out of the mold and served hot or cold with custard or whipped cream. The American type has the mold lined with ladyfingers or macaroons, with a center involving whipped cream, sometimes fruit, sometimes nuts; it is frozen, then unmolded and served with whipped cream or fruit garnish.

751. What is Charlotte Russe? A combination of sweetened, flavored whipped cream and stiffly beaten egg whites, put into a bowl lined with ladyfingers and chilled thoroughly before serving.

752. How do you make French Pancakes? Make a simple, very thin batter (about the consistency of light cream), using part water, part milk, eggs, and flour. Into a hot crêpe pan or skillet, with a bit of butter melted in it, pour just enough batter to coat the bottom of the pan, tipping to distribute it evenly. Cook until lightly browned. Turn and brown second side.

753. What are Crêpes Suzettes? Very thin French pancakes (see Question 752) are baked, folded in quarters, then placed in an orange-butter sauce in a chafing dish. Grand Marnier and cognac are poured over them and ignited. As soon as the flames die down, the crêpes are served.

754. Are French pancakes used for anything but Crêpes Suzette? Yes. They can be filled with jelly or jam, stewed fruits or fresh fruits. These may be flambéed with a liqueur or not, as you please. Crêpes (French pancakes) are also filled with meat, poultry, seafood, and vegetable mixtures, sometimes covered with a sauce, sometimes not, usually browned, after being rolled, under the broiler.

755. What is a Baba au Rhum? It is a light yeast cake which is soaked in a syrup of sugar, water, and dark rum, sometimes served with whipped cream.

756. What is a Savarin? It is a cake made of baba dough (see Question 755) and baked in a ring mold, soaked in a liqueur syrup (usually kirsch), and served with the center filled with whipped cream, custard, or fresh fruit.

757. What is a Bûche de Noël? It is a rich French Christmas dessert of chocolate with a mocha filling, covered with a chocolate glaze and shavings of chocolate, made in the form of a log (the Christmas log).

758. What is a Pot de Crème? A very rich chocolate pudding, made and served in little pots (custard cups). There is a variety of ways of making it, but one of the simplest and richest is to melt 12 squares of semi-sweet chocolate with 2 tablespoons of butter, then beat into it the yolks of 7 eggs, and finally fold into the mixture the stiffly beaten whites of 7 eggs. Put into the pots and refrigerate at least 2 hours. A pot de crème can also be vanilla, made with cream, sugar, eggs, and vanilla flavoring.

759. Is chocolate that has turned white spoiled? No. A whitish appearance in chocolate is due to the cocoa butter that has separated out. At a temperature of about 85° F. the cocoa butter in the chocolate melts and comes to the surface. When the cocoa butter hardens again it turns white. Only the appearance of the chocolate is affected; usually there is no loss of flavor or any other quality.

760. What is Blanc Mange? It is a cornstarch pudding which is served cold with chocolate or fruit sauce or maple syrup. Rather dull. (See Question 727.)

761. What is Cottage Pudding? It is a yellow cake baked in a square pan, or in individual muffin tins, and served hot with hot chocolate, butterscotch, or fruit sauce. (See Question 727.)

762. What is Syllabub? There is a variety of recipes for this, one of which starts out, "Take the mixture to the cow." However, it is easiest to make it with sherry and bottled raspberry juice, seasoned with lemon peel, nutmeg, and rosemary, left to stand in a bowl with sugar overnight, then incorporated into whipped cream. There are English recipes which make it with macaroons—a very different effect altogether!

763. Is fruit and cheese an adequate dessert? It is indeed. In fact, it is one of the best desserts possible and is rapidly becoming more popular in this country. (See Questions 215, 216, 217, 218, 220.)

764. What fruits are good with cheese? Almost all fruits, but especially pears and apples.

765. What is the most attractive fruit dessert you know? A half watermelon hollowed out, the fruit cut into chunks and mixed with other fruits, such as strawberries, cantaloupe and honeydew balls, blueberries, orange and grapefruit sections, sliced peaches, blue, red, and white grapes—anything you can find to vary the color, flavor, and texture. The fruits are heaped into the watermelon shell and may be flavored with wine or kirsch. They may also be flambéed with cognac. If they are ice cold when this is done, they will not be too much warmed, and the effect is spectacular.

766. What is a Cobbler? Fresh fruit, sugared, put into a baking dish, and covered with rich biscuit dough, then baked until the top is golden. A cobbler is served with whipped or plain cream.

767. How are Fruit Dumplings made? European fruit dumplings are made of a simple dough wrapped around a piece of fruit or some jam and steamed or boiled. Fruit dumplings here are usually made with pastry wrapped around the fruit and baked in the oven.

768. What are Beignets? Fritters, frequently made of apples, strawberries, and other fruits and served for dessert with a custard type of sauce.

769. How many apples make a pound? Two large, three medium or four small apples.

770. What varieties of apple are best for eating raw? Delicious, McIntosh, Jonathan, Winesap, and Golden Delicious. Most of these are also satisfactory for cooking.

771. What are the best apples for baking? Rome Beauty, Rhode Island Greening, and Northern Spy.

772. How can you keep apples from turning brown when you have peeled them, cut them up, and are not quite ready to use them? Put them into a bowl of cold water.

773. What are Crêpes Normandes? French apple pancakes (the apples incorporated into the batter), which are absolutely delectable, served for dessert with a sprinkling of powdered sugar.

774. What is a Brown Betty? A hot pudding made of apples, soft bread crumbs, sugar, and spice, served usually with hard sauce. (See Question 727.)

775. What is Apple Pan Dowdy? A Pennsylvania Dutch dessert of apples, peeled, cored, sliced, and seasoned with spices, butter, sugar, and molasses, covered with a biscuit crust and baked.

776. What is Ozark Pudding? Chopped apples and chopped pecans are mixed with beaten egg, sugar, and a very little flour. The mixture (which may be flavored with rum) is turned into a shallow dish and baked. The pudding rises while baking, then falls (it is supposed to) and has a macaroon-like top. It is served hot or cold with whipped cream.

777. Will peaches ripen after they are picked? It is possible that they may ripen quite satisfactorily if they were not picked at entirely too immature a stage. A creamy or yellowish ground color usually indicates that they are likely to ripen well.

778. Which is better, a white-fleshed or a yellow-fleshed peach? This is a matter of personal taste. Either has wonderful flavor if it is ripe.

779. How do you poach peaches? If you have perfectly ripe peaches, make a sugar and water syrup (half and half) and pour it, hot, over peeled halved or sliced peaches. Then chill them. This way they are not overcooked, and the fresh flavor is beautifully preserved. You can also poach them the way you do apricots. (See Question 787.)

780. What is a Peach Melba? Half a canned peach with a serving of vanilla ice cream in the center, covered with a raspberry sauce.

781. How do you make Peach Shortcake? Just like strawberry shortcake (see Question 813), except that you may either crush the peaches, as you do the strawberries, or just slice them and sugar them.

782. What is Pêches Cardinal? Peaches are poached in sugar syrup (see Question 779), cooled, and chilled, then served with a purée of fresh raspberries poured over them.

783. What pears are good to eat raw? Bartlett pears, available from early August through November, are probably the best known in this category. Bose, Comice, Anjou, and Winter Nelis come along later, are firmer and keep better. The last four are all good for poaching and other cooking uses.

784. How do you poach pears?   Peel, core, and halve the pears and cook them at a simmer in sugar syrup (half sugar, half water) until they are just tender but not mushy.

785. What are Pears Hélène?   Poached pear halves (see Question 784) topped with vanilla ice cream and covered with chocolate sauce. (See Question 727.)

786. Are tree-ripened apricots best?   Yes, but they are exceedingly hard to find unless you live near where they are grown. Most apricots available elsewhere are picked when "mature" but still hard. They are very perishable when fully ripe and do not travel well.

787. What is the best way to poach apricots?   Peeled, either halved or whole, cooked in half sugar, half water, until just tender but not mushy.

788. How can you tell a ripe plum?   A plum of good quality is plump, clean, and fresh in appearance. It is fully colored for the variety and soft enough to yield to slight pressure. Immature fruit does not ripen satisfactorily.

789. What are prunes?   They are dried purple plums.

790. How can bananas be best used at their various stages of ripeness?   When green-tipped, they should be cooked. When all-yellow, they may be either cooked or eaten as is. When flecked with brown, they are fully ripe and best for eating out of hand and for blending into cakes, cookies, and breads.

791. If we could get bananas ripened on the plant, would they be better than those we allow to ripen at room temperature?   No. Plant-ripened bananas have little flavor and are unpleasantly mealy. Even in the tropics where they grow, the natives cut bananas green and allow them to ripen in a shady place.

792. Should bananas be kept in the refrigerator?   Only if you wish to retard their ripening. First let them ripen to the degree you like, then if you want to keep them several days, put them into the hydrator or vegetable compartment.

793. How can sliced bananas be kept from darkening when they must stand before serving? Either sprinkle them with, or dip them into, pineapple, orange, grapefruit, lemon, or lime juice.

794. How can bananas be made into a hot dessert? They can be baked (usually halved lengthwise) with fruit juice or rum or wine. Or they can be sautéed, sprinkled with sugar, and flambéed with rum. They are also very good sliced, enclosed in pastry, and baked. These are called banana dumplings and are best served with whipped cream.

795. What is the difference between a plantain and a banana? A plantain is used as a vegetable and must be cooked to be palatable. It is longer and bigger around than a banana. When fully ripe it is black.

796. Do fresh ripe figs keep well? No, they are very perishable. Therefore, when you find them, plan to use them at once or they will be wasted. Never buy fresh figs with bruises on the skin, as they will probably have deteriorated already.

797. How do you serve fresh figs? Just "as is" to eat from the hand, or with cream if you like. Or they are absolutely wonderful each wrapped in a slice of prosciutto ham (see Question 394).

798. If one puts grapes which have seeds into a mixed fruit dish, must one take out the seeds? It is certainly much nicer and pleasanter for the guests if you cut such grapes in half and remove the seeds before mixing them with other fruits.

799. Can you suggest a dessert made with grapes? One of the best is of little seedless white grapes, well washed and chilled, sprinkled with brown sugar and topped with sour cream.

800. How do you know when a melon is ripe? There is a slight softening of the area around the "eye" at the blossom end, and it yields slightly to moderate pressure. Some melons have a very distinctive aroma when ripe. In some, the color is indicative of ripeness. No indication is infallible. So the best answer to this question is, find one of those magical market men who *can* tell when a melon is ripe and cling to him for dear life—you will never have a better way of being certain, as most of us are not so gifted.

801. How can you tell whether a pineapple is ripe?   The fruit should be firm, bright, and clean, golden-yellow, orange-yellow or reddish-brown in color (except the Mexican "sugar loaf," which remains green when ripe). Usually the heavier the fruit is in relation to its size, the better the quality, provided it is mature. Pineapples picked when immature will not ripen properly. The mature fruit has a fragrant, highly characteristic odor, and a leaf pulled from the top comes out easily.

802. What is a stuffed pineapple?   Cut a ripe pineapple in half, right through the plume. Cut out the flesh, leaving a shell about an inch thick. Cube the flesh and combine it with other fruits which make a happy contrast of color, texture, and flavor. Pile back in the halves and flavor with kirsch or other liqueur if you like. Chill well before serving. Beautiful on a buffet table.

803. Can you use fresh pineapple in a jellied mold?   No, it liquifies gelatin, so always use canned pineapple when you want to "jell" the dessert.

804. Should oranges be orange?   Most oranges which are bright orange in hue are artificially colored. This in no way affects the quality of the fruit. But most shoppers in the East and Midwest will buy far more colored than uncolored oranges, even though aware that the coloring is artificial, because they *look* as though they would be juicier and sweeter!

805. What is Ambrosia?   A mixture of orange sections and banana slices, sugared lightly and chilled. Before serving, it is topped with shredded coconut.

806. What is Lemon Snow?   It is a gelatin dessert flavored with lemon rind and juice, with stiffly beaten egg whites folded in before chilling. It is usually served with a custard sauce.

807. How do you broil grapefruit?   Cut it in half, remove the seeds, and cut the sections neatly. Next, put over each half either honey or brown sugar, dot with butter, and broil until nicely browned and bubbling. You may also add sherry or rum to the grapefruit before broiling if you like.

808. What are Cherries Jubilee?   Pitted black cherries in a hot sauce made from their juice, flambéed with cognac and served over vanilla ice cream.

809. How can you tell whether a box of berries is in good condition? Always insist on having the berries turned out so that you can see down to the bottom of the box. There may be spoiled, moldy berries or unripe ones underneath the handsome top layer.

810. What can you do with blackberries which are not quite ripe? A good question because it is so hard to find really ripe ones. Poach them as you do apricots (see Question 787), or make them into a fruit pie.

811. What are fresh blueberries best served with?   Cream or sour cream and sugar.

812. What is a Gooseberry Fool?   Gooseberries are cooked in sugar and water until soft, then puréed and cooled. They are then combined with whipped cream and chilled. "Fools" can be made from other fruits also.

813. How do you make Strawberry Shortcake?   Shortcake of any kind should be made of flaky biscuit dough (see Question 850), sweetened with sugar. This is baked, split, and buttered. Meantime, mash strawberries coarsely and sugar them to taste. When ready to serve, pour strawberries between halves of the shortcake and over the top and cover with whipped cream.

814. What is a Raspberry Whip?   It is made by combining half a pint of raspberries with a cup of sugar and an egg white in a bowl and beating with a rotary beater (½ hour) or an electric mixer (15 minutes) until the mixture forms stiff peaks. Never try to do this

with a blender because the one thing it cannot do is beat egg whites
—it goes too fast.

815. What is Rote Grütze? It is a German and Scandinavian dessert made from cooking raspberries and red currants together briefly
in a little water, sieving them, then boiling them, stirring constantly,
with sugar. Gelatin is added and the whole is chilled and served with
cream or milk (which the Germans prefer).

816. How do you cook rhubarb? You can bake, stew, or poach it.
I like it best stewed with about a cup of sugar to a pound of cut-up
rhubarb and just a few tablespoons of water. Cover and simmer until tender (18 to 20 minutes). And it is best of all when you add strawberries for the last half of the cooking.

XIII. BEVERAGES

817. What is the best container to use for storing ground coffee?
A vacuum can, kept tightly closed in the refrigerator. If you pour ground coffee into a canister, it is aerated and flavor escapes. When you buy ground coffee in a bag and the bag is not self-sealing, pour it into another container with a tight cap. Put the open end of the bag deep inside the container and pour as gently as possible. The less contact ground coffee has with air, the better.

818. How long can ground coffee be kept? It will stay comparatively fresh for a week in a tightly sealed container in a cool place.

819. What grind of coffee do you use in a percolator? "Regular."

820. What grind of coffee do you use in a drip pot? The special, fine "Drip" grind.

821. What grind of coffee do you use in a vacuum coffee-maker? The "Fine" grind, which is even finer than the "Drip," though the latter may also be used in a vacuum maker.

822. How much coffee should you use per cup? The first answer to that is *plenty*. Coffee cannot be stretched. Therefore, for each cup of coffee you plan to serve you should use 1 approved coffee measure (2 level tablespoons) of coffee to ¾ of a measuring cup of water. Here is a chart to help you remember:

Basic Coffee-to-Water Measure

Number of 5½ ounce servings	Approved coffee measure	Tablespoon measure (level)	Measuring cups of water	Fluid ounces of water
2	2	4	1½	12
4	4	8	3	24
6	6	12	4½	36
8	8	16	6	48
20	½ pound			1 gal. water
40	1 pound			2 gal. water

823. Must one start coffee-making with cold water? Yes. Hot water pipes are likely to have mineral deposits in them which alter the flavor of a beverage. Let the cold water run for a minute to flush out stale water from the pipe before you put it into your coffee-maker.

824. Should water be boiling when it is poured into a glass maker with a filter paper? No. It should be hot but not boiling. The grounds should be dampened with a little water first, then more water poured in.

825. Should you bring water to the boil before putting the filled coffee basket into a percolator? It is much more convenient because you can then time the perking action from the minute the basket goes in.

826. Is it all right not to brew the coffee-maker's full capacity? Do not brew less than three fourths of the capacity. If you make a small amount of coffee often, get a smaller pot for such brewings.

827. What happens if you let coffee boil after it is made? It becomes bitter and oily, and the flavor is ruined.

828. Is chicory good in coffee? That is entirely a matter of taste. Chicory for coffee is the roasted root of the chicory plant and has a quite decidedly bitter taste. In this country it is used largely in the New Orleans area. It appears to greater or less extent in most French coffee.

829. What kind of coffee is served for demitasse? It should be made double the strength of ordinary coffee. The espresso roast makes an excellent after-dinner brew.

830. What is Espresso Coffee? It is coffee made from a very dark roast—almost burned. It is made in a special machine using steam pressure, when you have it in a coffee shop. There are also home "espresso" pots, some using steam, some not. But you can make adequate espresso for demitasse with the right roast in any kind of pot.

831. What is Café au Lait? It is a combination of hot coffee and hot milk, usually half and half, served always for breakfast in France.

832. What is Viennese Coffee?   Strong black coffee, topped thickly with sweetened whipped cream.

833. What is Cappuccino?   An Italian drink, half espresso coffee, half hot milk, with a piece of cinnamon stick put into the cup so that the liquid absorbs the cinnamon flavor as one drinks it.

834. What is Irish Coffee?   A combination of Irish whiskey and strong, hot coffee, slightly sweetened and served with whipped cream on top.

835. What is Turkish Coffee?   It is a thick, sweet brew, made by mixing ground coffee and sugar, adding boiling water and letting it foam up and settle, which process is repeated three times. A dash of cold water is added as it is settling for the last time.

836. Are Café Diable and Café Brulot the same thing?   Essentially, yes. They are a mixture of flamed cognac with sugar, spices, orange and lemon rind, and strong black coffee.

837. How should tea be made?   It should be made, in the first place, in a china or an earthenware pot. Silver or other metal spoils the flavor. The pot should be heated by putting scalding hot water into it. Bring cold water to the boil. Pour the hot water out of the tea pot and into it put a teaspoon of tea for every cup you want to make, plus "one for the pot." Pour in a little boiling water, cover the pot, and allow the tea to steep for a minute. Then pour in the number of cups of hot water you need to make the desired quantity of tea. Steep until it has the desired strength.

838. Are tea bags as good to use as loose tea?   No purist would answer "yes." However, it is obviously a losing battle, because not enough people care that much. In my opinion, the chief charm of tea bags is that they can be lifted from cup or pot, whereas getting steeped tea leaves out is often quite a chore.

839. How should tea be made for iced tea?   It should be strong to allow for the dilution by melting ice. Use 50 per cent more tea than you do to make hot tea. It should then be kept at room temperature until used. Refrigerating it will make it turn cloudy.

840. Is there anything to be done about iced tea which has turned cloudy? Yes. Add a little boiling water to it.

841. Is tea a good ingredient to use in punch? Yes. It gives interest and good flavor to punches, both alcoholic and non-alcoholic. It should be made double strength, as for iced tea.

XIV. BAKING

842. What is the best way to measure flour? Sift it into a cup measure (there are small sifters which do this expeditiously) which stands on a piece of waxed paper. Hold the sifter up above the cup and fill it heaping full. Then even the top off lightly with a flat knife.

843. What is leavening? It means, literally, to lighten, and refers in baking to one of three methods for making baked goods rise—and *lighten*. First, leavening is air. It is achieved by beating egg whites or by sifting flour. Next, it is steam, which is the leavening for popovers and cream puffs. And third, it is carbon dioxide, which is derived from yeast, baking soda, and baking powder.

844. What is the best kind of yeast for use for bread-making? Paula Peck, whom I regard as the greatest authority on baking in this country, says that fresh yeast (also known as "compressed" yeast) is the best. But sometimes, nowadays, it is hard to get, and one can get good results from dry yeast.

845. When a recipe calls for one ounce of fresh yeast, how much dry yeast is substituted? Two packages of dry yeast is the equivalent of one ounce of fresh.

846. Can you substitute one cup of butter or margarine for one cup of vegetable shortening in recipes for baked goods? You may substitute butter or margarine for vegetable shortening, but add two tablespoons of the former in substituting for one cup of the latter. This is because butter and margarine contain only about 80 per cent fat, while vegetable shortening is 100 per cent fat.

847. How do you substitute sweet milk and baking powder for sour milk and soda in a baking recipe? Use the same amount of fresh milk as of the sour milk called for in the recipe and substitute one teaspoon of baking powder for each one-fourth teaspoon of baking soda.

848. When you are making whole wheat or buckwheat baked products, is it necessary to use some white flour as well? Yes. A proportion of white flour is always added in such recipes and usually when rye flour is used, also.

849. What causes poor texture in quick breads made with baking powder? Overmixing is often the cause. A batter, such as muffin batter, which contains about twice as much flour as liquid, should be mixed only enough to moisten the dry ingredients, as recipes often instruct you. Too much stirring or beating develops the gluten in the flour, and as a result tunnels are formed. Too high a baking temperature also may cause poor texture in quick breads.

850. How do you make baking powder biscuits that are flaky? By not mixing the flour and shortening too finely.

851. Should a baking powder biscuit be flat or tall and puffy? The answer depends upon what you like and, sometimes, on where you come from. In the South flat, flaky biscuits are preferred, but the North seems to like the tall, puffy kind. Roll them about ¼-inch thick for the Southern kind, thicker for the Northern!

852. Why do baking powder biscuits sometimes turn out to be tough? Probably because the dough is overhandled. Biscuits must be made quickly with a delicate touch if they are to be tender. They are kneaded, of course, but only for a few seconds.

853. What makes biscuits dry and small in volume? Biscuits may be dry and have poor volume because too little liquid or baking powder was used, or they may have been mixed too much or baked at too low a temperature.

854. What are drop biscuits? The milk in a baking powder biscuit recipe is increased slightly and the dough dropped from a teaspoon onto an ungreased baking sheet.

855. What is the most important factor in bread-making? The temperature at which the dough rises is of the greatest importance. It should be from 80° to 90° F. and the dough should be placed in a bowl, floured lightly, covered, and the bowl placed in a draft-free place. If all these conditions maintain, it should double in bulk in 40 minutes to an hour. If the temperature is too low, the rising period is too long, and you will get coarse bread. If the temperature is too high, the yeast may be killed, and thus the volume will be small and the bread not tender.

856. What is the difference between straight-dough bread and sponge bread? In the straight-dough method, all the flour and other ingredients of the bread are mixed together at the start. The sponge method is done in two steps. First, a sponge is prepared by combining the softened yeast, sugar, and part of the flour and liquid and allowing this to ferment until it is full of bubbles. The remaining ingredients are then added to make a dough stiff enough to knead.

857. Just how should bread dough be kneaded? The dough should be placed on a lightly floured board. With lightly floured hands fold the dough in half and press it with the heels of your hands about ten times. Now give the dough a quarter turn, fold, and repeat the process. Continue this until the dough is firm and elastic. Add a very little more flour to the board if necessary. This takes 5 to 7 minutes.

858. What is the cold-oven technique in bread-making? Before the dough has doubled in bulk (either the first or the second rising) it is placed in a cold oven to bake, the oven being turned on at that time to 350°. The bread then rises as the oven heats up.

859. What causes coarse texture in homemade yeast bread? Allowing the loaf to rise too much before baking is the most common cause of coarse texture in bread.

860. What causes a sour flavor to develop in yeast bread? A sour flavor will develop in bread if a poor yeast is used, or if the dough has been allowed to rise too long or at too high a temperature. Insufficient baking or baking at too low a temperature will also affect the flavor of yeast bread.

861. How can you correct lack of volume in homemade bread? If your bread lacks volume, you may have used too little yeast, allowed too little time for rising, or held the dough at too low a temperature. Or you may have added the yeast to liquid that was too hot or let the dough rise at too high a temperature. Under the right conditions, yeast produces carbon dioxide gas which leavens the bread. Warmth is needed for the process, but too much heat kills the yeast cells. A temperature of about 80° F. is best. Overkneading the dough, which may injure the baking quality of the gluten in the flour, is another possible cause of poor volume in bread.

862. What causes bread to have a flat top and sharp corners? The dough has been overmixed, or not enough time has been allowed for rising.

863. What is salt-rising bread? It is made from a fermented "starter," achieved by mixing scalded milk with sugar, salt, and cornmeal and keeping it in a warm place until it ferments. It is then used as the leavening agent in loaves of bread. It is a bit heavier than yeast bread, and moist and crumbly.

864. What is sourdoughbread? A bread in which part of the leavening is fermented yeast dough. If you like to make this bread, you will keep some of the fermented dough going all the time so it will be ready for use.

865. What are Cloverleaf Rolls? They are rolls made of yeast dough shaped into small balls, three of which are placed into each section of a muffin pan.

866. What is a Parker House Roll? It is a roll made from yeast dough, rolled out and cut into rounds, then folded over from the middle, so that in the end it bakes to look rather like a rounded envelope.

867. Why do people say that what we buy here as "French bread" is not French at all? Because it is certainly not like that which is baked in France. Their flour is different from ours, for one thing. Another major factor, in my opinion, is that they make their crusty loaves with water and we insist upon using milk because the bread will keep longer. To be sure, proper French bread does not keep over 24 hours, if that, but the flavor is incomparable and much better than that which we produce. If you want good French bread in this country, better make it yourself!

868. What is Crackling Bread?   Corn bread with bits of "tried-out" salt pork stirred into it. Fried chopped salt pork with the fat drained off it is known as cracklings.

869. What is Spoon Bread?   It is not really bread at all. Cornmeal, eggs, milk, and baking powder are mixed and baked in a casserole. The resulting product is served with a spoon from the dish, usually as a side dish for meat.

870. What is Panettone?   It is an Italian fruit bread, cylindrical in shape, which is achieved by letting the dough rise with a paper collar surrounding it, then baking it on a baking sheet.

871. What is a Croissant?   It is sometimes called, in this country, a crescent roll, but the ones we buy commercially are usually of a much less flaky and rich dough than the original French ones. A croissant is made of a yeast dough, with butter rolled into it. After chilling, it is shaped into crescents and baked.

872. What is a Brioche?   It is a slightly sweetened yeast bread, baked in a shape which makes it look rather like a mushroom with a very thick stem. It is usually served as a coffee bread or cake for breakfast.

873. What are Schnecken?   They are little cakes made from a sweet dough, which is rolled out, sprinkled with sugar, spices, currants, and nuts and rolled up like a narrow jelly roll. Muffin tins are arranged with a bit of corn syrup and sugar and some nut meats in the bottom of each. Then slices are cut off the roll and placed in the muffin tins. When the schnecken are baked, they are turned out at once and each is covered with a sticky glaze from the mixture in the bottom of the pans. They are called schnecken (snails) because of their rolled form. They are most frequently served with coffee.

874. What is a Kugelhopf?   It is a coffee cake made from yeast dough with raisins in it, in a fluted tube pan made especially for the purpose. It is generally credited to Alsace, but is certainly more commonly served in Austria, where I think it probably originated.

875. What is a Stollen? A German coffee cake made of a rich yeast dough filled with fruit and nuts, shaped into an oval loaf, folded like a Parker House roll. After baking, the cake is heavily sugared.

876. Should you grease a waffle iron? Only the first time you use it. You should brush it well with unsalted fat, then bake one waffle until it is good and brown. Throw that waffle out. From then on, wipe the waffle iron out after use. Never wash it.

877. How much batter should you put into a waffle iron? The compartments should not be full or the batter will overflow. Put about a tablespoonful of batter in the center of each compartment (depending upon the size of your waffle iron). The batter will then flow out to cover the entire compartment.

878. How can you tell when a waffle is done? Unless you have an electric iron which signals when the waffle is done, the best test is to watch for the moment when steam stops escaping.

879. Is it necessary to beat popover batter very thoroughly? No. It is not the air which you beat into them which makes popovers successful, but the steam caused by the sudden high heat they encounter while baking. Therefore it is necessary only to beat the batter until it is smooth, and it will not be harmed by standing 20 to 30 minutes before it is put into the pans.

880. What makes popovers refuse to pop? It is usually the baking, rather than the preparation. Since popovers pop because of steam caused by the high heat into which they are put, the heat of the oven is of prime importance. It should be preheated to 450°. Though it is possible to make popovers in custard cups, I much prefer a heavy iron popover pan, which should be heated in the oven sufficiently so that it sizzles when buttered. The batter must then be poured in quickly and the popovers put instantly into the oven, where they are cooked for 20 minutes without the oven door being opened, no matter how curious the cook may be! The oven heat is then reduced to

350° and the popovers cooked until they are done (10 to 15 minutes). (If you bake popovers in tin or glass pans, these need not be preheated.)

881. How full should you fill a muffin pan?   About two-thirds.

882. Why are muffins sometimes soggy?   Muffins may be soggy if their dough contained too much liquid or if they were baked at too low a heat.

883. Should muffins stand in the pan after baking?   No. They should be removed at once.

884. Why does fruit, such as blueberries or chopped dates, so often sink to the bottom of muffins?   Probably because enough flour was not saved out from the batter to coat the fruit well before stirring it in. This is done to hold the fruit suspended all through the muffin.

885. Is it all right to slice English muffins in half before toasting them?   It is much better to tear them apart with a fork. Slicing squashes the crumb of the muffin and makes it far less interesting to eat.

886. Is there any way to toast English muffins so that they do not burn in spots and not brown in others, as happens in a toaster?   Yes. In fact, the very best way to toast English muffins is to split them, butter them, and put them into a shallow pan, then place them in a 350° oven until they are browned to your taste. The browning is even and the butter melting into them gives them wonderful flavor.

887. What causes a cake to fall?   A cake is likely to fall if too much sugar or fat or baking powder or liquid is used. Undermixing or insufficient baking, too low an oven temperature, or moving a cake during baking before it has "set" also may cause a cake to fall and be soggy.

888. What causes a cake to have a peaked or cracked top?   If the batter is low in shortening or has been overmixed, the cake may form a peak while baking. Too little leavening (baking powder or soda) or too much flour may also cause a peaked top. Cracking of the top crust may result from baking the cake in too hot an oven.

889. What causes excessive shrinking in a cake? It may result from too much liquid or too much fat in the recipe or from too much batter in the pan. Also, a cake may shrink if the pan is too heavily greased. Baking in too hot or too cool an oven may result in poor volume in a cake.

890. How can cake failures be prevented at high altitudes? Special recipes are required at high altitudes. Usually a decrease in the amount of leavening (baking powder or soda) or sugar, or both, and an increase in the amount of liquid, are needed. It is also sometimes necessary to reduce the shortening when making very rich cakes at high altitudes.

891. Why do some sponge and angel cakes turn out to be tough and smaller than they should be? It is usually because the cake has been baked in too hot an oven. They should be baked in a 325° oven. If you are getting such results at that heat, have your oven regulator checked.

892. What is a Gênoise? A sponge cake made with butter.

893. What is a pound cake? This simple cake received its name from the fact that it was made from a pound of flour, a pound of sugar, a pound of butter and a pound of eggs, plus seasonings. To-day's recipes do not require you to weigh all the ingredients.

894. What is Lady Baltimore cake? It is a white layer cake, filled and iced with a boiled frosting containing figs, raisins, and nuts.

895. What is a Dobos Torte? It is an Austrian cake of many thin layers (usually seven) sandwiched together with chocolate butter cream and topped by a hard layer of caramelized sugar.

896. What is a Sachertorte? A very, very rich Austrian chocolate cake, glazed with apricot jam (see Question 897) and iced with chocolate. The Sacher Hotel in Vienna has never given the recipe to anyone, but there are many versions of it to be found in many cooking books!

897. What is an apricot glaze? Apricot jam is melted and put through a sieve and used to glaze various cakes and fruit tarts. It is usually applied lightly with a pastry brush.

898. What are Madeleines? Very rich, deceptively simple little cakes containing a great deal of butter, which should be baked, to be quite authentic, in shell-shaped molds.

899. What are Florentines? Rich, lacy cookies with orange peel and nuts in them, coated on the bottom with chocolate.

900. What kind of cheese is best for making cheese cake? It depends upon what sort of cheese cake you like. You can use cream cheese only for a rich, smooth product, cottage cheese for a fluffier cake, or a combination of both.

901. What is the best pan in which to make an upside-down cake? A skillet, because it is so simple to melt your butter, dissolve sugar, and arrange the fruit, then pour the batter over and bake all in one pan.

902. What is the best way to blend fat and flour for pastry? Pastry can be blended with two knives or with a pastry blender. If you use the latter, get one made of stainless steel, rather than the wire type, which bends too much and gets out of shape. However, you can also blend flour and fat with an electric mixer. The U. S. Department of Agriculture now thinks this is the easiest way, and furthermore that it requires less fat to make a flaky pastry. Fat should be at room temperature and should be blended into the flour for 2 minutes, with the electric mixer at lowest speed. Then sprinkle in water and blend 1 minute. By breaking the solid fat finely and adding the water by sprinkling, an even distribution of water and fat is achieved. The dough will look dry and crumbly, but will hold together in a ball.

903. Can one use liquid oil in place of solid fat in making pastry? Yes. The U. S. Department of Agriculture suggests that for making a two-crust pie pastry you shake together ½ cup (minus 1 tablespoon) cooking oil and ¼ cup of water, both at room temperature. Sprinkle this into the dry ingredients while blending with an electric mixer at lowest speed for 3 minutes. Or stir it in with a fork. The dough appears dry, but can be easily molded by hand. Corn, cottonseed, soybean, and safflower oil work equally well.

904. What is best to use as a container for sprinkling water and/or oil into dry ingredients for making pastry? Use an ordinary laundry sprinkler. The first time you use it, put in the oil and mark the level with nail polish. Then add the right amount of water and mark it. If you make your pastry with solid fat, use the sprinkler for adding water.

905. What is the best way to roll out pastry? A board covered with a floured pastry cloth makes rolling pastry simple. So does a rolling pin with ball bearings. Some people cover the rolling pin with a cloth jacket too, though I have never found that necessary. Cloths and pin covers can be purchased in housewares stores and departments.

906. How cold should pastry be when it is rolled out? Pastry dough which is rich in fat should be well chilled, but not so cold that it is hard to roll. On the other hand, if it is warm and sticky, the dough will be hard to handle and will probably require your adding more flour than you should in order to roll it out, thus changing its eventual texture.

907. Is it necessary to roll pastry with hard pressure? It is not only unnecessary, it is unwise. Too hard rolling makes shaping difficult and also may make the dough thick in some spots and thin in others. The pressure should be even, but relatively gentle.

908. Is there an easy way to make a piece of dough roll out into the desired shape? Yes. Turn the dough on the board or cloth occasionally, so that you go at it from different angles to make it into the shape you want.

909. How can you tell whether your dough is sticking to the board or cloth? If you are rolling on a well-floured cloth, this is unlikely to happen, but it may stick to a board. You should check occasionally by lifting the dough up. If it is sticking, lift the piece of dough up on one hand and add a light dusting of flour to the board before proceeding with the rolling.

910. What is the best way to keep an unfilled pastry shell from buckling while it is cooking? Butter lightweight foil and line the shell with it, pressing it well against the pastry, then fill it with dried beans. Or prick the bottom well with a fork. If this method is used and the sides of the shell start to sink at the beginning of the baking, just press them back with a fork. You can also place another pan or mold like the one in which you are baking your shell, buttered on the bottom, inside the shell and weight it down with a few dried beans.

911. What causes uncooked spots on the bottom of a pie? Usually one of these factors: inadequate blending of fat and flour; insufficient mixing after the water is added so that the dough is unevenly moistened, especially if too much water is used; combining warm dough with cold dough, or drops of water in the pie pan when the dough is put into it.

912. Can shrinkage of a baked pie crust be prevented? Some shrinkage is normal in a baked pie crust. Too much shrinkage may be caused by the use of too much water or by overhandling.

913. How can I get the bottom crust of a pie to brown? The pastry recipe and the baking temperature are important to the browning of pie crust. Pastry made by a rich formula which contains a large proportion of fat will brown more easily than one with less fat. For good browning, the dough must be evenly mixed and the pie plate must be dry before the crust is placed in it. An oven temperature of 400° to 450° at the start of baking is suggested, primarily to brown the bottom crust. (See Question 1007.)

914. What makes pastry "short"? An increase in the amount of fat used, relative to the quantity of flour. A very short pastry is made in the proportion of 2 cups of flour to 1 cup of fat.

915. What makes pie dough tough?   Pie dough is tough when too little fat or too much water is used or when the fat is not mixed properly. Overmixing pastry after the water is added will also make it tough.

916. What causes pastry dough to crumble?   Too little water or too much fat will cause pastry dough to crumble.

917. Is it possible to use frozen sour cherries to make a pie that does not run?   The home economists at Cornell offer this formula for a cherry pie which is not runny, but which also is not so thick that the cherries appear to be suspended in a jellied mass. Use a quart of frozen cherries for a well-filled 8- or 9-inch pie. Mix 2½ tablespoons of tapioca with 1⅓ tablespoons of cornstarch and add sugar to taste. Thaw the cherries only until most of the free ice has disappeared. Drain off the juice and add it to the thickener. Heat only until thickening is complete. Put cherries and juice into an unbaked pie shell and add a latticed cover. Bake at 400° on the lowest shelf of the oven for 25 minutes.

918. What is a Black Bottom Pie?   It is an open-faced pie with a crust made out of crushed ginger cookies, in the bottom of which is a layer of chocolate custard, topped by a layer of white custard, both flavored with either rum or brandy. The pie is often covered with whipped cream and decorated with shaved chocolate.

919. What is Pâte à Chou?   It is the pastry used to make cream puffs, and is made by turning the required amount of flour into a mixture of boiling water and melted butter and stirring vigorously until the mixture forms a ball, leaving the sides of the pan. Then eggs are added, one by one, off the heat. The mixture is shaped to the size you want and baked on a lightly greased sheet until puffed and delicately brown. When cool, the puffs are filled with Crème Pâtissière (see Question 735), whipped cream, or whatever else you like.

920. What is a Gateau St. Honoré?   A pastry confection ringed around with tiny sugar-glazed cream puffs and filled in the center with a Crème St. Honoré, which is a Crème Pâtissière (see Question

735) with beaten egg whites added to it. The Gâteau is usually decorated with marrons, sometimes with a sweet purée of same.

921. What is Pâte à Brisée? It is a rich French tart pastry made
with flour, butter, hard-cooked egg yolk, raw egg yolk, and flavorings. When baked it has a cookie-like quality.

922. What is puff pastry? It consists of many, many layers of flaky,
delicate, paper-thin dough. Its making involves incorporating a
large amount of butter into a flour-and-water mixture by means of
repeated rolling and turning. It is used in many ways, one of the most
familiar being to make patty shells.

923. Is puff pastry hard to make? Once you get the hang of it, it is
not hard, but it is exceedingly time-consuming. It is necessary to refrigerate the pastry dough after each "turn" (rolling out and refold-
ing) for a half hour—and there must be at least five turns. Of course
you can do other things between times, but the whole operation lashes
you to the mast, to say the least!

924. What is a Vol au Vent? A patty shell.

925. What is a Barquette? A tiny pastry shell in the shape of a
boat, which is usually filled with a bit of creamed fish, shellfish, mushrooms, or a cheese custard like Quiche Lorraine. (See Question 277.)

926. How is a typical French fruit tart made? It is usually a baked
shell with a Crème Pâtissière (sweet custard, see Question 735)
spread over the bottom, fresh fruit arranged on top and glazed.

927. What is a Linzertorte? An Austrian tart, the pastry for which
contains ground nuts and spices, filled with jam (usually raspberry),
covered with a lattice of the pastry, and baked.

XV. COOKING WITH HERBS, SPICES, AND WINES

928. With what foods are the following herbs used?

Basil, sweet:	Tomatoes, soups, salads, and sauces.
Bay leaf:	Meats, stews, and pot roasts. Strong. Use with discretion.
Chervil:	Eggs, salads, vegetables, soups, fines herbs. Delicate.
Chives:	Salads, omelets, potatoes, butter, fines herbs. Really a member of the onion family.
Dill:	Seafood, some salads, lamb, butter.
Fennel:	Salads, fish, duck. Licorice flavor, so to be used with thought.
Marjoram, sweet:	Peas, stuffings, soups, salads, meats, fines herbs.
Mint:	Carrots, sauce for lamb, pea soup, pot cheese, long cold drinks.
Oregano:	Sauces for meats, tomato dishes, other vegetables. Oregano is the name used in Italy and Spain for wild marjoram.
Parsley:	Fish, meat, sauces, salads, soups, vegetables, omelets, fines herbs. There are three kinds: the curly variety, which is commonest, the Italian, with a broader flat leaf and more distinctive flavor, and the Chinese, also broad-leaved and of strongish flavor and really not parsley at all, but fresh coriander.
Rosemary:	Lamb, poultry, sauces, vegetables, fines herbs.
Sage:	Stuffing, sauces. Should be used very sparingly, as it is strongly aromatic.
Savory, summer:	Vegetables (especially the cabbage family), dried peas and beans, and in soups.
Sorrel:	Soup (especially cold), salad, or vegetables.

Tarragon:	Chicken, fish, sauces (cold and hot), mushrooms, meats, fines herbs.
Thyme:	Chowders, tomatoes, cheeses, salads, fish, soups, other herbs.

929. Does it pay to buy dried herbs and spices in large quantity? It is not generally regarded as desirable, because they are inclined to lose flavor and potency with age. It is better to buy more frequently in small quantities.

930. What is the best way to keep dried herbs and spices? In jars with tops which can be screwed on tightly. Exposure to air depletes aroma and flavor quickly.

931. Are fresh herbs stronger than dried ones? Just the reverse! Dried herbs have stronger flavor and should be used in far less quantity than fresh ones. As with all herb cookery, you should taste as you add herbs, using great discretion at the start, and arriving at a seasoning which pleases you. Fresh herbs have, to be sure, better and more pleasing flavor than dried ones, and if you can grow them or find a shop in which to purchase them, you are in luck.

932. In learning to use herbs in cooking, how can one be sure of the right quantity? The best way is to use far less than you can possibly believe to be right (a tiny pinch at the start), taste, then add until you achieve subtle flavoring. Herbs should never be used in such quantity that their flavor overwhelms others in the dish.

933. What are fines herbs? A mixture of fresh parsley, chives, chervil, tarragon, and sometimes rosemary. Used, for instance, in an Omelet Fines Herbs. (See Question 262.)

934. What is a bouquet garni? A combination of parsley, thyme, and bay leaf used to flavor stews, soups, and sauces. If fresh, the herbs are tied together with string; if dried, they are put into a little cheesecloth bag and tied firmly. Sometimes other herbs, celery leaves, and the like are put into a bouquet garni, but in that case they are usually specifically mentioned in the recipe.

935. What is the best way to mince fresh herbs?   With a French cook's knife. Gripping the tip of the blade on top with the left hand, the handle with the right, and turning the knife about as you lift the handle end, come down on the herbs to be minced from the pointed end, which is never lifted. Use the knife also to scrape the minced bits back into a pile. Once you master this technique it is very speedy and thoroughly satisfactory, as it does not *mash* the herbs, merely gets them into as fine a mince as you desire.

936. With what foods are the following seeds used?

Anise:	Cookies, pastry, sauerkraut, coleslaw. Licorice flavor, so use with discretion.
Caraway:	Sauerkraut, rye bread, cookies, soups, pork, and beef.
Cardamon:	Scandinavian cakes and cookies, curries, pea soup. (Also comes ground.)
Celery:	Pot roast, chowders, soups, stews, salads, sauces.
Coriander:	Curry, cookies (especially ginger ones). (Also comes ground.)
Cumin:	Curry, cheese, poultry, game, stews, chili dishes. (Also comes ground.)
Dill:	Cheese, salad dressing, lamb stew.
Fennel:	Bread (sprinkled on top), Bel Paese cheese, beef, pork, seafood (in the cooking water), sauerkraut.
Juniper berries:	Game, beef stew. Strong, so use with discretion.
Mustard:	Curry, pickling and preserving.
Poppy:	Breads (sprinkle on top), cookies, canapés, cake fillings, sauces, noodles.
Sesame:	Breads (sprinkle on top), casseroles (mixed with, or instead of bread crumbs on top), topping for soups or vegetables.

937. With what foods are the following spices used?

Allspice:	Fruit pies, fruit salads, red cabbage, boiled fish, some meat dishes.
Cayenne:	Cheese dishes, sauces, meat dishes. Very hot.

Chilies, whole:	Curry, Mexican dishes, meat dishes, sauces. Very hot.
Cinnamon:	Applesauce, many desserts, especially rice pudding, toast, some meats, fruit pies, blended into chocolate ice cream, dessert sauces, hot beverages. Comes ground or in stick form.
Clove:	Ham, tongue, desserts, pies, soups, hot or iced tea, mulled wine. Comes ground or whole.
Ginger, fresh root:	Curry, Chinese dishes, chutneys.
Ginger, ground:	Baking, meats, poultry, puddings, sauces, vegetables, cooked fruits.
Ginger, preserved:	Dessert sauces, cakes, puddings.
Ginger, candied:	After-dinner coffee.
Mace:	Desserts, seafood stews, sweet spiced cakes and cookies. Mace is the outer shell of the nutmeg. To be used with discretion, as the flavor is most distinctive.
Mustard:	Sauces, especially for fish, with meats, cheese dishes, deviled eggs, salad dressings. Comes dry or prepared in many variations.
Nutmeg:	Desserts, applesauce, beverages, cakes and cookies, cooked fruits, meat dishes, sauces, vegetables (especially spinach). Comes ground, but much more flavorful if bought whole and ground fresh at home.
Paprika:	Stews, sauces, chicken and veal dishes, eggs, fish, meats, salads, vegetables. Hungarian paprika, which is the best, comes sweet or hot.
Pepper, black:	Good on or in any dish which is not sweet! Buy whole and grind it fresh for greatest flavor.
Pepper, white:	White or light sauces. White pepper is sweeter and less pungent than black, though they can be used interchangeably. If you use white pepper, have a grinder devoted to it and grind it fresh—much tastier!
Saffron:	Rice, Spanish and Italian dishes, sauces, breads, and cakes. Used more for color than

flavor, for if you use too much the dish will become bitter. Comes ground and in leaves (much cheaper) of which you make an essence for cooking.

Turmeric: Curry, fish, rice, sauces, pickles, and chutneys.

938. What is curry powder?   A mixture of ground spices. It contains always turmeric and chili peppers. Other spices sometimes included are cumin, coriander, cardamon, mustard, cinnamon, allspice, black pepper, and minced fresh ginger. (See Questions 437, 720.)

939. Is it possible to make one's own curry powder?   Yes. You can grind the spices with a mortar and pestle, or whirl the dry ones in the blender. This mixture of spices for curry is called, in India, the masala.

940. What wines should one have for cooking?   Dry white, dry red, dry white vermouth, sherry, Madeira, port, and Marsala are the basic ones, to be used with the following *types* of food:

Dry white: Fish and chicken.
Dry red: Meats and chicken.
Dry white vermouth: Fish, chicken, and soups.
Sherry, dry: Fish, chicken, soups (added at the end of cooking).
Sherry, sweet: Desserts.
Madeira: Chicken livers, brown sauces, ham.
Port: Meats, duck, chicken.
Marsala: Veal, desserts.

941. Are there definite rules for using wine in cooking?   No. There are suggestions to help guide you in regard to which wines are best with which foods, but as in all flavoring situations, you must experiment and taste to discover what suits you best. You may be quite unorthodox in your choices and still feel pleased with the results. Just remember, as you start to use wines in your cooking, that the guide lines have been developed over a long time by people who know how to cook with wine, and they are therefore worth following, at least at the start.

942. Is it all right to use cheap wines for cooking?   There could be several meanings behind this question. If by "cheap wines" you mean wines of inferior quality, the answer is no. On the other hand, there are lots of relatively inexpensive wines which are delightful to drink and thus fine for cooking. The premise, in general, is that you do not use wines in cooking which you would not care to drink. It is better not to use wine in your dishes at all than to ruin their flavor with inferior wines.

943. Is one adding a lot of alcohol to dishes by using wine or liqueur in them?   Practically none, as the process of cooking or flambéing evaporates the alcohol, leaving only the flavor. This would, of course, not be true in the case where you simply pour a liqueur over dessert, but you do not use enough to make it very alcoholic!

944. How much wine should one use in a sauce or gravy?   As a guide, I would suggest one or two tablespoons per cup of the sauce or gravy.

945. How much wine should one use in marinating meat?   A good guide line is: use half wine and half water, though the proportion may vary. If you use all wine, the flavor is likely to be too strong.

946. Is sauterne a good dry white wine to use in cooking?   This question points up a great American illusion. Sauterne is a sweet dessert wine, not dry. It can be used in making desserts, but would spoil the taste of any entrée.

947. Should one always serve the same wine to drink as has been used in cooking?   That is a pretty good rule to follow. If you do so, there will be no conflict of taste between the wine you serve and that used in the sauce. For instance, it would be a mistake to cook a chicken in white wine and then serve a red to drink at the meal. The red would overwhelm the white in the sauce. On the other hand, if you have cooked the chicken in red wine, you will do well to serve the same red to drink with the meal.

948. What liqueurs are particularly good for cooking?

Kirsch:	Especially to flavor mixed fresh fruit and the like.
Grand Marnier:	Orange flavor which is wonderful in soufflés, other desserts, and sauces.
Cognac:	Indispensable for flambéing meat dishes, as well as desserts, also for flavoring all sorts of sauces. Almost impossible to do fine cooking without it.
Crème de Menthe:	To flavor various desserts, and to pour over ice cream or ices.
Cherry Heering:	A Danish cherry liqueur which is delectable poured over desserts.

949. How are liqueurs used in cookery?   Largely to flavor fruits and desserts and occasionally in a sauce for duck or other meat dishes. Remember that, on the whole, liqueurs are quite sweet, thus not appropriate for flavoring most entrées.

XVI.   CANNED FOODS

950. Is canned food more economical to buy than fresh or frozen?
At certain times of the year the same food is cheaper canned than
fresh or frozen, but this varies with the size of crops, the weather,
and various other factors. In mid-winter, for instance, canned corn
is invariably less expensive than fresh, and almost always less expensive than the frozen product. However, the only way to be absolutely sure is to check prices, compare, and make your decision.
There is also the taste factor to consider. For instance, canned, frozen,
and fresh peas are really three different vegetables. Which taste you
like best can be an overwhelming matter in your decision. There are
people who would rather not eat peas at all than eat canned ones,
others who love them dearly.

**951. How do I translate the can numbers given in some of my favor-
ite old recipes into the weights shown on the cans?**   See Question
952 for a chart which gives you this information, together with the
approximate cup measurement of the various sizes of cans. The can
numbers which cookbooks formerly used are industry terminology.
Some years ago it was realized that the weight or designation of
fluid ounce contents would be more meaningful to the home cook,
and all food writers were asked by the canning industry to change
the terminology. All cans are marked with the weight or fluid ounce
measure of the contents, so it is easy for you to find the one you want
in the market.

**952. What are common can and jar sizes and their approximate cup
measurements?**   The labels of cans or jars of identical size may
show a net weight for one product that differs slightly from the net
weight on the label of another product, owing to the difference in
the density of the food. An example would be pork and beans (1 lb.),
blueberries (14 oz.), in the same size can.

Meats, fish, and seafood are almost entirely advertised and sold
under weight terminology.

Infant and Junior foods come in small cans and jars suitable for the
smaller servings used. Content is given on label.

Industry Term	Container (Approximate Net Weight or Fluid Measure)	Approximate Cups	Principal Products
8 oz.	8 oz.	1	Fruits, vegetables, specialties* for small families. 2 small servings.
Picnic	10½ to 12 oz.	1¼	Mainly condensed soups. Some fruits, vegetables, meat, fish, specialties.* 3 servings.
12 oz. (vacuum)	12 oz.	1½	Principally for vacuum pack corn. 3 servings.
No. 300	14 to 16 oz.	1¾	Pork and beans, baked beans, meat products, cranberry sauce, blueberries, specialties.* 3 to 4 servings.
No. 303	16 to 17 oz.	2	Principal size for fruits and vegetables. Some meat products, ready-to-serve soups, specialties.* 4 servings.
No. 2	1 lb. 4 oz. or 1 pt. 2 fl. oz.	2½	Juices,** ready-to-serve soups, some specialties,* pineapple, apple slices. No longer in popular use for most fruits and vegetables. 5 servings.
No. 2½	1 lb. 13 oz.	3½	Fruits, some vegetables (pumpkin, sauerkraut, spinach and other greens, tomatoes). 6 servings.
No. 3 cyl. or 46 fl. oz.	3 lb. 3 oz. or 1 qt. 14 fl. oz.	5¾	"Economy family size" fruit and vegetable juices,** pork and beans. Institutional size for condensed soups, some vegetables. 10 to 12 servings.
No. 10	6½ lb. to 7 lb. 5 oz.	12–13	Institutional size for fruits, vegetables, and some other foods. 25 servings.

* Specialties: Food combinations prepared by manufacturer's special recipe.
** Juices are now being packed in a number of other can sizes including the 1 quart size.

953. How long will canned foods keep? Indefinitely, if nothing happens to the cans to cause leaks.

954. Where should canned foods be stored? Preferably in a cool, dry place. Rust does not damage canned foods unless it is sufficient to penetrate the cans. However, if your cellar is damp, it is best to store canned foods in a tight cupboard or closet. High temperatures for stored canned foods may impair the color and flavor of some of them, though not their wholesomeness.

955. Is anything added to canned foods to make them keep? No. Heat is the only thing used to make canned foods keep. In the process of canning, they are sterilized in airtight containers, and thus microorganisms which would cause spoilage are destroyed.

956. How does freezing affect canned foods? It may possibly break down the texture of some canned foods. Also, some foods of creamy consistency may curdle or separate, owing to freezing, but heating usually restores the original smooth consistency.

957. Does damage to the outside of a can indicate damage to the food inside? Stains on labels, rust, and dents do not affect the contents of a can, so long as there are no leaks. Any container which leaks should be discarded. If a can has bulged or swelled at either end, it is suspect.

958. How can you tell whether the contents of a can or jar has spoiled? In the same way you judge any home-cooked food: by appearance, odor, and taste. If any of these is off, it is probably best to discard the can.

959. Is it safe to leave unused canned foods in their cans after the cans have been opened? It is entirely safe if you cover and refrigerate the can, just as you would store any other cooked food for future use.

960. Why are some cans lined with gold-colored enamel? Enamel-lined cans help certain foods to retain an attractive appearance; for example, to preserve the color of red fruits or to prevent sulphur-staining of the can interior.

961. If a can or jar hisses when it is opened, what does it mean?
Simply that because there is a vacuum in the container, when air rushes in it fills the vacuum and makes the hissing sound.

962. Should food be heated in its can? It is best to remove food from the can before heating, but if circumstances make it necessary to heat the food in the can, it is most important to remove the lid or puncture it. Also, the can should be heated in boiling water, not directly on the heating unit.

963. What are dietetic canned foods? They are foods canned without the addition of salt or sugar. They are intended primarily for persons who are on low-sodium, low-sugar, or low-calorie diets.

964. Can anything be done to prevent pimientos in open can or jar from molding fast in the refrigerator? Yes. They will keep longer if you pour off the liquid in which they were packed, cover them with water, and store them in the refrigerator in a tightly sealed jar.

965. Is it possible to prevent an opened can of olives from molding fast in the refrigerator? Yes. Put them, with the liquid from the can, into a jar with a tight-sealing lid and store them in the refrigerator. They keep much longer that way, but try to remember to use them *fairly* soon.

966. What can be done with the remains of a 6½-ounce can of tomato paste, after using one tablespoon? Put the remainder of the paste into a small plastic container with a tight seal and freeze it. It keeps indefinitely this way, but molds very fast in the refrigerator.

XVII. FROZEN FOODS

967. What are the maximum storage periods for frozen foods at zero degrees?

	Storage Time (Months)		Storage Time (Months)
Butter	6–8	Crabmeat	2
Cheese	4–6	Shrimp	4
Eggs	6–10	Asparagus, beans, peas	8
Beef roasts and steaks	12	Cauliflower, corn, spinach	10
Lamb roasts	12	Fruits	12
Veal roasts	8	Fruit juice concentrates	12
Veal cutlets and chops	6	Bread and rolls	3
Fresh pork roasts	8	Cinnamon bread and rolls	2
Cured pork	2	Doughnuts	3
Bacon	2	Angel or chiffon cake	2
Sausage and ground meat	2–3	Fruit cake	12
Chicken, whole	12	Layer cake	4
Chicken, cut up	6	Pound or yellow cake	6
Chicken livers	3	Pastry shells	2
Duck, goose and turkey, whole	6	Pies (unbaked)	8
		Prepared main dishes	3–4
Fish	2–3	Sandwiches	½
Cooked fish and shellfish	3	Soups	4

968. What are the defrosting times for frozen foods?

	In Refrigerator	At Room Temperature
Meat	5 hours per pound	2–3 hours per pound
Shellfish	6–8 hours for 3 pounds	1 hour per pound
Poultry	6–10 hours	3 hours
Fish	8 hours	4 hours

969. At what temperature must frozen foods be stored to be safe?
Zero degrees or lower. You can, of course, keep frozen foods for brief periods in the freezer compartment of a refrigerator, but the temperature there is never as low as zero.

970. What is the best packaging material for home-frozen foods?
To retain the highest quality in frozen food, packaging materials

should be moisture-vapor-proof to prevent evaporation, which dries out the food. Many of the materials obtainable for packaging frozen foods are moisture-vapor-*resistant* (not proof), and some of them can retain satisfactory quality in the food, but ordinary waxed paper, household aluminum foil, and cartons for cottage cheese and ice cream are not suitable. Rigid containers made of aluminum, glass, plastic, tin, or heavily waxed cardboard are suitable for all packs and especially for liquid packs. Bags and sheets of moisture-vapor-resistant cellophane, heavy aluminum foil, pliofilm, or laminated papers and duplex bags consisting of various combinations of paper, metal foil, cellophane, and rubber latex are suitable for dry-packed fruits and vegetables. Bags are less convenient for liquid packs than are rigid containers. Remember that bags without a protective carton are difficult to stack. Rigid containers that are flat on top and bottom stack well in the freezer. Round containers waste space.

971. What is the best way to seal containers of frozen foods? Rigid containers are usually sealed by pressing or screwing on the lid. Some need to have freezer tape applied after sealing, to make them airtight. Glass jars must be sealed with a lid containing composition rubber or with a lid and a rubber ring. Many bags can be heat-sealed, or twisted at the top and secured with string, a good quality rubber band, or other sealing device.

972. What is best for labeling frozen packages? Gummed labels, colored tape, special crayons, pens, and stamps are made for the purpose. Every label should carry the name of the food and the date on which it was packed and frozen.

973. Is it all right to pile packages of food on top of one another to freeze them? No. Food cannot be frozen properly unless it is in direct contact with the freezing surface. After it is frozen, it can be stored in the door rack of your freezer or piled up to conserve space.

974. Why do the tops on rigid frozen food containers sometimes rise up in the freezer? Almost invariably because enough head room was not allowed for the food to expand as it froze, which it always does.

975. Is it safe to refreeze totally defrosted foods? If foods have thawed slowly and warmed gradually over a period of several days to a temperature of 40° F. they are not likely to be fit for refreezing. This can happen when the current fails and the freezer is not operating. Under such conditions meats, poultry, most vegetables, and some prepared foods may become unsafe to eat. Fruits and fruit products develop a bad flavor and odor, at which point they should not be refrozen.

976. If the frozen meat I have brought home is slightly thawed, can I refreeze it? Frozen meat can be safely refrozen if it has not been thawed completely. However, the meat may be less tender and juicy.

977. Why do some commercially frozen fruits and vegetables seem to have lost color and flavor when one opens them up to cook them? This is due to improper handling at any time after they are packaged. You should check at the market to make sure that the packages you buy are clean and firm, not torn, crushed, or juice-stained. If possible, also check the temperature of the food case. It should register zero or lower. It should be stacked with food no higher than the fill line. Buy frozen foods last when you market, and ask to have them put into a double bag or an insulated one. Take them home at once and put them immediately into the freezer. Consult the storage time chart (see Question 967) to see how soon you should use them up.

978. Is it all right to freeze leftovers, meats, and others foods in the freezing compartment of a refrigerator? It is, but you must not be under any illusion that you have "frozen" these foods in the same way you would have if you had done the job in a freezer. The foods you buy in packages are *quick* frozen at temperatures of zero or less. The same result is impossible to achieve in a freezing compartment.

979. Are there foods which cannot be frozen, and if so, which are they? There are a very few, and perhaps one day we will even figure out a way to freeze them! Lettuce and other greens which are best eaten crisp do not freeze well. Neither do raw tomatoes, onions, celery, and green peppers. However, when these last are cooked or used as seasonings they may be frozen without damage to texture or flavor. Cooked egg whites get tough when frozen, but can be grated and then frozen. Boiled potatoes get soggy when frozen. Bananas in their skins should not be frozen. Custard and cream pies do not freeze well. Mayonnaise, as is, will separate when frozen, but can be frozen in combination with other foods. With these exceptions the sky and your freezer's capacity is the limit.

980. Is it economical to freeze fresh fruits and vegetables? It is if you grow them yourself or if you buy local produce when it is most abundant. It is if you take care to prepare and freeze them at once upon purchase. They must also be packaged properly to avoid waste and spoilage. It is also economical if you keep your freezer well filled and rotate the products, using first the earliest ones frozen and filling in with other frozen foods so that space is not wasted.

981. Is the quality of beef improved by freezing? For a long time it was said that freezing in no way changed the quality of beef. Thus, one was always advised to buy good grades of beef for freezing, since one would take from the freezer exactly as good beef as one had put in. Very recent experiments in Oklahoma, however, showed that an impartial taste panel rated frozen steaks better than steaks which had not been frozen, the only complaint being that the frozen ones were not as juicy.

982. Why is it unsafe to stuff poultry and freeze it at home? It is impossible to insure, in the home, the rapid handling and freezing necessary to produce a safe product. When poultry and stuffing are held at temperatures from 50° to 120° F., microorganisms associated with food poisoning may multiply and produce toxins. Even a bird taken directly from the refrigerator may reach room temperature while it is being prepared for freezing, and the stuffing is likely to be still warmer. At zero, the temperature of most home freezers, the freezing process is so slow that portions of the bird and the stuffing may remain in the danger zone too long, especially if the bird is a large one. It is better, therefore, to freeze poultry without stuffing, and stuff it just before cooking.

983. Can butter be frozen? Yes, it can be frozen in the wrapping (or box) in which it comes from the market.

984. Is it possible to freeze cheese?   Yes, with the possible exception of cream cheese, which does not yield a very acceptable product when frozen. However, cheese should be frozen in small pieces of a pound or less in weight and not over an inch thick. If properly covered and sealed, it may be held in the freezer for 4 to 6 months. The foil or other moisture-proof wrapping should be pressed tightly against surfaces to eliminate air and to prevent evaporation, then frozen promptly. It will retain exactly the ripeness and flavor it had when you put it into the freezer.

985. Can you freeze eggs?   Yes, eggs freeze very well, either whole or separated. Most people are likely to freeze either egg whites or yolks, each left from dishes requiring the other. Egg whites can be frozen in those little plastic containers sometimes used for freezing ice cubes. When they are hard they can be put into a plastic bag, sealed well, and used as desired—for instance, one of these is very handy to add to a soufflé. That extra egg white is often the secret of a soufflé's success. Egg whites do not take long to defrost, but should be removed from the freezer in time not only to defrost but to reach room temperature, if they are to be beaten so that they will achieve peak volume.

986. Does pork freeze well?   Pork fat tends to get rancid much faster than other animal fats, and so pork, unless it is very lean, should not be held long in the freezer.

987. Does game freeze well?   Yes. It should be handled just like meat or poultry.

988. Can nut meats be frozen?   Yes, they freeze well and keep well, too.

989. Do herbs freeze well?   They freeze very well, minced, and are a handy thing to have available at any moment. Freeze minced fresh herbs in season in small packages and enjoy them all year round.

990. Should meat be defrosted before cooking?   For best results it most certainly should. Therefore, try to remember to remove meat from the freezer in time for it to defrost at room temperature or in the refrigerator. See Question 968 for defrosting times.

991. Should poultry be defrosted before cooking? Yes, with the exception of dishes containing cooked poultry in a sauce. (See Question 968 for defrosting times. Also see Question 472.)

992. Should fish be defrosted before cooking? Yes, and not by putting it into running water, either. It should be defrosted for exactly the right amount of time either in the refrigerator or at room temperature and cooked as soon thereafter as possible, for best results. See Question 968 for defrosting times.

993. Should fruits be defrosted before serving? Yes, though many frozen fruits are exceedingly good when served just barely defrosted.

994. Should vegetables be defrosted before cooking? In general, not, but cooked from the frozen state, as most commercial packages instruct. However, there is a way of cooking frozen vegetables in a very little chicken stock until they absorb all of it, for which one should defrost at least until the pieces in the package separate.

995. What prepared dishes freeze well? Meat loaves, pot roast, stews, hash, stuffed peppers, meatballs in sauce, meat birds, meat turnovers, creamed chicken or turkey, fish loaves or puddings, lobster or shrimp in sauce, chili con carne, Spanish rice, lasagna, macaroni and cheese (with or without ham)—these are a few of the many which freeze well.

996. Is it all right to season dishes just as you ordinarily would before freezing them? It is better to underseason and then to add seasonings during the reheating. Pepper, cloves, and synthetic vanilla have a tendency to get strong and bitter. Curry sometimes acquires a musty flavor.

997. Should prepared dishes be thawed before reheating? No, they are best reheated without thawing and take a bit longer to cook than if you had just put them together without freezing.

998. What soups freeze well?   Vegetable (without potatoes), split pea, pea, navy bean, chicken, onion, beef or chicken stock, and chowders all freeze well.

999. What is the best way to freeze leftover turkey?   As soon as possible after the turkey has been served, remove meat from the carcass in large pieces. Wrap in plastic film, heavy aluminum foil, or other moisture-vapor-resistant packaging material. Freeze at once. The turkey pieces will hold their quality a full month. Smaller pieces covered with gravy to keep out air should be frozen in rigid plastic, glass, or metal containers, allowing a half-inch of space per pint at the top for expansion, tightly sealed, and frozen at once. Turkey thus frozen with gravy has a storage life of six months at zero or lower.

1000. Do stews freeze well?   Yes, but if the one you wish to freeze contains potatoes, put them in during the reheating, since whole potatoes, or quartered ones, do not freeze well.

1001. Does rice freeze well?   Yes, and it is a good binder for casseroles. "Converted" rice is preferable to the quick-cooking variety for freezing.

1002. Can crumb and cheese toppings be added to casseroles before freezing?   It is better to add them when the food is about to be reheated for serving.

1003. Do milk sauces freeze well?   Sometimes sauces containing a relatively large amount of milk separate during freezing and thawing, but usually they can be stirred or beaten smooth again.

1004. Do fried foods freeze well?   In general, they do not. French fried potatoes and fried onion rings are exceptions.

1005. Is it possible to freeze meat pâté successfully?   Not in my opinion, for though they may taste quite like the original mixture, they will have a certain *wet* quality which is far from attractive. But they will keep ten days in the refrigerator, and in most households they will not last that long!

1006. Do most baked goods freeze well? Yes, but they are bulky and take a good deal of space, which is a consideration. Most baked goods freeze well, whether baked or unbaked. If you want to freeze a frosted cake, do so before wrapping. Most cookies keep longer than other baked goods in the freezer—from 6 to 12 months. They should be cooled completely before freezing.

1007. Is it good to put an unbaked pie shell in the freezer before baking? Yes. If you possibly can, you will get a better result if you put such a shell into the freezer for at least an hour before baking. The pastry browns more evenly and lightly, and if there is a liquid filling in it, is less likely to get soggy.

1008. Does pastry freeze well? Yes, it does, and this includes puff pastry.

1009. Should you bake meat pies or turnovers before freezing? No. It is best to freeze them unbaked, then bake them from the frozen state.

1010. Does bread freeze well? Beautifully. Commercially made bread can be frozen in the container in which it was purchased and kept for two weeks. Homemade bread and rolls and brown-and-serve bakery products can be kept, properly wrapped, for three months in the freezer.

1011. Must bread be defrosted for use? It can be toasted from the completely frozen state (if it is sliced bread, that is!), just taking a little longer than it would have if it had not been frozen. But for most other uses it wants defrosting, which does not take long, especially if you separate the slices and lay them out on the counter.

1012. Is it a good idea to freeze sandwiches? Freezing sandwiches is a great time-saver and quality-keeper. Use day-old bread because it is easier to slice and spread (and sometimes cheaper) and it is freshened by freezing. Make a lot of sandwiches at a time, using the "drug-store wrap" or plastic sandwich bags. Label them carefully, with the kind of bread, type of filling, and date frozen clearly marked. The variety of fillings is infinite and limited, really, only by your imagination. It is better to use salad dressing rather than mayonnaise; or else to send the mayonnaise along in a little separate container when the sandwiches go into their box. Since frozen sandwiches take 2 to 4 hours to thaw, they are perfect at lunch time if they are placed, frozen, in the lunch or picnic box in the morning—or if they are brought into the kitchen far enough ahead of mealtime.

RECOMMENDED COOKBOOKS

Basic

America's Cook Book. The New York Herald Tribune Home Institute. Charles Scribner's Sons.

The Joy of Cooking. Irma S. Rombauer and Marion Rombauer Becker. Bobbs-Merrill Company.

General

The Fireside Cookbook. James A. Beard. Simon and Schuster, 1949.

The James Beard Cookbook. James Beard and Isabel E. Callver. E. P. Dutton & Company, 1961.

The Good Housekeeping Cook Book. The Editors of *Good Housekeeping.* Holt, Rinehart & Winston, 1955.

Woman's Day Collector's Cook Book. The Editors of *Woman's Day Magazine.* E. P. Dutton & Company, 1960.

The Art of Fine Baking. Paula Peck. Simon and Schuster, 1961.

Foreign

Mastering the Art of French Cooking. Beck, Bertholle, Child. Alfred A. Knopf, 1961.

The SAS World-Wide Restaurant Cookbook. Charlotte Adams. Random House, 1960.

The Talisman Italian Cookbook. Ada Boni. Crown Publishers.

Polish Cookery. Marja Ochorowicz-Monatowa. Crown Publishers, 1958.

Indonesian Cookery. Lie Sek Hiang. Crown Publishers.

100 Most Honorable Chinese Recipes. Yu Wen Mei and Charlotte Adams. Thomas Y. Crowell Company, 1963.

Viennese Cooking. O. and A. Hess. Crown Publishers.

INDEX

References are to question numbers

(Glossary of Cooking Terms and Tables of Equivalent Weights and Measures are not indexed.)

Aioli Sauce, 723, 725
Allspice, 937
Aluminum cookwear, 4–8
Aluminum foil
  for turkey, 475
Ambrosia, 805
Angel cake, 891
Angels on Horseback, 574
Anise seeds, 936
Anna, potatoes, 620
Apple Pan Dowdy, 774
Apples
  for baking, 771
  Brown Betty, 774
  discoloration, 772
  for eating, 770
  number per pound, 769
  Ozark Pudding, 776
  Waldorf Salad, 700
Applesauce
  in aluminum, 8
Appliances, electric, 48
  blender, 49
  coffee-maker, 57
  mixer, 50, 51
  rotisserie, 53
  sauce pan, 52
  skillet, 54–56
  toaster, 58
  waffle baker, 59
Apricot glaze, 897
Apricots, 786
  poached, 787
Arroz con Pollo, 462
Artichoke
  bottoms, 591

Globe, 589, 590
Jerusalem, 592
Asparagus, 593
  Milanese, 594
Aspic, tomato, 702
Aurore Sauce, 726

Baba au Rhum, 755
Bacon, 382
  Canadian, 383
Bacon Sauce, 724
Bagna Cauda, 724
Baked Alaska, 744
Baked goods
  biscuits, 850–854
  breads, 855–864, 867–870
  cake, 887–901
  coffee cake, 873–875
  flour, 842, 848
  to freeze, 1006–1011
  leavening, 843
  muffins, 881, 884
  pastry, 902–927
  popovers, 879, 880
  substitutions, 845–847
  texture, 849
  yeast, 844, 845
Baking powder, 843, 847, 849
Bananas, 790–795
  Ambrosia, 805
  dessert, 794
Barbecue Sauce, 720
Barquette, 925
Basil, sweet, 928
Baster, bulb, 24
Bavarian Cream, 747

Bay leaf, 928
Bay Scallops, 581
Beans
    dried, 108, 287
    green, 586, 595
Beárnaise Sauce, 720, 723
Beater, rotary, 38
Bechamel Sauce, 645, 708
Beef
    amount per person, 291
    Birds, 327
    blade roast, 320
    Boeuf à la Mode, 323
    boiled, 321
    Bourguigonne, 328
    braised, 322, 415
    Carbonnade, 326
    carving, 285
    Chili Con Carne, 335
    chuck roast, 320
    corned, 339
    Cornish pasty, 337
    fat, 290
    Empanadas, 338
    filet, 295, 318
    Fondue Bourguigonne, 312
    frankfurters, 387
    frozen, 981
    ground, 279, 332
    hamburger, 333
    Hotchpotch, 331
    Hungarian Goulash, 329
    kidney, 403
    London broil, 314
    New England boiled dinner, 340
    one-rib roast, 317
    Pasticha, 336
    prime, 289
    Red Flannel hash, 341
    refrigerator, removal from, 292
    roast, 285, 316, 317, 319, 320, 413
    round, 319
    sauerbraten, 325
    steak, 293–311, 414
    Stifaido, 330
    Stroganoff, 313
    Swedish meatballs, 334

Yankee pot roast, 324
Beet Soup (Borsht), 152
Beetroot salad, 688
Beets, Harvard, 596
Beignets, 768
Bellevue, Consommé, 153
Bel Paese cheese, 216
Benedict, Eggs, 275
Berries, 809
    blackberries, 810
    blueberries, 811
    gooseberries, 812
    raspberries, 814, 815
    strawberries, 813
Beurre Manié, 207
Beurre Noir, 206
Beverages
    beer, 141, 437
    carbonated, 140
    coffee, 817–836
    tea, 837–841
Billi Bi, 173
Bird's Nest Soup, 179
Birds, Beef, 327
Biscuit Tortoni, 746
Biscuits
    baking powder, 850–853
    drops, 854
Bisque, 147
Black Bottom Pie, 918
Black Cherry Sauce, 722
Blackberries, 810
Blanc Mange, 760
Blanquette de Veau, 354
Blender, 49
    for cheese, 44, 226
    ice-crushing attachment, 46
    for mayonnaise, 666
    for nuts, 44
Blending pastry, 902
Bleu cheese, 220
Blintzes, Cheese, 229
Blueberries, 811
Blue cheese, 220
Bob White, 499
Boeuf à la Mode, 323
Boeuf Bourguignonne, 328

Boiling
  beef, 321
  coffee, 827
  corn, 599
  duck, 481
  eggs, 251
  lobster, 560
  potatoes, 616
Bombe, 742
Borsht, 152
Bordelaise Sauce, 720
Bouillabaise, 171
Boula-Boula Soup, 166
Bouquet garni, 934
Bouquetierre, steak, 310
Bourguigonne, Fondue, 312
Brains, 405
  au beurre noire, 406
Braising
  beef, 322
  pheasant, 509
  quail, 502
  time chart for meats, 415
Bread. *See also* Baking.
  cold-oven technique, 858
  flavor, 860
  kneading, 857
  shape, 862
  texture, 847, 859
  rising temperature, 855
  volume, 861
Bread Pudding, 749
Bread Sauce, 510, 718
Breads
  Brioche, 872
  crackling, 868
  French, 867
  frozen, 1010
  salt-rising, 863
  sponge, 856
  spoon bread, 869
  straight-dough, 856
  sourdough, 864
  Panettone, 870
  popadums, 437
  poories, 437
Breakfast, 62

Brick cheese, 216
Brie cheese, 217
Brioche, 872
Broiler, chicken, 441
Broiling
  chart for meat, 414
  chicken, 442
  grapefruit, 807
  in rotisserie, 53
  steak, 302, 303
  venison, 517
  wild duck, 494, 497
Broth
  clarify, 144
  to keep, 281
  Scotch broth, 145
Brown Betty, 775
Brown rice, 653
Brown Sauce, 716, 717
Brunswick Stew, 529
Brussels Sprouts, 597
Bûche de Noël, 757
Buckwheat baked products, 848
Budget, food, 80, 81
Bulb baster, 24
Bulk in menu, 71
Butter
  Beurre Manié, 207
  Beurre Noir, 206
  to clarify, 205
  frozen, 983
  grades, 199
  refrigerator, removal from, 204
  shrimp, 208
  storage, 202, 203
  as substitute, 846
  sweet, 200
  whipped, 201
Butterfly Shrimp, 568
Buttermilk, 185
Butterscotch Sauce, 727
Buying, impulse, 83

Cabbage, 117
  Coleslaw, 689
Cacciatore, chicken, 445
Caciocavallo cheese, 215

Caesar Salad, 683
Café au Lait, 831
Café Brulot, 836
Café Diable, 836
Cakes
    Angel, 891
    Cheese, 900
    Cracked top, 888
    Dobos Torte, 895
    Genoise, 892
    falling, 887
    at high altitudes, 890
    Lady Baltimore, 894
    Madeleines, 898
    pans, 18
    pound, 893
    Sachertorte, 896
    Shrinkage, 889
    Sponge, 891
    Upside-down, 901
Calories, 125–127
Calves' liver, 398
Camembert cheese, 217
Can opener, 45
Canadian bacon, 383
Canard à la Presse, 483
Canelloni, 632
    with crèpes, 642
Caneton à la Bigarade, 484
Caneton à l'Orange, 484
Canned foods
    can sizes, 951, 952
    dietetic, 963
    freezing, 956
    heating, 962
    menus, 74
    soup, 142
    spoilage, 957, 958, 960, 961
    storage, 953–955, 959, 964–966
    values, 950
Caper Sauce, 720
Capon, 439
Cappuccino, 833
Caraway seeds, 936
Carbonnade of Beef, 326
Cardamon seeds, 936
Cardinal, Pêches, 782

Carrots, 112
    Purée Crécy, 162
Carving roast beef, 285
Cashkavallo cheese, 215
Casino (clams or oysters), 576
Cassoulet, 287
Caviar, eggplant, 604
Cayenne, 937
Celerie Rémoularde, 690
Celery seeds, 936
Charlotte
    (dessert), 750
    Russe, 751
Chasseur, chicken, 444
Chasseur Sauce, 720
Chaud Froid, mayonnaise, 670
Cheddar cheese, 215
Cheese
    Blintzes, 229
    Cheese cake, 900
    classifications (charts), 215–220
    Coeur à la Crême, 234
    to cook, 227
    Fondue, 228
    freezing, 984
    Fried, 230
    graded, 209
    grated, 224–226
    Liptauer, 235
    mold on, 223
    natural, 210
    processed, 211
    refrigerated, 221, 222, 224
    ripened, 212, 215–217, 219–220
    Soufflé, 232, 233
    types, 214
    unripened, 213, 218
    uses, 215–220, 763–764
    Welsh Rarebit, 231
Chef's Salad, 681
Cherries Jubilee, 808
Cherry Heering, 948
Cherry pie, 917
Chervil, 928
Chicken. See also Poultry.
    amount per person, 418
    Arroz con Pollo, 462

Chicken (*cont'd*)
  breast, 449–452
  broilers and fryers, 441
  broiling, 442
  Cacciatore, 445
  Chasseur, 444
  City, 352
  Coq au Vin, 465
  dressed, 419
  French Fricassee, 455
  Fricassee, 454
  fowl, 453
  Grill outdoors, 446
  Hash, 456
  Jeanette, 452
  Kiev, 451
  à la King, 457
  Legs, mock, 353
  livers, 468
  Marengo, 464
  Maryland, 463
  Mole, 466
  Paella, 461
  Paprika, 460
  in parts, 447, 448
  Pie, 459
  ready-to-cook, 419
  roast, 416, 440
  Salad, 439, 467
  Sauté, 443
  stewing, 453
  Supreme de Volaille, 450
  Tetrazzini, 458
Chicory, 828
Chiffonade salad, 687
Chili Con Carne, 335
Chilies, 937
Chitterlings, 384
Chives, 928
Chocolate, 759
  Bûche de Noël, 757
  Pot de Crème, 758
  sauce, 727
Chopper, 41
Chops. *See* lamb, pork, veal
  broiling time chart, 414

Chowder, 168
  Manhattan clam, 170
  New England clam, 169
Cinnamon, 937
City Chicken, 352
Civet de Lapin, 526
Clabber, 186
Clam sauce, 641, 724
Clams, 577
  Casino, 576
  in chowder, 169, 170
  cleaning, 578
  steamed, 579
Clarify
  broth, 144
  butter, 205
Cleaver, 31
Clove, 937
Cloverleaf rolls, 865
Cobbler, 766
Cock-a-Leekie, 146
Coeur à la Creme, 234
Coffee, 819–827
  Brulot, Café, 836
  Cappuccino, 833
  with chicory, 828
  demi-tasse, 829
  Diable, Café, 836
  Espresso, 830
  Irish, 834
  au lait, 831
  storage, 817, 818
  Turkish, 835
  Viennese, 832
Coffee cake, 873–875
Coffee-maker
  drip, 47
  electric, 57
  glass, 11
  vacuum, 821
Cognac, 948
Colbert Sauce, 723, 726
Cold soups
  Cold Cream Senagalese, 176
  Gaspazcho, 174
  Madrilene, 159
  Vichyssoise, 175

Coleslaw, 689
Colander, 39
Collop (lobster), 559
Condensed milk, 188
Consommé
  à la Reine, 156
  Bellevue, 153
  Double, 154
  Madrilene, 159
  Petite Marmite, 161
  Printaniere, 155
  Royale, 157
Converted Rice, 649, 650
Cooking equipment, 1, 2
  aluminum, 4–8, 18, 19
  baster, 24
  beater, rotary, 38
  chopper, 41
  cleaver, 31
  coffee maker, 11, 47, 57, 821
  colander, 39
  cooky sheets, 17
  copper, 9, 10
  corkscrew, 43
  Dutch oven, 20
  electric, 1, 45–59
  enamelware, 12–14, 20
  flan ring, 22
  garlic press, 32
  glass, 11
  grater, 44
  grinder, 26
  ice crusher, 46
  iron, 12, 20
  knives, 28–30, 40
  measuring spoons, 27
  opener, can, 45
  opener, jar top, 36
  pans, 3, 52
  pans, cake, 18, 23
  pans, omelet, 19, 263–265
  parsley mincer, 40
  pressure cooker, 21
  reamer, 33
  roaster, 284, 430
  scissors, 34
  shears, game, 42
  sifter, 35
  spatula, 25
  strainer, 39
  tin, 15–17
  wire whisk, 37
Cooky sheets, 17
Copper cookware, 9, 10
Coq au Vin, 465
Coquilles St. Jacques, 585
Coral (lobster), 557
Coriander seeds, 936
Corkscrew, 43
Corn, 598–600
  Fritters, 601
  New England Pudding, 602
Corned Beef, 339
  New England Boiled Dinner, 340
  Red Flannel Hash, 341
Cornish Pasty, 337
Cornish Rock Hen, 416, 489
Cottage cheese, 218
Cottage Pudding, 761
Court bouillon, 542
Cracklings, 385
  bread, 868
Cream
  Cheese, 218
  Crème Fraiche, 197
  Bavarian, 747
  Devonshire, 198
  sour, 195, 196
  Spanish, 748
  Sweet, 194
Cream puffs, 919
Cream Sauce
  with chicken, 721
  with eggs, 726
  with fish, 723
  preparation, 704
  to prevent lumps, 705
  to thicken, 706
  to thin, 707
Cream Senagalese, 176
Crécy, Purée, 162
Crème Brulée, 736
Crème de Menthe, 948
Crème Fraiche, 197

Crème Pâtissière, 735
Creole Gumbo, 172
Creole sauce, 726
Crêpes, 752, 754
    for Canelloni, 642
    Normandes, 773
    Suzettes, 753
Crescent rolls, 871
Croissants, 871
Crown roast
    lamb, 363
    pork, 377
Crusher, ice, 46
Cucumbers
    cooked, 603
    with trout, 548
    wilted, 684
Cumberland Sauce, 720
Cumin seeds, 936
Curry
    Cold Cream Soup, 176
    Sauce, 436, 720, 721, 726
    served with, 437
    powder, 938, 939
Custard, 276, 733–737
    Quiche Lorraine, 277
    Royale, 158
    sauce, 737

Deep-fat frying
    fish, 545
    saucepan, 52
Defrosted foods, 975, 976
Defrosting
    bread, 1011
    fish, 992
    fruits, 993
    meat, 990
    poultry, 991
    prepared dishes, 997
    times, 968
    vegetables, 994
Dehydrated soups, 142
Delmonico Steaks, 300
Demi-tasse, 829
Dessert Sauces
    Butterscotch, 727

Chocolate, 727
Custard, 727
Foamy, 727
Fruit, 727
Hard, 727
Lemon Mousseline, 727
Zabaglione, 727
Desserts
    Ambrosia, 805
    Apple Pan Dowdy, 775
    Baba au Rhum, 755
    Baked Alaska, 744
    Bavarian Cream, 747
    Beignets, 768
    Biscuit Tortoni, 746
    Blanc Mange, 760
    Bombe, 742
    Bread Pudding, 749
    Brown Betty, 774
    Bûche de Noël, 757
    Cherries Jubilee, 808
    Charlotte, 750
    Charlotte Russe, 751
    Cobbler, 766
    Cottage Pudding, 761
    Crème Brulée, 736
    Crème Pâtissière, 735
    Crêpes Normandes, 773
    Crêpes Suzettes, 753
    English Trifle, 733
    Floating Island, 737
    French pancakes, 752
    fruit dumplings, 767, 794
    Gooseberry Fool, 812
    ice cream, 738–740, 742–746
    Indian Pudding, 728
    Jelly Roll, 729
    Lemon Snow, 806
    Ozark Pudding, 776
    Parfait, 743
    Peach Melba, 780
    Peach Shortcake, 781
    Pears Hélène, 785
    Pêche Cardinal, 782
    Pot de Crème, 758
    Profiteroles, 745
    Raspberry Whip, 814

Desserts (*cont'd*)
  Rote Grütze, 815
  Salzburger Nockerl, 731
  Savarin, 756
  sherbet, 741
  soufflé, 732
  Strawberry Shortcake, 813
  Syllabub, 762
  Zabaglione, 730
  Zuppa Inglese, 734
Devonshire Cream, 198
Diane, steak, 308
Dietetic canned foods, 963
Dill, 928
  seeds, 936
Dobos Torte, 895
Doria, trout, 548
Dutch oven, 20
Dove, 511, 512
Dressings
  French, 660
  Mayonnaise, 663–671
  Lorenzo, 674
  Russian, 673
  Thousand Island, 672
  Vinaigrette, 661
Drip coffee
  pot, 47
  coffee, 820
Duchesse potatoes, 619
Duck
  boiled, 481
  Caneton à la Bigarade, 484
  Caneton à l'Orange, 484
  Caneton à la Presse, 483
  grilled outdoors, 482
  roast, time table, 416
  number served, 480
  weight, 479
  Wild, 490–498
Dumplings, fruit, 767

Economy in buying, 63, 73, 82, 87,
  89–91, 950
Edam cheese, 215
Egg Sauce, 723
Eggplant Caviar, 604

Eggs
  baked, 256
  Benedict, 275
  blood spots, 240
  boiling, 251
  breaking, 246
  double-yolked, 241
  Florentine, 273
  food value, 105–107, 238, 239
  freezing, 244, 985
  frozen, 245
  frying, 253
  grades, 236
  Mollet, 272
  number to cup, 249
  omelet, 257–266
  poaching, 252
  refrigeration, 242–243
  in sauce, 250, 723
  scrambling, 254, 274
  separating, 247, 248
  shirred, 255
  Soufflé, 267–271
  Scotch Woodcock, 274
  by weight, 237
Electric appliances, 1, 48–59
  blender, 49
  coffeemaker, 57
  mixer, 50, 51
  rotisserie, 53
  saucepan, 52
  skillet, 54–56
  toaster, 58
  waffle iron, 59
Emergency meals, 74, 75, 76
Emmenthaler cheese, 215
Empanadas, 338
Enamel-covered iron cookware, 12
Enamelware, 13, 14
Endive, Belgian, 605
English muffins, 885, 886
English Trifle, 733
Equipment, cooking. *See* Cooking
  Equipment.
Espagnole, Sauce, 716
Espresso coffee, 830
Evaporated milk, 189, 190

Farmer cheese, 218
Fat
  in beef, 290
  food value, 128
Fat back, 386
Fennel, 928
  seeds, 936
Feta cheese, 218
Fettucini, 632, 636, 637, 639
Figs, fresh, 796, 797
Filé powder, 172
Filet of Beef, 295–297, 312, 318
Filet Mignon, 295
Finnan Haddie, 553
Fish, 530–555. *See also* shellfish.
  baked, 539–541
  broiled, 537, 538
  Finnan Haddie, 553
  food value, 100, 101, 126
  fried, deep fat, 545
  Gravad Lax, 550
  Kedgeree, 546
  kippers, 552
  Norwegian Fish Pudding, 554
  poached, 542
  salmon, smoked, 551
  sautéed, 544
  Seviche, 555
  soup and chowder, 147, 168–173
  trout, 547
  Trout Doria, 548
  Truite au Bleu, 549
  Quenelles, 543
Flan ring, 22
Floating Island, 737
Florentine, eggs, 273
Florentines, 899
Flour
  to measure, 842
  sifter, 35
Foamy sauce, 727
Fondue
  Bourguignonne, 312
  Cheese, 228
"Fools," fruit, 812
Fowl, 453
Fra Diavolo, lobster, 564

Frankfurters, 387
"French bread," 867
French chicken fricassee, 455
French cook's knife, 1, 935
French dressing, 660
French fruit tart, 926
French omelet, 257–259
French pancakes. *See* crêpes.
Fresh ham, 374
Fricassee, chicken, 454
  French, 455
Fried Cheese, 230
Fried food, 79
  freezing, 1004
Fried rice, 655
Fritters, 768
  Corn, 601
Frozen foods, 967–1012
  baked goods, 1006
  beef, 981
  bread, 1011
  butter, 983
  casserole topping, 1002
  cheese, 984
  containers, 971, 984
  defrosting times, 968
  eggs, 244, 985
  foods not to freeze, 979
  fruits and vegetables, 977
  fruits, 980
  fried foods, 1004
  labeling, 972
  leftovers, 978
  meat, 976
  meat pâtés, 1005
  meat pies, 1009
  menus, 75
  milk sauces, 1003
  packaging, 970
  pastry, 1007–1009
  prepared dishes, 995
  pork, 986
  poultry, 982
  refrigerator freezer, 978
  rice, 1001
  sandwiches, 1012
  stews, 1000

Frozen Foods (*cont'd*)
  storage, 973
  storage periods, 967
  storage temperature, 969
Fruit
  with cheese, 763, 764
  as dessert, 765–768, 773–776, 779–
    782, 784, 785, 794, 799, 802, 803,
    805, 806, 808, 812–815
  food value, 112, 119–121
  to freeze, 980
  in muffins, 884
  salad, 699
  sauce, 727
  soups, 148
  tart, 926
Fryer, chicken, 441
Frying, deep-fat, 52, 545

Game, 490–529
  freezing, 987
  shears, 42
Garlic press, 32
Garnishing, 433
Gaspazcho, 174
Gâteau St. Honoré, 920
Genoise, 892
Giblet gravy, 434
Ginger, 937
Gjetost cheese, 218
Glace de Viand, 715
Glass cookware, 11
Glaze, apricot, 897
Globe Artichoke, 589, 590
Gnocchi, 646
Goose, 485
  roast, time table for, 416
Gooseberry Fool, 812
Gorgonzola cheese, 220
Gouda cheese, 215
Goulash, Hungarian, 329
Grain products, 110, 111
Grand Marnier, 948
Grapefruit, broiled, 807
Grapes, 798, 799
Grater, 44
Gratin Dauphinoise, 621

Gravad Lax, 550
Gravy
  giblet, 434
  to keep, 281
Greek salad, 685
Green Mayonnaise, 671
Green sauce, 724
Gruyere cheese, 215
Guacamole, 701
Gumbo, Creole, 172

Hablé Crème Chantilly cheese, 217
Ham, 390
  Braising, time table for, 415
  Canned, 396
  Fresh, 374
  Fully cooked, 391
  Jambalaya, 571
  Picnic, 395
  Prosciutto, 394, 797
  Ready-to-eat, 391
  Roast, time table for, 413
  Slice, 392
  Smithfield, 393
Hamburger, 333
Hanging game
  partridge, 503
  pheasant, 506
  quail, 500
  venison, 513
  wild duck, 491
Hard sauce, 727
Hare, 520, 521
  to cook, 522
  Hassenpfeffer, 525
  Jugged, 523
Harvard beets, 596
Hash
  chicken, 456
  Red Flannel, 341
Heart, 407
Hélène, Pear, 785
Herbs, 928–935
  Bouquet garni, 934
  fines, 933
  freezing, 989
  to mince, 935

Herbs (*cont'd*)
  in omelet, 261
Hollandaise Sauce, 709
  with asparagus, 593
  cracked, 710
  with eggs, 725
  to keep warm, 714
  too thick, 713
  too thin, 711, 712
  with vegetables, 725
Homard, 556
Home Freezing, 970–974
Homogenized milk, 182
Horseradish
  cream sauce, 723
  sauce, 720
Hotchpotch, 331
Hungarian Goulash, 329

Ice cream
  Baked Alaska, 744
  Bombe, 742
  to freeze, 738–740
  Parfait, 743
  Profiteroles, 745
Ice crusher, 46
Iced tea, 839, 840
Indian Pudding, 728
Instant rice, 651
Irish coffee, 834
Irish stew, 365
Iron cookware, 12, 20
Italian Salad, 692

Jack cheese, 215
Jack rabbit, 520
Jambalaya, 571
Jar-top opener, 36
Jeannette, chicken, 452
Jelly Roll, 729
Jerusalem artichoke, 592
Jugged Hare, 523
Juniper berries, 936

Kaskaval cheese, 215
Kedgeree, 546

Kidneys, 400
  Beef, 403
  Lamb, 402
  number per person, 400
  Pork, 404
  Veal, 401
Kiev, chicken, 451
Kippers, 552
Kirsch, 948
Kitchen, 1
Kitchen equipment. *See* cooking
  equipment.
Kneading bread, 857
Knife racks, 29
Knife sharpener, 30
Knives, 28
Köttbullar, 334
Kugelhupf, 874

Lady Baltimore Cake, 894
Lamaze sauce, 723, 726
Lamb, 359
  Amount per person, 358
  Chops, 360, 414
  Crown roast, 363
  Grades, 357
  Kidneys, 402
  Navarin Printanier, 366
  Shashlik, 368
  Shish Kebab, 367
  Stew, 364, 365, 415
  Roast, 361–363, 413
Langouste, 556
Lasagna, 632
  Verdi al Forno, 645
Lax, Gravad, 550
Leavening, 843
Leeks, 606
Leftover foods
  to freeze, 978
  for lunch, 62
  sauces, 719
  to use, 73
Lemon
  Butter sauce, 725
  Mousseline sauce, 727
  Snow, 806

Liederkranz cheese, 217
Limburger cheese, 217
Linguine, 632
Linzertorte, 921
Liptauer cheese, 235
Liqueurs, 948, 949
  in desserts, 753, 756, 802
Liver, 399
  Calves, 398
  Chicken, 468
  Steer, 398
  Pork, 404
Lobster, 556
  a l'Americaine, 563
  to boil, 560
  Collop, 559
  Coral, 557
  Fra Diavolo, 564
  Liver, 557
  Newburg, 561
  Rock tails, 558
  Roe, 557
  Scallop, 559
  South African, 558
  Thermidor, 562
London Broil, 314
Lorenzo Dressing, 674

Macaroni, 632
  and cheese, 640
Mace, 937
Macedoine, salad, 691
Madeleines, 898
Madeira, 940
  sauce, 720
Madrilène, 159
Manhattan Clam Chowder, 170
Manicotti, 632, 643
Marengo, chicken, 464
Margarine, 846
Marinara sauce, 724
Marinating
  beef, 323, 325
  hare, 521–523
  lamb, 367
  rabbit, 524–526
  venison, 514, 515

Marjoram, sweet, 928
Marketing, 63–65, 80–93
Marsala, 940
Maryland, chicken, 463
Matelote sauce, 723
Mayonnaise
  in blender, 666
  Chaud-Froid, 670
  cracking, 668
  curdling, 669
  Green, 671
  to make, 663
  preparation, 663
  proportions, 664, 665
Meals. *See* menu planning.
Measuring spoons, 27
Meat
  broiling time chart, 414
  Cassoulet, 287
  grades, 278
  grinder, 26
  ground, 279
  Loaf, 286
  Pies, frozen, 1009
  refreeze, 976
  roasting time chart, 413
  sauce, 724
  storage, 280
  thermometer, 283
  to wash, 282
Melon, 800
Menu planning, 60–64, 67–72, 76, 78, 79
  leftovers, 73
  list of foods, 65
  menus, 66, 74, 75, 77
  nutrition, 94–138
  timing of meal, 77
Meuniere sauce, 723
Milanese
  Asparagus, 594
  Risotto, 657
Milk
  Buttermilk, 185
  Clabber, 186
  Condensed, 188
  Evaporated, 189, 190

Milk (cont'd)
  Homogenized, 182
  Non-fat dry, 184
  Pasteurized, 181
  Raw, 180
  Sauces, 192, 1003
  Skim, 183
  Sour, 187, 847
  Storage, 191
  Yoghurt, 193
Mimosa, salad, 682
Minestrone, 150
Mint, 928
  sauce, 720
Minute steak, 301
Mixer, electric, 49, 50, 51
Mock chicken legs, 353
Molasses, 132
Mole, 466
Mollet, eggs, 272
Mongole, Purée, 164
Monosodium glutamate, 134
Mornay sauce, 721, 723, 726
Mouli grater, 44
Mousseline sauce, 725
Mozzarella cheese, 218
Müenster cheese, 216
Muffins, 881–886
  with fruit, 884
Mulligatawny Soup, 160
Mushroom sauce, 725, 726
Mushrooms, 607, 608
Mussels
  Billi Bi, 173
  cleaning, 578
  serving, 580
  steaming, 579
Mustard, 937
  sauce, 720
  seeds, 936

Nantua, Sauce, 543, 723, 726
Navarin Printanier, 366
Neufchatel cheese, 218
New England
  Boiled dinner, 340
  Clam Chowder, 169

Corn Pudding, 602
New Orleans Oyster Loaf, 575
Newburg
  lobster, 561
  sauce, 723
Nicoise, salad, 686
Nokkelost cheese, 215
Noodles, green, 639
Normandes, Crêpes, 773
Norwegian Fish Pudding, 554
Nut meats, freezing, 988
Nutmeg, 937
Nutrition
  beans, 100, 108
  bread, 104
  calories, 125–127
  dairy products, 95–97
  eggs, 105–107
  fish, 100, 101
  fruit, 112, 119–121
  fats, 128–131
  grain products, 110–111
  liver, 102
  meat, 100, 101
  menu, balanced, 94
  molasses, 132
  onions, 136
  parsley, 136
  peanut butter, 103
  peas, 100, 109
  proteins, 100, 101, 103, 126
  salt, 134, 135
  sugar, 133
  vegetables, 112–118
  vitamins, 122–124
  yoghurt, 98

Oka cheese, 216
Olive oil, 660, 662–664
Olive sauce, 722
Olives, 965
Omelet pan, 19, 263
  seasoning, 264
  for soufflé omelet, 267
  sticking prevented, 266
  washing, 265

Omelets
  directions, 257–259
  filling, 261
  other ingredients, 262
  seasoning, 260
  soufflé, 267
Opener, jar top, 36
Orange sauce, 722
Oranges, 804
  Ambrosia, 805
  food value, 119, 121
Oregano, 928
Osso Buco, 355
Outdoor cooking
  Chicken, 442, 446
  Corn, 600
  Duck, 482
  Steak, 303
Oxtail, 408
Oyster plant, 625
Oysters
  Angels on Horseback, 574
  Casino, 576
  New Orleans Loaf, 575
  Rockefeller, 573
  Stew, 572
Ozark Pudding, 776

Paella, 461
Palm, Hearts of, 609
Pancakes
  French, 752
  Potato, 622
Panettone, 870
Pans, 3, 6, 7, 18, 19
Paprika, 937
  chicken, 460
  sauce, 721
Parfait, 743
Parisienne, salad, 693
Parkerhouse rolls, 866
Parmesan cheese, 219
Parsley, 40, 928
Pasta, 631, 635, 639
  amount per person, 636
  to cook, 637, 638

  forms of, 632, 642–646
  to make, 633
Pasticha, 336
Pastina, 632
Pastry
  baking, 910–913
  Barquette, 925
  Black Bottom pie, 918
  blending, 902
  French fruit tart, 926
  ingredients, 903, 914–916
  Gâteau St. Honoré, 920
  Linzertorte, 927
  Pâte à Brisée, 921
  Pâte à Chou, 919
  Puff, 922–923
  to roll, 905–909
  Vol au Vent, 924
Pasty, Cornish, 337
Pâte à Brisée, 921
Pâte à Chou, 919
Pâté, meat, 1005
Partridge, 499, 504
  to cook, 505
  to hang, 503
Patty shell, 924
Peaches, 777, 778
  Cardinal (Pêches), 782
  Melba, 780
  Poached, 779
  Shortcake, 781
Peanut butter, 103
Pears, 783, 784
  Hélène, 785
Peas, 610
  food value, 108, 109
  French, 612
  purée, 611
  Snow, 613
Pêches Cardinal, 782
Pepper, 937
Percolator, 819
Perigueux sauce, 720
Perigourdine sauce, 318, 721
Pesto sauce, 724
Petite Marmite, 161

Pheasant, 506, 507
  to cook, 508, 509
  to serve with, 510
Philadelphia Pepperpot, 149
Pie. *See also* pastry.
  chicken, 459
  frozen, 1007
  meat, 337, 338
Pig's knuckles, 379
Pilaf, 654
Pimientos, 964
Pineapple, 801–803
Piroshki, 635
Plantain, 795
Plat, 255
Plum, 788
Poaching
  Apricots, 787
  Eggs, 252
  Fish, 542
  Peaches, 779
  Pears, 783
Au Poivre, steak, 309
Pont l'Eveque cheese, 216
Popovers, 879, 880
Poppy Seeds, 936
Pork, 369–389
  Amount per person, 370
  Bacon, 382
  Canadian bacon, 383
  Chitterlings, 384
  Chops, 378
  Cracklings, 385
  Crown roast, 377
  Fat back, 386
  Frankfurters, 387
  Freezing, 986
  Fresh ham, 374
  Grades, 369
  Hungarian Goulash, 329
  Kidneys, 404
  Liver, 404
  Pig's knuckles, 379
  Roast, time table for, 413
  Roasting, 375, 376
  Sausage, 388

Scrapple, 389
Spareribs, 380, 381
Swedish Meatballs, 334
Port, 940
Port du Salut cheese, 216
Pot cheese, 218
Pot de Crème, 758
Pot Roast of beef, 324, 325
Potage St. Germain, 163
Potatoes, 614–623
  Anna, 620
  Baked, 615
  Boiled, 616
  Duchesse, 619
  food value, 118
  Gnocchi, 646
  Gratin Dauphinoise, 621
  Pan-browned, 618
  Pancakes, 622
  salad, 695–698
  Soufflé, 623
  waxy, 617
Pot-au-Feu, 151
Poulette sauce, 723
Poultry. *See also* Chicken, Turkey, Duck.
  amount per person, 418
  garnish, 433
  grades, 417
  freezing, 982
  preparation, 423
  refrigeration, 420
  roasting, 416, 428–432
  Salmis, 437
  seasoned, 421
  stuffed, 424–426
  singe, 422
  truss, 427
  wash, 421
Press, garlic, 32
Pressure cookers, 21
Printanière, Consommé, 155
Prosciutto, 394
Profiteroles, 745
Provolone Cheese, 215
Prunes, 789

Pudding,
  Cottage, 761
  Corn, New England, 602
  Indian, 728
  Ozark, 776
Puff Pastry, 922, 923
Pulao, 656
Purée Crécy, 162
Purée Mongole, 164

Quail, 499–501
  to cook, 502
Quenelles, 543
Quiche Lorraine, 277
Quick breads, texture, 849

Rabbit, 524
  Civet de Lapin, 526
  Hassenpfeffer, 525
Ragù Bolognese, 645, 724
Raisin sauce, 720
Raspberry whip, 814
Ratatouille, 588
Ravigotte sauce, 580, 725
Ravioli, 632, 635, 644
Reamer, 33
Red Currant sauce, 722
Red Flannel Hash, 341
Refreezing food, 975, 976
Remoulade sauce, 723
Rhubarb, 816
Rice, 647–659
  amount per person, 647
  brown, 653
  converted, 649, 650
  to cook, 648, 649
  freezing, 1001
  fried, 655
  instant, 651
  long grain, 649, 650
  Pilaf, 654
  Pulao, 656
  Rijsstafel, 659
  Risotto, 657
  in salad, 703
  Spanish, 658
  Wild, 652

Ricotta cheese, 218
Rijsstafel, 659
Risotto
  Milanese, 657
  allo Sherry, 657
Roaster, 430
Roasting time chart, 413, 416
Robert, Sauce, 720
Rock Lobster tails, 558
Rockefeller, oysters, 573
Rolls
  Cloverleaf, 865
  Croissant, 871
  Parker House, 866
Romano cheese, 219
Roquefort
  Cheese, 220
  Steak, 311
Rosemary, 928
Rote Grütze, 815
Rotisserie, 53
Royal jelly, 139
Royale
  Consommé, 157
  Custard, 158
Russian Dressing, 673
Russian Salad, 694

Sachertorte, 896
Saffron, 937
Sage, 928
St. Germain, Potage, 163
Salad, 76, 676–703. *See also* Dress-
      ings.
  Beetroot, 688
  Caesar, 683
  Chef's, 681
  Chicken, 439, 467
  Chiffonade, 687
  Coleslaw, 689
  Fruit, 699
  Greek, 685
  Italian, 692
  Macedoine, 691
  Mimosa, 682
  Nicoise, 686
  Parisienne, 693

Salad (cont'd)
  Potato, 695–698
  Rice, 703
  Russian, 694
  Tossed green, 677, 679
  Waldorf, 700
  Wilted green, 680
Salad bowl, 675
Salmis, 438
Salsify, 625
Salt-free diet, 135
Salzburger Nockerl, 731
Sap Sago cheese, 219
Sauces, 704–726
  Aioli, 723, 725
  Aurore, 726
  Bacon, 724
  Bagna Cauda, 724
  Barbecue, 720
  Béarnaise, 720, 723
  Bechamel, 708
  Black Cherry, 722
  Bordelaise, 720
  Bread, 510, 718
  Brown, 716, 717
  Caper, 720
  Chasseur, 720
  Clam, 641, 724
  Colbert, 723, 726
  Cream, 593, 704–707, 721, 723, 725,
    726
  Creole, 726
  Cumberland, 720
  Curry, 720, 721, 726
  Egg, 723
  Espagnole, 716
  Green, 724
  Hollandaise, 593, 709–714, 725, 726
  Horseradish, 720
  Horseradish Cream, 723
  Hot, adding egg yolks to, 250
  Lamaze, 723, 726
  Lemon butter, 725
  Left-over, 719
  Madeira, 720
  Marinara, 724
  Matelote, 723
  Meat, 724
  Meuniere, 723
  Mint, 720
  Mornay, 721, 723, 726
  Mousseline, 725
  Mushroom, 725, 726
  Mustard, 720
  Nantua, 543, 723, 726
  Newburg, 723
  Olive, 722
  Orange, 722
  Paprika, 721
  Perigeux, 720
  Perigourdine, 318, 721
  Pesto, 724
  Poulette, 723
  Ragù Bolognese, 724
  Raisin, 720
  Ravigote, 580, 725
  Red Currant, 722
  Remoulade, 723
  Robert, 720
  Smitane, 720
  Soubise, 720, 723
  Steak, 307
  Supreme, 721
  Sweet and sour, 720
  Tartare, 723
  Tomato, 720, 724
  Tomato and Mushroom, 724
  Veloute, 725
  White wine, 723
Sauces, dessert, 727
Sauerbraten, 325
Sauerkraut, 626, 627
Sausage, 388
Sauternes, 946
Savarin, 756
Savory, Summer, 928
Scallop (lobster), 559
Scallops, 581–585
  to cook, 583
  Coquilles St. Jacques, 585
  raw, 584
Scallops, veal, 347, 348
Schnecken, 873

Schnitzel
  a la Holstein, 350
  Wiener, 349
Scotch Broth, 145
Scotch Woodcock, 274
Scrapple, 389
Seeds, 936
Semolina gnocchi, 646
Senagalese, Cream, 176
Sesame Seeds, 936
Seviche, 555
Shallots, 624
Shark's Fin Soup, 178
Shashlik, 368
Sherbet, 741
Sherry, 940
  in English Trifle, 733
  in Risotto allo Sherry, 657
Shish Kebab, 367
Shortcake,
  Peach, 781
  Strawberry, 813
Shrimp, 565–571
  Butter, 208
  Butterfly, 568
  Jambalaya, 571
  to prepare, 566, 567
  Tempura, 570
  Toast, 569
Skillet, 54, 55, 56
Smitane sauce, 720
Smithfield ham, 393
Snapper Soup, 167
Snert, 165
Snow peas, 613
Sorrel, 928
Soubise sauce, 720, 723
Soufflé, 268–271
  cold, 732
  omelet, 267
  Salzburger Nockerl, 731
Soups, 142–179
  Billi Bi, 173
  Bird's Nest, 179
  Bisque, 147
  Borsht, 152
  Boula-Boula, 166

  Bouillabaise, 171
  Cock-a-Leekie, 146
  cold soups, 174–176
  Consommé, 153–161
  Creole Gumbo, 172
  fruit soups, 148
  frozen, 998
  Minestrone, 150
  Mulligatawny, 160
  Petite Marmite, 161
  Philadelphia Pepperpot, 149
  Pot-au-Feu, 151
  Potage St. Germain, 163
  from poultry carcass, 143
  Purée Crécy, 162
  Purée Mongole, 164
  Scotch Broth, 143
  Shark's Fin, 178
  Snapper, 167
  Snert, 165
  Won Ton, 177
Spaghetti, 632, 636
  with clam sauce, 641
Spaghettini, 632
Spanish Cream, 748
Spanish Rice, 658
Spareribs, 380
  to cook, 381
Spatula, 25
Spätzle, 635
Spices, 929, 930, 937
Spinach, 628, 629
Sponge bread, 856
Sponge cake, 891, 892
Spoon bread, 869
Squab, 486
  to cook, 488
  to roast, 416, 487
Squirrel, 527, 528
  Brunswick Stew, 529
Staples, 64
Steak, beef, 293–311
  Bouquetierre, 310
  Broiling, 303
  Broiling, time table, 414
  Club, 299
  Delmonico, 300

Steak (*cont'd*)
  Diane, 308
  Filet Mignon, 295
  Hotchpotch, 331
  London Broil, 314
  Minute, 301
  New York cut, 298
  Planked, 302
  Au Poivre, 309
  Roquefort, 311
  Sauces for, 307
  Sautéing, 306
  Swiss, 315
  Tournedos, 296
  Tournedos Rossini, 297
Stifaido, 330
Stilton Cheese, 220
Stollen, 875
Storage,
  Butter, 202, 203
  Canned foods, 954, 959
  Cheese, 221
  frozen foods, 967
  Mayonnaise, 667
  Meat, 280
  Milk, 191
  Pork, 371
  Salad greens, 676
Strainer, 39
Strawberry Shortcake, 813
Stroganoff, beef, 313
Stuffing
  poultry, 424–426, 435
  turkey, 473
Supermarkets, 87, 88
Suprême de Volaille, 450
Supreme sauce, 721
Swedish Meatballs, 334
Sweet and Sour sauce, 720
Sweetbreads, 405
Swiss cheese, 215
Swiss steak, 315
Syllabub, 762

Tarhonya noodles, 635
Tarragon, 928

Tartare sauce, 723
Tea, 837–841
  Iced, 839, 840
  in punch, 841
Tempura, 570
Tetrazzini, chicken, 458
Thermidor, lobster, 562
Thermometer, meat, 283
Thousand Island Dressing, 672
Thyme, 928
Timing in preparing meal, 77
Tin cooking ware, 15, 16
Toast,
  prevent browning, 58
  Shrimp, 569
Tomalley (lobster), 557
Tomato
  Aspic, 702
  food value, 112, 119
  and mushroom sauce, 724
  paste, 966
  sauce, 720, 724
Tomatoes, green, 630
Tongue, 409, 410
Tortoni, Biscuit, 746
Tournedos, 296
  Rossini, 297
Trifle, English, 733
Tripe, 411, 412
Trout, 547–549
  au Bleu, 549
  Doria, 548
Truite, au Bleu, 549
Trussing poultry, 427
Turmeric, 937
Turkey
  in aluminum foil, 475
  amount per person, 469
  frozen, 472, 999
  half, 476
  in parts, 471
  roast, 416, 474
  roll, 477
  size to buy, 470
  smoked, 478
  stuffed, 424–427, 473
Turnovers, 1009

Turtle
  Snapper Soup, 167
  Boula Soup, 166

Upside-down cake, 901

Vacuum coffee-maker, 821
Variety Meats, 397–412
  Beef kidney, 403
  Brains, 405
  Calves liver, 398
  food value, 102
  Heart, 407
  Kidneys, number per person, 400
  Lamb kidneys, 402
  Oxtail, 408
  Pork kidneys, 404
  Pork liver, 404
  Sweetbreads, 405
  Tongue, 409, 410
  Tripe, 411, 412
  Veal kidneys, 401
Veal, 342–356
  Blanquette de Veau, 354
  Braising, 415
  Chops, 351, 414
  City Chicken, 352
  Kidneys, 401
  Mock Chicken Legs, 353
  Osso Buco, 355
  Roasting, 346, 413
  Scallops, 347, 348
  Schnitzel a la Holstein, 350
  Shanks, 355
  Vitello Tonnato, 356
  Wiener Schnitzel, 349
Vegetable shortening, 846
Vegetables, 586–630. See also Menu
    Planning, Nutrition.
  asparagus, 593, 594
  artichoke, 589–591
  beets, 596
  Brussels sprouts, 597
  cucumbers, 603
  corn, 599–602

  eggplant, 604
  endive, 605
  green beans, 595
  Jerusalem artichoke, 592
  leeks, 606
  mushrooms, 607, 608
  peas, 610–613
  potatoes, 615–623
  Ratatouille, 588
  salad, 679
  salsify, 625
  sauerkraut, 626, 627
  shallots, 624
  snow peas, 613
  spinach, 628, 629
  tomatoes, 630
Veloute sauce, 725
Venison, 513–519
  Broiled, 517
  Marinating, 514, 515
  Roast, 516
  Stewed, 518
Vermicelli, 632
Vermont Sage cheese, 215
Vichyssoise, 175
Viennese coffee, 832
Vinaigrette dressing, 661
Vitamins, 122–124
Vitello Tonnato, 356
Vol au Vent, 924

Waffle iron, 876
Waffles, 877, 878
  to prevent breaking, 59
Waldorf Salad, 700
Wiener Schnitzel, 349
Wellington, filet of beef, 318
Welsh Rarebit, 231
Wheat germ, 138
Whisk, wire, 37
Whole wheat baked products, 848
Wild rice, 652
Wines, 940–947
  in desserts, 730, 733, 762, 765
  with meat, 297, 307, 323, 367, 945
  white wine sauce, 723

Won Ton, 635
  Soup, 177

Yankee Pot Roast, 324
Yeast
  in bread-making, 844
  substitution, 845

Yoghurt, 98, 193

Zabaglione
  dessert, 730
  sauce, 727
Zuppa Inglese, 734